# CRIMINAL THEORY PROFILES

This book brings to life the major theories of crime and deviance by presenting detailed profiles that help readers differentiate each theory and its major propositions by better understanding how, when, and by whom the theory was formed.

Criminology is based on strong theoretical foundations that attempt to answer the question of why people commit crime. Criminological theory is especially complex in that theorists come from a variety of disciplines including medicine, sociology, psychology, economics, and law. While not an exhaustive list of each theorist's works, nor an in-depth review of the empirical work that has been done on each theory, this text tracks the intellectual development of a theory by profiling the theorists who are responsible for the major ideas in criminological thought. By viewing the field in the context of the social conditions of the time and the personal histories of the theorists, students can better understand the intellectual history of each theory and the relationship between criminology and other fields, to grasp a better appreciation of how the science of crime and the study of criminals have evolved.

All chapters are organized with a brief overview of the theorist and their significant ideas, a biographical profile of the theorist, coverage of the theoretical developments and contributions of the theorist, a list of major works by the theorist, and a summary detailing the overall legacy of the theorist in the field. This book is ideal for courses on criminology, criminological theory, and criminal behavior.

**Joshua D. Behl**, Ph.D., is an assistant professor of criminology at Flagler College in Saint Augustine, Florida. He has a B.A. and M.A. in Criminology and a Ph.D. in Criminology, Law, and Society from the University of Florida. He teaches Criminological Theories, Sociology of Law, and Psychology and Law. He has also authored and co-authored empirical articles, encyclopedia chapters, and book reviews. When not teaching, Dr. Behl enjoys sharing his research with practitioners and attorneys in his role as a litigation consultant.

**Leonard A. Steverson**, Ph.D., is associate professor emeritus of sociology at South Georgia State College and currently an adjunct professor of sociology at Flagler College in Florida. He has a B.S and M.S. in Sociology and a Ph.D. in Human Services. He has authored three books, co-authored two more, and contributed seven chapters in edited volumes. His publications include *Policing in America: A Reference Handbook* (ABC-CLIO, 2007), *Debating Social Problems* (with Jennifer E. Melvin, Routledge, 2018), *Madness Reimagined: Envisioning a Better System of Mental Health in America* (Vernon Press, 2018), and *Addiction Reimagined: Challenging Views of an Enduring Social Problem* (Vernon Press, 2020). In addition to a long academic career, he has worked as a mental health and substance abuse program director, a correctional counselor, and probation officer.

# CRIMINAL THEORY PROFILES

## Inside the Minds of Theorists of Crime and Deviance

*Joshua D. Behl and Leonard A. Steverson*

Routledge
Taylor & Francis Group

NEW YORK AND LONDON

First published 2022
by Routledge
605 Third Avenue, New York, NY 10158

and by Routledge
2 Park Square, Milton Park, Abingdon, Oxon OX14 4RN

*Routledge is an imprint of the Taylor & Francis Group, an informa business*

*Library of Congress Cataloging-in-Publication Data*
Names: Behl, Joshua D., author. | Steverson, Leonard A., author.
Title: Criminal theory profiles : inside the minds of theorists of crime and deviance / Joshua D. Behl & Leonard A. Steverson.
Description: New York, NY : Routledge, 2022. | Includes bibliographical references.
Identifiers: LCCN 2021010710 (print) | LCCN 2021010711 (ebook) |
ISBN 9780367478148 (hardback) | ISBN 9780367472733 (paperback) |
ISBN 9781003036609 (ebook)
Subjects: LCSH: Criminology. | Criminologists. | Criminal behavior. |
Deviant behavior. | Crime–Sociological aspects.
Classification: LCC HV6018 .B44 2022 (print) | LCC HV6018 (ebook) | DDC 364.01–dc23
LC record available at https://lccn.loc.gov/2021010710
LC ebook record available at https://lccn.loc.gov/2021010711

ISBN: 978-0-367-47814-8 (hbk)
ISBN: 978-0-367-47273-3 (pbk)
ISBN: 978-1-003-03660-9 (ebk)

DOI: 10.4324/9781003036609

Typeset in Bembo
by Taylor & Francis Books

Joshua D. Behl:
To my wife, Taylor, my biggest cheerleader

Leonard A. Steverson:
To the love of my life, Betty, and our wonderful family

# CONTENTS

# FIGURES

# ACKNOWLEDGEMENTS

Together, the authors would like to thank the various faculty and staff at Flagler College who made this project possible. As we suggest that we are all a product of our social and historical context, the Proctor Library staff are a major contributor to the social and historical context of this text. Without their hard work and dedication in helping us retrieve the materials we needed in the middle of the Covid-19 pandemic, this work would have never been possible. We would also like to acknowledge Taylor Stearns, for helping us prepare this manuscript; we would be nowhere without her detailed and diligent work. Finally, we want to acknowledge all of our students, past and current, who were the true inspiration of this text.

# BY JOSHUA D. BEHL

It is a true joy to publicly thank my family for the love and support that they have continued to pour on me for years: my wife, Taylor, and dog, Ruby; parents, Helen Carnegie and Chuck and Nicole Behl; my siblings, Bryan and Marissa Behl, Amanda and Jared Chute, Jessica and Dan Moose, and Jacob Vondran; my in-laws, Ruth and Daryl Reimer, and Mark and Julie Allegood as well as a host of siblings-in-law, uncles, aunts, cousins, and many more. Anyone could count themselves lucky to have any one of these individuals in their lives; I have somehow been blessed with all of them. Of particular note are the debts I owe to my wife, Taylor, for being the greatest thrill in my life; it is an honor to be your husband, and to my parents, Helen and Chuck, for their unfailing love and support, and instilling in me a real belief that I could do anything I set my mind to – a belief I know they had in me from the day I was born.

# BY LEONARD A. STEVERSON

This book was partially written as a global pandemic changed the way the world operates. COVID-19 presented many challenges to academics, such as limiting access to the reservoirs of knowledge needed for a project such as this. It also created challenges to families who have struggled (and still struggle) in their attempts to adjust. I am blessed to have a family that made living in this environment, especially while writing a text, more tolerable. To Betty, Nikki, Misty, Ashton, Trent, Colin, Alden, Maely, my big sister, Millie, and the rest of the family, I love and appreciate you all.

# 1

# INTRODUCTION

## Goals of this Text

Criminology as a field – and Sociology of Deviance is included in this definition – is based on strong theoretical foundations to answer the question of why people commit crime. This question has been vexing researchers for centuries. The ideas that have been developed to answer this seemingly unanswerable question range from viewing crime as an individual choice, to viewing crime as caused by societal factors that are forced onto individual members of society. Regardless of the answers developed, the question of why people commit crime is still one of great interest to researchers and students today.

Most textbooks on criminological or sociological theories of deviance are either focused heavily on the Criminal Justice System and how the theories of crime fit into the system more broadly (see Larry Seigel's entire series of theory textbooks published under Cengage Publishing) or go into great detail on the theories themselves (e.g., operational definitions of variables, how they have been measured, etc.), while providing little in the way of criminal justice application and detail (See Akers, Sellers, & Jennings, 2016; Kubrin, Stucky, & Krohn, 2009). This text attempts to achieve neither goal. Rather than add another option to the already crowded theory text market, this text attempts to view theories from the lens of the theorist. In other words, this text's primary focus is on the theorists and their theories.

*Criminal Theory Profiles* has the potential to connote a lot of different ideas. When criminologists and sociologists hear profiling, they may think of racial profiling, criminal profiling, crime scene profiling, or a host of other ideas. That is not at all what we mean. A profile can be defined as an outline, or a short biographical sketch that brings certain aspects of a biography into sharper focus. C. Wright Mills (1959) implored readers of *The Sociological Imagination* to seek to understand the connection between a person's individual biography and the larger social history, the environment in which that biography was formed. Therefore, we hope to provide students with a text that places each theorist in their larger historical and social context to better explain how the theorists developed their respective theories. The authors of this text have noticed over the years that students tend to study certain theories and view with skepticism how they were ever widely accepted by the field. Once the historical context of the theories is explained, the students understand the significance. For example, similarities can be seen between the Jewish Holocaust and

DOI: 10.4324/9781003036609-1

Lombroso's theory of crime, even though Lombroso wrote the theory nearly 50 years before the outbreak of World War II. The logic of eugenics and extermination is quite similar. This reinforces the sociological idea that we are all a product of our social environment (Mills, 1959). Social science theorists are no different in that regard. To celebrate this idea, this text is an attempt to place the theorists in their social contexts to give students a more complete understanding of how the most popular theories of crime and deviance were developed.

It is also important to be quite clear as to what this text is hoping to accomplish. This is not an exhaustive list of each theorist's works, nor is it an in-depth review of the empirical work that has been done on each theory. Rather, this text tracks the intellectual development of a theory by profiling the theorists who are responsible for each major idea in criminological thought. Of course, major theoretical works will be discussed, but so will the social conditions of the time and the personal histories of the theorists. This will allow for a more holistic view of the theory while also making the theorists more accessible to the readers rather than as giant intellectuals that seem out of touch with society.

## What is a Theory?

To many in our society, the term "theory" connotes nothing more than an idea or hypothesis that has yet to be explored in any real way. Some have gone so far as to refer to theory as a "controlled fantasy" (Cuzzort, 1989, p. 10). However, in social sciences, theories are much more concrete than that. Akers, Sellers, and Jennings (2016), in their introductory chapter to a theory text, refer to theories as "tentative answers to the commonly asked questions about events and behaviors" (p. 1). In other words, theories are answers to questions that help us make sense of our everyday lives.

It is important to note that in social sciences, theories are inherently probabilistic – they do not suggest that if certain social factors are present, a certain behavior is inevitable. In fact, quite the opposite. Theories simply suggest that given a certain set of facts, a behavior is probabilistically more likely. This reliance on probability and testability is a key factor that theories of crime and deviance rely on to determine their value. As most theories are in competition with one another as to what the causes of crime or deviant behavior are, it is important that those who study theories of crime and deviance also know how best to evaluate the theories before adopting policies that support the ideas set out in the theory.

Akers et. al. (2016) lay out in great detail the best way to evaluate a theory to assess its value to the field (read Akers, et al., 2016 for a complete overview of this process). Basically, they suggest that a theory should be logically consistent, have broad scope, be parsimonious, testable, empirically valid, and have actionable policy implications. Testability and empirical validity are the most important criteria for theory evaluations because without those two things, theories would be scientifically useless.

It is also important when discussing theories of crime and deviance to make a distinction between theories of law creation and theories of criminal and deviant behavior. In the first category – theories of law creation – theorists, such as Donald Black, Max Weber, and Émile Durkheim (two of whom have sections in this text as well), define why certain acts and individuals are defined as criminal while other, seemingly similar acts are not defined as criminal. For example, tobacco and marijuana are both plants that grow in the ground and can be smoked. Theories of law creation may attempt to explain why one is legal to smoke while the other, up until recently, was completely outlawed in America. Contrast this with theories of criminal and deviant behavior that attempt to explain why social and legal norms are violated. These theories, with their theorists, attempt to explain why certain individuals (micro–level) or societies (macro–level) are more criminogenic compared to other individuals or groups. This text's focus is on the latter type of theories and will focus exclusively on theories of law violation rather than theories of law creation.

## Sociology of Deviance or Criminology

This text is meant to be accessible to a wider audience than just those interested in criminology or criminal justice – it is also geared to be used by those interested in deviance more broadly defined. To that end, it is important to note the difference between the two seemingly inter-changeable terms. Criminology, as a definition, is the scientific study of crime and criminal behavior. Therefore, of particular interest to criminologists is one specific, formal type of deviance – crime. Contrast that with the term "sociology of deviance", whose definition could reasonably be the scientific study of norm violation, either formal (e.g., crime) or informal (e.g., rules set by parents, schools, etc.). While these definitions are certainly close, in fact, some scho-lars refer to the study of deviance as the "Sociology of Crime and Deviance", the sociological definition is clearly broader in scope compared to the criminological (Downes, Rock & McLaughlin, 2016). The best theorists, and therefore theories, should be able to explain both types of behavior since both deal with violations of social control in some capacity.

## Topic Areas

Since this text is a combination of both criminological and sociological ideas about crime and deviance, the chapters have contributions from both disciplines. The text begins with a chapter on the foundations of criminological thought and the origins of both the Classical School and the Positivist School of thought on crime and deviance (Chapter 2). It moves on to the most common usages of the Classical School in crime prevention (Chapter 3). The three major sociological explanations of crime and deviance – Control Theories, Learning Theories, and Anomie/Strain Theories – are then discussed (Chapters 4, 5, and 6). The text than shifts to macro-level theories and discusses societal explanations in deviance (Chapters 7 and 8). One specific macro level theory, Conflict Theory (Chapter 9), suggests that laws are created by those in power; therefore, laws are used as a hegemonic strategy to maintain that power. Using this conflict paradigm, gender (Chapter 10) and race (Chapter 11) are also discussed. Finally, the text discusses the newest trends in criminological and deviance research with the focus being on crime over the life course (Chapter 12).

The reader will notice that each chapter follows the same basic format. The chapter begins with an overview of the theoretical orientation that will be discussed. Then, the chapter is broken down into each theorist. Each section will begin with a brief introduction and a biography of the theorist. This allows for the primary goal of this text to be accomplished – namely, identifying the historical and social context that had an influence on each theorist. The second section will provide an overview of the theory that is credited to each theorist or theorists. (As is often the case in social science research, more than one theorist may be credited with the theory that was developed. For example, Mike Gottfredson and Travis Hirschi coauthored *A General Theory of Crime* where they outlined self-control theory. In these cases, both theorists may be discussed simultaneously.) The third section is an overview of the theoretical works that were written by each theorist. Finally, there is a legacy section that discusses the impact each theorist had on the larger field of Criminology and Sociology. As is often the case in research, some legacies are positive while others are a bit more critical. However, every attempt is made to be as fair as possible in evaluating the legacy of each theorist. Therefore, the authors do not discuss personal preference for theories but leave it up to each reader to decide which explanations they find most desirable.

## References

Akers, R.L., Sellers, C.D.S., & Jennings, W.G. (2016). *Criminological Theories: Introduction, Evaluation, & Application* (7th ed.). New York: Oxford University Press.

Cuzzort, R.P. (1989). *Using Social Thought*. Mountain View, CA: Mayfield Publishing Company.

Downes, D., Rock, P.E., & McLaughlin, E. (2016). *Understanding Deviance: A Guide to the Sociology of Crime and Rule-breaking*. New York: Oxford University Press.

Kubrin, C.E., Stucky, T.D., & Krohn, M.D. (2009). *Researching Theories of Crime and Deviance*. New York: Oxford University Press.

Mills, C.W. ([1959]2000). *The Sociological Imagination*. New York: Oxford University Press.

# 2

# FOUNDATIONS IN CRIMINOLOGY AND THE SOCIOLOGY OF DEVIANCE

## Beccaria & Bentham, Lombroso

## Introduction

From Adam and Eve eating the apple to the modern day, rule violation has been a central focus of civilization. This chapter will introduce you to some of the earliest scientific thoughts on rule violation and criminal behavior. Beginning with Beccaria and Bentham, readers will be exposed to the idea of law as a deterrent – or using punishment to control human behavior. Readers will note that neither Beccaria nor Bentham were trained sociologists or criminologists, but they still made a huge impact on the field and study of deviance. In fact, their contributions are commonly referred to as the "Classical School".

Next, readers will note Cesare Lombroso, an Italian physician, who was also interested in the study of crime, but viewed rule violation as a sign of evolutionary relapse. He argued that crime was due to inborn abnormalities and that the causes of crime could be traced back to the individual. Lombroso is credited with the forming of a "Positivist School" that shifts the focus of crime causation from society to innate differences within the individual offenders.

While Beccaria and Bentham are typically grouped with other crime prevention and deterrence theorists, and Lombroso is grouped with other biological/biosocial theorists, we are more interested in the social climate and intellectual impact of the theorists. Therefore, we grouped these seemingly disparate theorists together, as they are founders of different schools of thought in the study of crime and deviant behavior.

## Cesare Beccaria (1738–1794) & Jeremy Bentham (1748–1832)

### Introduction

Considered the "Father of Criminal Justice", Cesare Beccaria's influence over the field of criminology and the sociology of deviance is perhaps the greatest of everyone in this text – the closest challenger is Jeremy Bentham. Both men were philosophers who were concerned with the legal and penal systems and demanded reform (Akers, Sellers, & Jennings, 2016). While neither intended to formulate an explanation of criminal behavior, they developed a theory that is at the heart of the United States system of justice to this day. In fact, the writings of Beccaria and Bentham are believed to have had a direct impact on the

DOI: 10.4324/9781003036609-2

Constitution of the United States, including the Bill of Rights (Akers, et al., 2016; Snipes, Bernard, & Gerould, 2010) and played a role in the French Revolution of 1789 (Snipes, et al., 2010). While the scholarship of these two men extends well beyond explanations of crime, the focus of this section will be limited in scope to what has been referred to as the "Classical School" of criminology, namely Deterrence Theory.

## Biographical Profile

### Cesare Beccaria (1738–1794)

Born in 1738, the eldest son of an aristocratic family, Beccaria was an heir to an estate at a time when the church was losing some power as a legal institution and the remnants of some of the cruel practices of previous generations remained (Hostettler, 2011). Shy and sensitive, Beccaria had empathy for those who suffered from injustice and wrote a short, but influential text challenging the status quo of legal decision-making. Not an academic or legal scholar, Beccaria's text was intended as a work of advocacy rather than an academic, theoretical study of the law. His text was initially published anonymously for fear of retribution by the church and the state; later it was published in several different languages, giving it widespread reach. His first wife, for whom he had endured house arrest to marry, died unexpectedly when Beccaria was 36, leaving him with two daughters. A few months later he remarried and fathered a son. The general opinion was he could not be alone but in fact he mourned his late wife terribly (Hostettler, 2011). Beccaria died suddenly of apoplexy in November of 1794. Not widely mourned in death due to his shy demeanour, Beccaria's writings were anything but shy as he took on the established legal and religious institutions of the time, shifting the focus from simply penal law to social and moral principles – quite literally changing the world.

### Jeremy Bentham (1748–1832)

Born in 1748, the eldest of seven children, Bentham was one of only two siblings to survive to adulthood (Rosen, 2014). With an attorney as a father, Bentham was exposed to education from a young age – learning Latin at age 3 and attending Oxford at age 12. Much younger and smaller in stature than his peers, Bentham did not enjoy his time at Oxford as he was often lonely. Under pressure from his father, Bentham entered the study of law where he studied under William Blackstone – a prominent English legal scholar. After being admitted to the London Inn, Bentham, despite his father's wishes, never took up the practice of law, preferring to be a philosopher and critic of what he saw in society. Occupied with the French Revolution, prison preform, and legislation, Bentham continued to write until a month before his death. In June of 1862, Bentham breathed his last; he had committed his body to dissection and it was placed on display as an auto-icon. Bentham is credited as being the founder of Utilitarianism and recognized as one of Britain's greatest jurists (Rosen, 2014).

## Profiling the Theory

Beccaria was focused on what he perceived as an arbitrary, biased, and capricious criminal justice system (Akers, et al., 2016). His advocacy for a more just, rational, and fair system stemmed not only from his philosophical beliefs, but from practicality as well. Known today as Deterrence Theory (also known as the Classical School of Criminology), Beccaria's (1764) theory suggested that individuals are rational beings who will try to minimize their pain and maximize their pleasure. These desires would naturally lead to crime if there were not adequate threats of punishment to deter the behavior – hence deterrence theory.

According to Beccaria (1764), for punishment to truly deter would-be offenders the punishment must be swift, certain, and sufficiently severe. On swiftness (also known as celerity), Beccaria (1764) stated, "the more immediate after the commission of a crime a punishment is inflicted, the more just and useful it will be…An immediate punishment is more useful; because the smaller the interval of time between the punishment and the crime, the stronger and more lasting will be the association of the two ideas of crime and punishment". This idea is similar to the idea of operant conditioning (Skinner, 1965) wherein a consequence for a behavior needs to be closely tied to the behavior in order for that behavior to be either reinforced or punished (however, Beccaria developed his theory centuries before B.F. Skinner was born).

For certainty, Beccaria (1764) believed that the probability of apprehension and punishment needs to be high in order to deter deviant behavior. Believing certainty to be connected with severity, Beccaria and Bentham believed certainty of punishment to be more effective in deterring behavior than severity. This is because the more severe the punishment, the less likely it is to be applied (and therefore less certain). However, the less certain the punishment, the more severe it must be in order to deter. "The certainty of a small punishment will make a stronger impression, than the fear of one more severe, if attended with the hopes of escaping" (Beccaria, 1764). We can see an example of the importance of certainty easily in our lives if we consider when one is driving down the highway. The average driver will exceed the speed limit – until a police officer is spotted. As the certainty of punishment increases with the presence of the police, the rate of speed decreases.

The final aspect of punishment that Beccaria (1764) and Bentham thought important in deterring crime is severity. Using the principal of proportionality, the belief is that the punishment should be proportional to the offense committed. The goals of this are twofold, first, to "make the strongest and most lasting impressions on the minds of others" while also causing "the least torment to the body of the criminal" (Beccaria, 1764). However, Beccaria (1764) warns that the punishment cannot be too severe as it could have the opposite effect of deterrences. "That a punishment may produce the effect required, it is sufficient that the *evil* it occasions should exceed the *good* expected from the crime; including in the calculation of the certainty of the punishment, and the privation of the expected advantage. All severity beyond this is superfluous, and therefore tyrannical" (emphasis in original). In simplified terms, a punishment that is too light will not deter, in much the same way that a punishment that is too severe, will equally not deter.

One important element of this deterrence approach is the classification of two different forms of deterrence – specific and general. Specific deterrence refers to the deterrence of the specific individual engaged in the deviant act (Zimring, 1971; Akers, et al., 2016). In other words, the punishment should be used to keep the specific offender from offending again. In the previous example of speeding down the highway, a police officer giving a hasty driver a ticket would be specific deterrence, as that driver is being punished. General deterrence refers to the state's punishment of the offender to serve as an example to the general public. The consequences of the offender's deviant act serve as an example to the rest of society. Returning to the speedy driver, general deterrence is the idea that all those who pass the stopped car will change their own deviant behavior (speeding) in order to not suffer a similar fate.

One point of clarification between specific and general deterrence needs to be made – and one that confuses students on a regular basis. Specific deterrence does NOT mean that any specific individual is deterred – rather that the specific individual who received the punishment is deterred from recommitting the act. Anyone else who is deterred, be it the general public or only one witness, by seeing/hearing about the punishment someone else receives would be subject to general deterrence. This is a point that often confuses students in their study of deterrence and one which the authors hope to conclusively clarify.

Although it is the theoretical underpinning of the United States system of justice, the empirical validity of the deterrence doctrine is decidedly mixed (Kubrin, Stucky & Krohn, 2009). In fact, as a variable, severity is seldom found to have a crime reducing effect on the criminal (Akers, et al., 2016). Even when focusing on specific types of punishments (e.g. the death penalty), the relationship between certainty of death or even the existence of the death penalty has no relationship to homicide rates. Where the deterrence doctrine seems to have the strongest effect is when combined with other, informal social consequences (e.g., parental or teacher disappointment, loss of friendship, etc.).

### Profiling the Literature

### On Crimes and Punishments *(1764)*

What has been defined as Beccaria's major contribution to the field, this text was originally outlawed in Italy upon pain of death (Hostettler, 2011). The text challenges the "existing bleak inhumanity of the penal law to startling effect" (Hostettler, 2011, p. 21). However, Beccaria does not just criticize, he offers solutions. Suggesting that punishments should be set by the state, clearly expressed, proportionate to the crime, swift, and certain, he challenged the commonplace reality of arbitrary and biased judges handing down random sentences from the bench (Cullen, Agnew, & Wilcox, 2011). In so doing, Beccaria changed the legal landscape of much of the world.

### An Introduction to the Principles of Morals and Legislation *(1780)*

Introducing the idea of utilitarianism, or the greatest happiness principal, Bentham laid out in *An Introduction to the Principles of Morals and Legislation* his ideas of pleasure versus pain in achieving happiness. Beginning his text, Bentham (1780, p. 11) says, "Nature has placed mankind under the governance of two sovereign masters, pain and pleasure. It is for them alone to point out what we ought to do, as well as to determine what we shall do. On the one hand the standard of right and wrong, on the other the chain of causes and effects, are fastened to their throne. They govern us in all we do, in all we say, in all we think." Bentham's "highly original" writings were used "to create a philosophical system which he could bring to bear on hitherto largely emotive issues of crime and punishment" (Rosen, 2014).

### Legacy

The legacies of Beccaria and Bentham are much more wide reaching than the fields of Criminology and the Sociology of Deviance. The United States and modern France can trace their legal routes back to these two philosophers (Snipes, et al., 2010; Akers, et al., 2016; Kubrin et al., 2009). While the effectiveness of their theoretical idea has been shown to be ineffective, there is no doubt that their writings caused a shift in focus from the arbitrary and cruel judicial decisions of the time to the more equal and fair ideals that we strive for today. Their ideas about human rationality and the ability of the system to work for the good of society are also at the philosophical heart of many of the perspectives on justice that we still utilize today.

## Cesare Lombroso (1835–1909)

### Introduction

Cesare Lombroso, an Italian Army Physician, professor, and anthropologist, is most well known for his ideas that saw the biological make-up of criminals as the primary cause of crime. What Bentham and Beccaria were to the Classical School of Criminology, Lombroso was to the Positivist School – in which the focus was shifted from the crime to the criminal (Gibson, 2006). Specifically, Lombroso focused on the physical make-up of individuals as a predictor of deviance. While his work has largely been unsupported by the empirical literature, his impact on the field justifies his inclusion as a giant in Criminology.

### Biographical Profile

Cesare Lombroso was born in Austrian controlled Verona in 1835 as the son of Jewish parents (Martin, Mutchnick, & Austin, 1990). Fortune smiled upon young Lombroso as had Verona been under Italian control at the time, he would not have been able to attend school due to his Jewish heritage. A precocious child, Lombroso excelled in school, eventually graduating from medical school with a specialty degree in surgery (Wolfgang, 1973; Kurella, 1910; Martin, et al., 1990).

Over the course of his life, Lombroso had a variety of jobs, which included being an army physician, psychiatrist, and professor of varying subjects (including medical jurisprudence, psychiatry, and anthropology; Martin, et al., 1990). It was during his time as an army physician that Lombroso first noticed the positive correlation between soldiers with tattoos and soldiers who were involved in violations of military and civilian rules of law. This was the foundation for Lombroso's development of a biological theory of crime and what first piqued his interest in the relationship between physical manifestations and behavior.

Lombroso was held in high regard throughout his life, in both Europe and the United States. Due to this popularity, one of Lombroso's daughters, Gina, helped him translate *L'Uomo delinquente* into English. This text became his seminal work *Criminal man*. On October 19, 1909, Lombroso died. As requested, his body was autopsied, and his brain was placed in the Institute of Anatomy (Wolfgang, 1973).

### Profiling the Theory

Lombroso grew up in an age that was marked by vast scientific advancements where the basic assumptions of humankind were being challenged (Martin, et al., 1990). Ideas such as "free will" and man being created in "God's own image" were being challenged by the likes of Charles Darwin, Benjamin Rush, and Rudolf Virchow (Martin, et al., 1990; Wolfgang, 1973). In fact, Darwin, in *The Descent of Man* first used the idea of "atavistic man", which Lombroso adopted in his theory of criminal behavior. A lot of these new ideas were viewed as radical, yet it is clear that Lombroso adopted a great many of them.

The main idea behind Lombroso's work, *The criminal man*, one reiterated in other writings, was that criminals are born, not made (Akers, et al., 2016). Lombroso theorized that crime is caused by biological differences between criminals and law-abiding citizens. Extending his work on Italian soldiers from his time as an army physician, Lombroso determined that there were physical differences between soldiers and criminals. He therefore determined that the convict in prison was a "born criminal".

A born criminal is an atavism – or a throwback to an earlier stage in human evolution (Lombroso, 1911). These atavisms have the physical make-up, mental capabilities, and instincts of primitive man and therefore are unsuited for civilized life. So it is that born criminals have no choice but to be criminal. Identifying these atavisms was done through the measurement of visible stigmata, or physical characteristics that pointed toward deviance. These stigmata could included features like an asymmetrical face, large, monkey-like ears, large lips, a twisted chin and nose, protruding cheekbones, long arms, and extra fingers and toes. Men with five or more of these stigmata and women with three or more of these stigmata were marked as born criminals. Women exhibited fewer signs than men due to the evolutionary process of natural selection. Lombroso, along with his son-in-law Ferrero, proposed that men were less likely to breed with physically deformed women and therefore the degenerative traits in women would be less likely to be passed on compared to those traits in men. The born criminal, they considered, was the most dangerous of all the criminals and commited the most serious crimes.

In addition to the born criminal, Lombroso also identified two other types of criminals, the "criminaloid" and the "insane criminal". The criminaloid was motivated by passion or had an emotional make-up that compelled them, under the proper circumstances, to commit acts of deviance. These criminals were quick to confess when caught and were typically swayed to good or evil depending on the available circumstances. Criminaloids could become habitual offenders and therefore incarceration was to be avoided in favor of a fine or a labor sentence in order to avoid further socialization with born criminals (Lombroso, 1911). While the criminaloid typically committed minor offenses, the insane criminal included the idiot, imbecile, epileptic, and psychotic, and was mentally unfit for society. The insane criminal's make-up caused them to be unable to differentiate right from wrong. Lombroso believed them to be truly insane and therefore without responsibility for their actions (Lombroso, 1911).

The study of the criminal, while a widely acknowledged practice today, was quite revolutionary in the time of Lombroso. Experimental methodology became the model for positivists who rejected the classical ideas of deductive mathematical theories that were being utilized by Classical theorists like Cesare Beccaria. As one of, if not the first, to utilize this primitive model of experimental methodology, it is no wonder that flaws existed in the design of Lombroso's experiments. One of most frequent criticisms levelled at Lombroso is the absence of a control group in his research – or his choice of control group when he used one, namely, Italian soldiers.

Lombroso also broke from the Classical School in terms of his conception of punishment. His first deviation from the Classical School involved the idea of the sentence fitting the offender rather than the crime.

> Further, when a criminal is sentenced for 20 years but is reformed in 10, why keep him there for 10 years longer, when another, to whom it would be useful to remain in prison longer, is liberated at the end of 5 years? Crime is like sickness. The remedy should be fitted to the disease.
>
> *(Lombroso, 1911, p. 386)*

Although he initially opposed the death penalty, Lombroso came to realize that for the born criminal, the death penalty, sterilization, or life imprisonment accelerated natural selection, ridding society of delinquent biology. However, when it came to insane criminals, he wanted them placed in specialized mental institutions, where they could receive treatment but still being separated for life from the rest of society. For the criminaloid, Lombroso sought alternatives to corporal punishment and viewed incarceration and imprisonment as "schools of evil" where reformable inmates would be socialized with more serious offenders. Therefore, Lombroso advocated sanctions like fines, labor, house arrest, or judicial reprimands.

## Profiling the Literature

### The Criminal Man *(1863)*

Viewed as Lombroso's most important work (Wolfgang, 1961), *The Criminal Man* (*L'uomo delinquente*) is the text where Lombroso fleshed out his theoretical ideas about atavisms and the visible stigmata of degeneration necessary to identify criminals. Like most theorists, Lombroso released several additions to his book (which began at a modest 252 pages and eventually grew to over 2,000 pages and included the eventual standalone text *Crime: Its Causes and Remedies* [1911 translation printed after death]). Throughout these editions, Lombroso's ideas about criminals evolved and focused more on degeneration and the similarities between the criminal, the insane, and the epileptic (Wolfgang, 1961). The more Lombroso studied the criminal, the more he hadd to modify his theory, as too many examples arose that might falsify his original claims. To that end, Lombroso theorized that many abnormalities could not be explained by atavism, so he searched for some other causal mechanism – specifically that people with arrested development in their nerve centers could also be criminal. "The fusion of criminality with epilepsy and with moral insanity alone could explain the purely pathological and non-atavistic phenomena in the delinquent" (Lombroso, 1897). Regardless of how his work would later be received by the academic community, Lombroso did support it with a sort of research methodology, rudimentary though it was.

### The Female Offender *(1894)*

This follow-up work of Lombroso's was written specifically to address the issue of female offending. Written in collaboration with his son-in law Ferrero, Lombroso argued that anatomically, there is much more overlap between the sexes than there is variability (Wolfgang, 1961). Lombroso uses the specific example of prostitution as evidence of atavistic phenomena in women. Lombroso still argued that there were visible stigmata that identified female offenders. However, the sex difference in male versus female offending were due to natural selection – men were less likely to breed with physically deformed women and therefore the degenerative traits in women would be less likely to survive over time than such traits in men (Akers, et al., 2016).

## Legacy

Although the idea of an individual's physical make-up being a cause of crime and the basic idea of criminals as evolutionary throwbacks have been largely dismissed in modern day criminology, there is no doubt that Cesare Lombroso left his mark on the field of Criminology. "Any scholar who succeeds in driving hundreds of fellow students to search for the truth and whose ideas after half a century possess vitality, merits an honorable place in the history of thought" (Sellin, 1937, pp. 896–897). Due of the work of Lombroso, the basic concept of innate criminality became a dominant perspective on crime and triggered a plethora of biological theorizing about crime that still exists today. Any theory of crime that refers to factors like inherited traits, biological inferiority, physical abnormalities or categorizing people by body type, biochemical imbalance, or genetic make-up traces its origins back to Cesare Lombroso. "Before Lombroso, the study of crime fell into the domain of metaphysicians, moralists, and penologists; Lombroso turned it into a biological science" (Rafter, 2006, p. 39). Today, biosocial criminology is one of the major perspectives in Criminology.

## References

Akers, R.L., Sellers, C.D.S., & Jennings, W.G. (2016). *Criminological Theories: Introduction, Evaluation, & Application* (7th ed.). New York: Oxford University Press.

Beccaria, C. (1764). *On Crimes and Punishments*. New Brunswick, NJ: Transaction Publishers.

Bentham, J. (1780). *The Collected Works of Jeremy Bentham: An Introduction to the Principles of Morals and Legislation*. London: Clarendon Press.

Cullen, F.T., Agnew, R., & Wilcox, P. (2011). *Criminological Theory: Past to Present. Essential Readings*. New York: Oxford University Press.

Gibson, M.S. (2006). Cesare Lombroso and Italian criminology: Theory and politics. In P. Becker, & R.F. Wetzell, (Eds.). *Criminals and their Scientists: The History of Criminology in International Perspective*. New York: Cambridge University Press.

Hostettler, J. (2011). *Cesare Beccaria: The Genius of On Crimes and Punishments*. Sherfield: Waterside Press.

Kubrin, C.E., Stucky, T.D., & Krohn, M.D. (2009). *Researching Theories of Crime and Deviance*. New York: Oxford University Press.

Kurella, H. (1910). *Cesare Lombroso: A Man of Science*. New York: Rebman Co.

Lombroso, C. (1863). *The Criminal Man*. Duke University Press.

Lombroso, C. (1987). *L'uomo delinquente*, 5th edn. Vol. V., with an atlas. Turin: Fratelli Bocca. Trans as *Crime: Its Causes and Remedies*. Boston, MA: Little, Brown, 1913. Repr. Montclair, NJ: Patterson Smith, 1968.

Lombroso, C. (1911). *Crime, its Causes and Remedies* (Vol. 3), trans. H.P. Horton. London: Little, Brown.

Lombroso, C. & Ferrero, G. (1894). *The Female Offender*. New York,: Appleton.

Martin, R., Mutchnick, R.J., & Austin, W.T. (1990). *Criminological Thought: Pioneers Past and Present*. New York: Macmillan Publishing Company.

Rafter, N.H. (2006). Cesare Lombroso and the origins of criminology: Rethinking criminological tradition. In S. Henry & M.M. Lanier. *The Essential Criminology Reader*. New York: Taylor and Francis.

Rosen, F. (2014). Bentham, Jeremy. *Oxford Dictionary of National Biography* (online ed.). Oxford University Press.

Sellin, T. (1937). The Lombrosian myth in criminology (letter to the editor). *The American Journal of Sociology*, 42, 898–899.

Skinner, B.F. (1965). *Science and Human Behavior*. New York: Simon and Schuster.

Snipes, J.B., Bernard, T.J., & Gerould, A.L. (2010). *Vold's Theoretical Criminology*. New York: Oxford University Press.

Wolfgang, M. (1973). *Cesare Lombroso 1835–1909*. In H. Mannheim (Ed.), *Pioneers in Criminology*, second edition enlarged. Montclair, NJ: Patterson Smith.

Wolfgang, M.E. (1961). Pioneers in criminology: Cesare Lombroso (1825–1909). *Journal of Criminal Law Criminology, & Police Science, 52(4)*, 361–391.

Zimring, F.E. (1971). *Perspectives on Deterrence* (Vol. 2). National Institute of Mental Health, Center for Studies of Crime and Delinquency.

# 3

# CRIME PREVENTION

## Jeffery, Clarke

## Introduction

Extending from the "Classical School", crime prevention theories operate under the same basic assumption of the "rational criminal". Using this idea of rationality as the backdrop, the theorists in this chapter also developed policies to make crime or deviant behavior less attractive. By utilizing the theories and policies discussed below, one could successfully deflect, or block, being victimized. Basically, by either decreasing the pleasure or increasing the risk or pain of committing deviant acts in a specific location, one could reduce one's own victimization.

While these ideas do overlap with some of the foundational ideas presented by Beccaria and Bentham, the theorists in this chapter are shown to be more interested in what has been called "expected utility", or the idea of pleasure maximization and pain avoidance. Therefore, policies such as Crime Prevention through Environmental Design (Jeffery) and Situational Crime Prevention (Clarke) are primarily focused on increasing the pain or decreasing the pleasure that crime and deviance provide to the offender.

## C. Ray Jeffery (1921–2007)

### Introduction

C. Ray Jeffery was more interested in crime prevention than crime deterrence or rehabilitation. His idea of Crime Prevention through Environmental Design (CPTED) modernized and applied theory to the practice of criminal justice (Jeffery, 1971). While some applied this approach to the specific architecture of buildings and urban centers (see Newman, 1972), Jeffery intended this idea to go beyond just the physical environment to include the social, and, eventually, the biological/genetic environment of individuals. While Newman (1972) is more widely acknowledged as the reason CPTED is a common concept today, even he acknowledged that it was C. Ray Jeffery who created the idea.

DOI: 10.4324/9781003036609-3

## *Biographical Profile*

Born in 1921 in Pocatello, Idaho, Jeffery was surrounded by the criminal justice system at a young age (Fishbein, 1996). Jeffery's father was a criminal law attorney, working for a time as both a defense and prosecuting attorney, and his uncle was head of the Idaho state police. At Indiana University Jeffery received his undergraduate degrees in Economics and Philosophy. Beginning his graduate work in economics, Jeffery switched to sociology and studied under criminologist Edwin Sutherland. This influence, along with that of Jerome Hall and B.F. Skinner (all at Indiana University) helped to mold Jeffery's view of crime and made him inherently interdisciplinary while still in school (Fishbein, 1996). It was this interdisciplinary view of behaviorism that helped influence his theory of Crime Prevention through Environmental Design.

## *Profiling the Theory*

Jeffery's (1971) idea of Crime Prevention through Environmental Design consisted of constructing and locating buildings in such a way as to reduce criminal acts through concepts of "target hardening" and "defensible spaces" in order to make criminal behavior seem less appealing. Based on similar ideas of Situational Crime Prevention and rational choice, CPTED assumes that criminals are rational beings that will select crimes or victims in such a way as to increase their pleasure and minimize their pain. However, Jeffery (1971) suggested the social and physical environment may open up the opportunities to commit crime. This caused a change in focus from the offender to the environment (social or physical) in which the offender operates (Lab, 2010).

Challenging the ideas of deterrence and rehabilitation head on, Jeffery (1971) suggested that the primary methods of social control simply do not work at deterring or rehabilitating offenders. Jeffery was more focused on prevention rather than reactions to crime – the primary focus of deterrence and rehabilitation. Jeffery proposed that it was more effective, and therefore more important, to stop crime from happening in the first place, rather than reacting to it after the fact. Specifically, he argued that offenders were focused on the future consequences of their offending. Thus, by removing environmental cues to gain those consequences, offending would be reduced.

Jeffery (1971) was heavily influenced by the work of B.F. Skinner (1965) which posited that if the rewards of offending could be reduced or eliminated, the desire to offend would also be reduced. However, Jeffery did not stop with simple operant conditioning of the offender. He argued that the physical and social environments could help determine the pleasure or pain associated with deviant behavior. Unlike those who came after him who focused mostly on the physical environment (see Newman, 1972), Jeffery (1971) was equally focused on the social environment, such as involvement in prosocial activities and proactive programming by law enforcement to help increase social controls. In his 1977 edition of his text, Jeffery added a biological component to CPTED; he argued that there was a genetic and biological component to behavior that was interactive (e.g., A affects B which affects A, etc.), as opposed to a more traditional sequential ordering of events (e.g., A causes B). This was one of the first "biosocial" approaches taken to crime control and prevention (Lab, 2010). This approach took a while to catch on as the field of crime and deviance was largely unfamiliar with the field of biology (Lab, 2010). However, this new biosocial approach to criminology is quite popular today.

## *Profiling the Literature*

### Crime Prevention through Environmental Design *(1971)*

Described as an "invaluable thought provoking source of information" (Anderson, 1978, p. 58), *Crime Prevention Through Environmental Design* is a text that shifts the focus from physical space and architecture to psychological and genetic approaches to crime prevention. Arguing that the best approach to crime control is prevention, Jeffery suggests that criminologists should move on from target-hardening techniques and combine the psychological, sociological, and biological with the environmental in order to truly reduce crime. This new school of thought "ushered in a new way of looking at crime" (Lab, 2010, p. 494).

### Criminology: An Interdisciplinary Approach *(1990)*

*Criminology: An Interdisciplinary Approach* is the most comprehensive layout of Jeffery's theory; he argues for a fully integrated biological, sociological, psychological, and economic model for understanding human behavior and crime (Lab, 2010). He argues that without understanding the biological, one can never truly understand the physical and social environments, because an individual's physical and social environments are necessarily interpreted and influenced by their biology and genetics.

### *Legacy*

Even though C. Ray Jeffery's significant work was a tremendous advance in criminological theory, his legacy more closely matches that of an artist who was unappreciated in his/her time. "Most criminologists have ignored the seminal contributions made by Jeffery's original and subsequent work" and his ideas have "received minimal recognition in the field of criminology" (Robinson, 2013, pp. 427–428). His theoretical ideas were not as popular during his lifetime as those of other theorists (e.g., Ronald Akers, Travis Hirschi, or Robert Agnew), however, they have continued to be applied in a variety of disciplines today. Newman (1972) used these ideas for crime-reducing architecture. Timothy Crowe offers training classes in CPTED concepts for private security and industry professionals to reduce crime in their environments (see Crowe, 1991). In fact, a review of CPTED concepts suggests that there is a growing number of studies to support the concepts of CPTED in reducing crime and fear of crime in communities (Cozens, Saville, & Hillier, 2005). CPTED concepts are also at the heart of Clarke's Situational Crime Prevention (Clarke, 1995). Further, Jeffery's push toward integrating the biological sciences with the social as an explanation of crime has become mainstream in criminology today. However, he is often not given his due. However, in obituaries written by his former students and colleagues (https://asc41.com/obituaries/), there can be no doubt about the tremendous influence of this "modest and humble", "brilliant criminologist", "supportive colleague", and "loyal and trustworthy friend".

## Ronald Clarke (1941–)

### *Introduction*

A psychologist by training, Clarke abandoned the psychological explanations of crime when the research on the effects of psychological treatment on recidivism revealed no differences between the treatment and control groups (Clarke & Felson, 2011). Clarke, working with Derek Cornish, helped define Rational Choice Theory (Cornish & Clarke, 1986). It has been suggested by some that Rational Choice Theory is an extension of the deterrence perspective; however, rational choice theorists claim this is a general theory that encompasses the decision to commit a specific act and the development of or desistence from a criminal career (Akers, Sellers, & Jennings, 2016).

### Biographical Profile

A perpetual outsider, Clarke was born in Africa during World War II to a British colonial father and German missionary mother (Clarke & Felson, 2011). After having moved back to the UK at the age of ten, Clarke was often questioned about his white skin due to his being born in Africa. Being labeled as an outsider would have lasting effects throughout his personal and academic life – thus, the clinical psychologist would abandon the therapeutic approach to deviance, and instead favor a more sociological explanation of deviance.

Clarke obtained his undergraduate degree in behavioral psychology before training as a clinical psychologist in London (Clarke & Felson, 2011). Upon completion of his training, he obtained his first job as a research officer in a training schools for delinquent boys. This educational and vocational training, along with the results of a study done with Cornish (Clarke & Cornish, 1972) revealed to Clarke that most of the psychological interventions used to treat delinquent boys did not work. Utilizing the data obtained from these training schools, Clarke was able to work part-time towards his Ph.D. in Psychology, while also undertaking a job at the Home Office Research Unit (the UK's largest employer of criminologists).

At the Home Office Research Unit, Clarke was forced to only conduct research that could directly inform criminal justice policy, as the UK government's funding was strictly limited to such research endeavors (Clarke & Felson, 2011). While he did not appreciate the confinement of his research endeavors, it did influence how Clarke carried out his research agenda when entering the halls of academia – he always kept policy relevance to the fore. When evidence suggested that rehabilitation did not reduce crime and other research questioned the ability of law enforcement and the courts to do anything about the crime problem, two formative publications came out – Newman's (1972) *Defensible Space* and C. Ray Jeffery's (1971) *Crime Prevention through Environmental Design*. These publications further convinced Clarke of the effect of situational factors on criminal opportunity; if those factors could be controlled, so too, could crime.

### Profiling the Theory

Similar to the deterrence doctrine of Bentham and Beccaria's approaches, Rational Choice Theory suggests that offenders make an effort versus reward calculation of the cost of crime compared to the likelihood and severity of punishment – also called *expected utility* (Cornish & Clarke, 1986). This is a two-step process that begins with the individual deciding that they are going to become involved in crime to meet their needs (Cornish & Clarke, 1986; Cullen, Agnew, & Wilcox, 2011). Second, the individual must decide to commit a particular offense – this specific decision is situationally based, and consideration is given to the costs and benefits of the act (e.g., is the house to be robbed vacant or occupied?). An excess in perceived benefits with a deficiency in perceived risks will result in deviant behavior. "The cardinal rule of rational choice theories is never to dismiss a criminal act as wanton or senseless or irrational, but rather to seek to understand the purposes of the offender" (Snipes, Bernard, & Gerould, 2010, p. 50).

At face value, this seems like a very satisfying theory. It is logical, speaks to free will, and allows individuals to justify why they would never be criminal – one can choose to commit crime or not. However, the empirical evidence for this theoretical orientation is quite weak (Akers, et al., 2016; Kubrin, Stucky, & Krohn, 2009). When rationality is viewed as *pure* the empirical validity is basically non-existent. This has caused researchers to put forward a type of *limited* or *bounded* rationality, where the offenders do not require particularly high levels of rationality in order to be considered *rational*. In these tests of *bounded rationality* researchers typically combine elements of Rational Choice Theory with elements of other sociological or psychological variables (Akers, et al., 2016). Due to this, the empirical tests are no longer tests of Rational Choice Theory, but of some other theory (typically Social Learning or Social Bonding Theories) causing the empirical validity of Rational Choice Theory itself to remain weak.

While the theory may lack empirical evidence, the policy implications of it are quite clear – something Clarke was always cognizant of in his research (Clarke & Felson, 2011). One major policy is referred to as Situational Crime Prevention (Clarke, 1995). The basic idea of Situational Crime Prevention is to reduce opportunities for crime by increasing the risk of punishment from offending. Combined with ideas like defensible spaces (Newman, 1972) and crime prevention through environmental design (Jeffery, 1971), Situational Crime Prevention aims at reducing crime by making streets safer, reducing deteriorated housing, and changing the physical environment to reduce crime (e.g., better access control, locks on doors, low bushes, etc.). Following these practices to reduce crime may seem self-evident, however most researchers have found that doing so simply displaces crime rather than reducing it. In other words, it reduces crime in specific places, but not overall (Akers, et. al., 2016). While this may not be effective as a public policy, retail locations and neighborhoods utilize these types of policies to reduce crime in the areas that they are responsible for protecting.

### *Profiling the Literature*

### The Reasoning Criminal *(1986)*

Written with Derek Cornish, *The Reasoning Criminal* has been described as "impressive scholarship" that "no sociological criminologist can afford to miss". This edited volume aims to "promote a synthesis of the rational choice approaches" (England, 1988, p. 213) to deviant behavior by combining leading researchers' perspectives from the Rational Choice school of thought. Broken down into various sections, the book argues the theoretical basis of Rational Choice Theory while also attempting to offer policy prescriptions to help reduce crime. The major idea based on the theory is that "it is through strategic intrusions into would-be offenders' decision making that society can best hobble its tiger" (England, 1988, p. 213).

### Situational Crime Prevention: Successful Case Studies *(1992)*

While the empirical validity of Rational Choice Theory is weak, Clarke published a book of case studies to show that the theory does still have practical utility in the prevention of crime. Showing how crimes ranging from prostitution to pay phone toll fraud can be reduced with these strategies, Clarke makes an argument for the broad scope and application of a theory in reducing crime, at least in specific places at specific times.

## Legacy

Regardless of the validity of the Rational Choice approach, there is no question that Clarke has left his impact on the field. His applied view of crime prevention has been adopted in a variety of retail and employee theft applications (see the National Retail Security Survey that is published annually). Retail stores across America utilize the ideas provided by Clarke's Situational Crime Prevention in reducing stolen merchandise (shrink) while also balancing the ability of customers to shop and handle merchandise they may consider purchasing. This type of applied criminology, while rare, also allows for other exciting career paths for students who are interested in investigations.

## References

Akers, R.L., Sellers, C.D.S., & Jennings, W.G. (2016). *Criminological Theories: Introduction, Evaluation, & Application* (7th ed.). New York,: Oxford University Press.

Anderson, T.F. (1978). Review of the book Crime prevention through environmental design, by C. Ray Jeffery. *Criminal Justice Review*, 3(2), 57–58.

Clarke, R.V.G. (1992). *Situational Crime Prevention: Successful Case Studies*. New York: Criminal Justice Press.

Clarke, R.V. (1995). Situational crime prevention. *Crime and Justice*, 19, 91–150.

Clarke, R.V., & Cornish, D.B. (1972). The controlled trial in institutional research: Paradigm or pitfall for penal evaluators? *A Home Office Research Studies No.* 15. London: Home Office Research Unit.

Clarke, R.V., & Felson, M. (2011). The origins of the routine activity approach and situational crime prevention. *The Origins of American Criminology: Advances in Criminological Theory*, 16, 245–260.

Cornish, D.B., & Clarke, R.V.G. (1986). *The Reasoning Criminal*. New York: Springer-Verlag.

Cozens, P.M., Saville, G., & Hillier, D. (2005). Crime prevention through environmental design (CPTED): A review and modern bibliography. *Property Management*, 23(5), 328–356.

Crowe, T.D. (1991). *Crime Prevention through Environmental Design*. Stoneham, MA: Butterworth-Heinemann, 2000.

Cullen, F.T., Agnew, R., & Wilcox, P. (2011). *Criminological Theory: Past to Present. Essential Readings*. New York: Oxford University Press.

England, R.W. (1988). Heresies revived: Three vexing books. *Contemporary Sociology*, 17(2), 211–213.

Fishbein, D. (interviewer). (1996). C. Ray Jeffery – Oral history of criminology [Video file]. Retrieved from https://www.youtube.com/watch?v=vaaCAWOWUbk&feature=youtu.be.

Jeffery, C.R. (1971). *Crime Prevention through Environmental Design*. Beverly Hills, CA: Sage Publications, 1977.

Jeffery, C.R. (1990). *Criminology: An Interdisciplinary Approach*. Englewood Cliffs, NJ: Prentice Hall.

Kubrin, C.E., Stucky, T.D., & Krohn, M.D. (2009). *Researching Theories of Crime and Deviance*. New York: Oxford University Press.

Lab, S.P. (2010). C. Ray Jeffery: Crime prevention through enivronmental design. In F.T. Cullen, & P. Wilcox. (Eds.). *Encyclopedia of Criminological Theory*. SAGE Publications, Inc. (pp. 494–496).

Newman, O. (1972). *Defensible Space*. New York: Macmillan.

Robinson, M.B. (2013). The theoretical development of "CPTED": Twenty-five years of responses to C. Ray Jeffery. *The Criminology of Criminal Law*, 8, 427–462.

Skinner, B.F. (1965). *Science and Human Behavior*. New York: Simon and Schuster.

Snipes, J.B., Bernard, T.J., & Gerould, A.L. (2010). *Vold's Theoretical Criminology*. New York: Oxford University Press.

# 4

# THEORIES OF SOCIAL CONTROL
## Gusfield, Hirschi, Sykes & Matza, Cohen

## Introduction

Control theories are one of the major sociological explanations of deviant behavior. Control theories suggest that crime and deviant behavior happen due to a lack of social controls in our lives. However, control theorists also approach the study of crime and deviance in a different manner; they ask, "why do individuals conform", as opposed to "why do individuals offend" as most other theorists ask. In this way, control theorists argue that there is nothing specific in society that motivates an individual to offend, rather it is the society's controls over their lives that cause individuals to conform.

Due to this focus on social controls, control theorists are interested in both formal and informal methods of control (e.g., the police and law, as well as parental and school discipline). Further, control theorists are focused on how social controls are weakened or loosened in our lives. This chapter covers the creation of social controls (Gusfield) and how social controls can be strengthened or weakened (Hirschi; Sykes & Matza; Cohen).

## Joseph R. Gusfield (1923–2015)

### Introduction

Joseph R. Gusfield is best known for his work involving symbolic crusades, the title of his most famous book (1963). Part of the second generation of Chicago School theorists, which includes Howard S. Becker and Erving Goffman, Gusfield was a groundbreaking sociologist whose studies focus on how society defines and controls *public problems*, such as addiction-related offenses and other acts considered by society to be deviant (Fine, 1995). Understanding why these acts are so defined, who defines them, and the reasons for these definitions are a focus of Gusfield's theorizing.

Gusfield relates problems growing up in the 1930s; he described his Jewish heritage as being "more than what you were; it was the definitive statement of your place in history" (Gusfield, 1990, p. 106). He claims he was beat up by Polish American hoods for being Jewish and by Jewish hoods just for fun. His early engagement with politics in his youth

DOI: 10.4324/9781003036609-4

taught him that conditions promoting rule making and rule breaking (including violence) were tenuous; this would influence his thought as a social scientist (Gusfield, 1990).

### Biographical Profile

Gusfield was born into a middle-class Jewish family in Chicago and grew up during the Great Depression. He entered the University of Chicago where he enjoyed studying social theory, though he found it to be overly abstract. His education was interrupted when he joined the US Army in 1943, but resumed when he returned to Chicago to finish his undergraduate degree in 1946. He then entered Law School at the University, but found it stifling, so he dropped out to enroll in the Sociology Department. He received his Ph.D. in 1954 and was one of several scholars trained in the Chicago tradition, including Howard Becker and Erving Goffman; this group of scholars are sometimes referred to as the Second Chicago School, as they were the beneficiaries of training by the original members (Roizen, 2016).

Before completing his dissertation, he and his wife Irma moved to New York state where he taught at Episcopalian Hobart and Smith College. It was here that he was introduced to a difference in culture, one which fostered his interest in social movements, particularly those involving early anti-alcohol movements. This subject became his passion and the topic of his doctoral dissertation, which would culminate in his book on moral crusades – a classic in sociology (Roizen, 2016).

Gusfield left Hobart and Smith in 1955 to join the faculty at the University of Illinois, where he remained until 1969. He became involved in the Civil Rights movement, even participating in the 1965 Selma march. He left Illinois to develop a program at the University of California at San Diego, where he mixed ethnomethodological approaches with Chicago School methodology. He continued to research areas such as drunk driving, and later received awards and other accolades for his work (Conrad, 2017; Roizen, 2016). His wife Irma died in 2013 after 66 years of marriage and Gusfield died two years later. Gentle and ever inquisitive, he will be remembered as a pioneer in the study of deviance, social movements, and addiction studies (Roizen, 2016).

### Profiling the Theory

Gusfield's theoretical approach is normally described as social constructionism, which posits that social reality must be understood as developing from social and cultural influences, rather than as possessing objective truth. Therefore, from this perspective, human behaviors are defined by certain people who are able to designate these behaviors as normative or conversely (in the early language of deviance theory), *pathological*.

As Best (2017) notes, Gusfield's perspective is defined by 1) his insistence that deviance should be placed in its historical, cultural, structural, as well as social context; 2) the examination of alternatives that claims makers place on their selected types of action, in other words, an examination that requires claimsmakers to decide which options to pay attention to and which to disregard; and 3) an investigation of the language used by advocates. Gusfield uses history to provide support to the idea that activity considered deviant or criminal is constructed in relation to historical periods. Therefore, alcohol consumption, smoking, and other acts should be observed in relation to specific points in history. Understanding what is considered deviant also requires a focus on choices or alternatives regarding the deviant act; in other words, social scientists should examine all the potential explanations for a deviant act, as well as other circumstances or relationships that might have an influence. Gusfield also evaluates the claims by those endowed with the ability to classify actions as deviance, later exemplified in the process described by Best (1994). Media depictions, for example, project the claim of deviance (and often concern) to a wider audience – this idea appears in the later work of Stanley Cohen and others in the concept of the moral panic.

Gusfield encourages us to make critical observations of social phenomena, such as deviance and crime, observe the problem objectively, and consider the possibilities for alternative solutions. He states, "every perspective is a way of *not* seeing as well as a way of seeing" (Gusfield, 1981, p. 187, italics in text). Attention should be paid to broader cultural issues, such as those related to drunk driving, to keep people safe, rather than individual cases of drinking and driving incidents. This focus should include how meanings and motivations are constructed and maintained.

Gusfield's concept of "ownership" is important here and is defined as "the ability to create and influence the public definition of a problem" (Gusfield, 1981, p. 10). This concept can be understood as the connective tissue to Gusfield's theory, and is integral in understanding constructionism and social movement activity. Best (2017) notes the importance of "skepticism" in Gusfield's theorizing, suggesting that, as Gusfield felt, a healthy dose of skepticism is important for social scientists. This makes sense for someone who adopts a social constructionist perspective.

### Profiling the Literature

### Symbolic Crusade: Status Politics and the American Temperance Movement *(1963)*

This is a classic text in the sociology of deviance, released in 1963 when Erving Goffman's (1963) *Stigma* and Howard Becker's (1963) *Outsiders* were published, and years ahead of many other social constructionist works. It is not only a study of deviance, but a study of social movements as well (Best, 2017). It provides a richer examination to comparable works by introducing social status and class, social control and enforcement measures, alcohol abstinence, policy responses, and political ideology from a historical perspective on the temperance movement. The work examines the "moral indignation" that often accompanies the coercive nature of many social/moral movements. The issue of symbolism reflects Gusfield's Chicago School training, and he describes how prohibition signified "the superior power of the old middle class in American society" (1963, p. 122); indeed, the Temperance Movement itself was a symbolic, rather than an instrumental movement.

### Moral Passage: The Symbolic Process in Public Designations of Deviance (1967)

The article "Moral passage: The symbolic process in public designations of deviance" expands Gusfield's ideas on moral crusades and provides the core position of *Symbolic Crusade* (Best, 2017). Gusfield expresses the symbolic significance of norms and their enforcement by first distinguishing between the instrumental and symbolic functions of law – in the former the law requires enforcement by governmental agencies, and in the latter it reflects the internalized meanings that individuals attach to legal proscriptions. He also brings in the concept of the *patterned evasion of norms*, referring to the norms that are codified into law but rarely enforced, the function of which are to minimize conflict resulting from the enforcement of primarily symbolic laws. Further, Gusfield (1967) provides a typology of three types of people who engage in deviant behavior: 1) those who are "repentant" and sincerely seek reform for their behavior; 2) those who are "ill", such as those whose addiction has been redefined as a disease; and 3) those deemed the "enemy" who do not seek redemption and who choose to remain outside the normative structure.

### On Legislating Morals: The Symbolic Process of Designating Deviance (1968)

In "On legislating morals: The symbolic process of designating deviance", Gusfield discusses a type of deviance designation that exists in moral crusades he terms *moral indignation*, and defines as the "hostility directed against a norm violator despite the absence of direct or personal damage to the norm upholder and designator" (1968, p. 54). He mentions victimless acts such as homosexuality, prostitution, gambling, and abortion in this analysis. He also returns to his distinction between instrumental and symbolic law and his typology of deviants mentioned in *Moral Passage*, however he adds an extra type – the *cynical deviant* who is normally a professional criminal. In this analysis, he uses the deviant status of drug addict (which includes that of alcoholic) in his analysis of types. He explains how groups such as addicted persons attempt to influence the process of deviance designation by: 1) attempting to influence the police through bribery and personal affiliation; 2) joining groups such as Alcoholics Anonymous that seek to reframe addiction as an illness; and 3) seeking to redefine the use of addictive substances as a personal matter. A similar moral crusade, Gusfield concludes, is underway for homosexuality; from a twenty-first-century vantage point, this seems absurd, however it illustrates how understandings of deviance are related to historical periods.

### The Culture of Public Problems: Drink-driving and the Symbolic Order (1981)

In this book, Gusfield begins by explaining how the coupling of two issues – drinking alcohol and operating automobiles – is a microcosm of larger cultural issues and is constructed as a social, or public problem; he describes it in this way: "the existence of a drinking-driving problem is the result of a procedure by which the automobile and fatalities have been construed as a problem of societal concern, to be acted upon by public officials and agencies" (1981, p. 3). In an earlier study Gusfield conducted in the early 1970s to assist California officials with traffic safety control solutions, he became aware of how public agencies narrowly define problems and thus the solutions. From this he developed the concepts of *ownership*, the ability of officials to influence definitions of social problems, and *responsibility* which seeks both to answer the specific causes of problems and to define the policy obligations of institutions to alleviate these problems.

He draws on the work of art literacy critic Kenneth Burke and the dramaturgical approach of Erving Goffman to describe the construction of the drinking-driving problem and the *moral drama* of the drunk driver (constituting a type similar to Stanley Cohen's concept of *folk devil* – see p. 00), ruling out other potential contributors to the problem of auto fatalities in which alcohol was involved (e.g., the cultural reliance on cars, unsafe vehicles, availability of alcohol, and the cultural aspects of alcohol use).

Gusfield states this work is his favorite as the study of human behavior involving alcohol allows for intellectual discovery of social issues that lie beneath the surface and requires disciplinary perspectives of history, philosophy, law, and others (Gusfield, 1990); this certainly had been his philosophy since *The Symbolic Crusade*.

### Legacy

Gusfield's contributions were not only to the sociology of deviance, but also to social constructionism and the sociological subfields of social problems and social movements. He continues to influence scholars in all these areas. The sociology department at University of California at San Diego still maintains the foundations set by Gusfield in his years from 1969–1991 (Conrad, 2017).

Criminologists and sociologists of deviance are well advised to see criminal activity as it has been influenced by politicians (at all levels), regulators, and the media. And an objective approach (with the assistance of history) can help provide a more comprehensive view of offending behavior as well as expose hidden alternatives to its alleviation. Joel Best, contemporary sociologist says of Gusfield that "his work is a fine role model for sociologists who dare to explore the past" (Best, 2017, p. 16).

## Travis Hirschi (1935–2017)

### Introduction

Travis Hirschi is the most cited criminologist of the twentieth century (Laub, 2011). A contemporary, critic, and colleague of Ronald Akers while at University of Washington, Hirschi came to prominence during the golden age of criminological thought. Hirschi is the intellectual father of Social Bonding Theory and Self-Control Theory (also known as *A General Theory of Crime*, the title of a book he co-authored with Michael Gottfredson). What is most unique about Hirschi is the fact that he authored two major theories of deviance whose ideas subsumed all the previous control theories that came before them (Akers, Sellers, & Jennings, 2016). In terms of sociological theories, Hirschi's control theories are some of the most tested and examined, alongside Social Learning Theory and General Strain Theory.

### Biographical Profile

Born in Rockville, Utah to parents who never attended high school, Travis Hirschi was the fifth of eight children born to hard working parents (Laub, 2011). While his parents had not achieved much academically, Hirschi had older siblings and in-laws that rose to the ranks of successful careers such as physicians and attorneys. Because of this, Hirschi always knew that he was going to go to college. Selecting sociology as his major after his wife discouraged him from entering civil engineering, Hirschi knew he wanted to study deviance and race relations. Hirschi took a criminology course with Arthur Beeley whom he remembered as being a positivist who believed in rehabilitation. However, when finding a paper written by Beeley some years later (see Beeley, 1954), Hirschi discovered that Beeley was very much a theorist in the control tradition. Beeley's (1954) work and writing style had a strong influence on most of Hirschi's later work.

After completing his undergraduate degree, Hirschi began his MA in sociology and educational psychology. His thesis, with the pooled resources of all ten of his MA cohort, was a survey of a Salt Lake City suburb. A replication of a well-received article on anomie (see Srole, 1956), Hirschi found the results of the original work unreliable and yet widely accepted by the field. This began a career filled with "cynical lessons" that Hirschi came to learn during his illustrious career (Laub, 2011). While the reception of his thesis results was not as strong as he would have liked, the project led Hirschi to Durkheim. Hirschi said "Before I read *Suicide*, I had no idea what sociology was about" (Laub, 2011, p. 298). This began his lifelong foray into the sociological study of deviance.

However, Hirschi's academic career was temporarily interrupted by being drafted into the US Army. Fortunately, Hirschi scored high on the aptitude test and became a data analyst for the Army, analyzing attitudinal surveys of enlisted personnel. It was here that he learned about the clash between scientific data and ideology – something that a lot of social scientists struggle with today. After leaving the Army, Hirschi attended UC Berkeley to obtain his Ph. D. – he wanted to attend the School of Criminology at the University of California, but they only offered MA degrees. This was because criminology was still a nascent field that had not fully separated from sociology. Hirschi took a deviance course with Goffman that helped influence his view of crime. A book contract on quantitative research in deviance and a dedicated mentor who put Hirschi in touch with Sheldon and Eleanor Glueck (who turned down his request for data) and David Matza on his dissertation committee, Hirschi eventually graduated after accepting his first teaching job at the University of Washington. While the connections between Hirschi and many of the other profiles in this text are clear, Hirschi "rejects the idea that personal background matters much in understanding a person's views on crime or anything else for that matter" (Laub, 2011, p. 296). Whether he is correct or not, Hirschi's influence on the field of criminology and the sociology of deviance remains unquestioned.

### Profiling the Theory

Hirschi is the intellectual father of two major theories of crime and deviance (Hirschi, 1969; Gottfredson & Hirschi, 1990). Although viewed by most theorists as competing theories (Akers, Sellers, & Jennings, 2016), Hirschi (2004) suggests that they are complementary and made efforts to bring the theories closer together. Either way, these two theories now sit at the center of control theories and dominate criminology today (Akers, et al., 2016; Snipes, Bernard, & Gerould, 2010). Control theories, as a group, suggest that most theories of crime and deviance are asking the wrong question – "Why do people commit crime?" Rather, they should be asking "Why do people conform?" The basic answer is that we conform due to societal controls on our lives. When those controls break down, deviance develops (Akers, et al., 2016; Reiss, 1951). It is with that in mind that Hirschi developed the following theories.

### Social Bonding Theory

The main premise of social bonding theory is that "delinquent acts result when an individual's bond to society is weak or broken" (Hirschi, 1969, p. 16). The bond is made up of four primary elements – *attachment, commitment, involvement*, and *belief*. The stronger these variables are in the social bond with parents, peers, and authority figures, the more likely behavior will be controlled toward conformity. The weakening of any of these elements, the more likely behavior will be pushed toward delinquency. As these variables are intercorrelated, the weakening of one variable causes the weakening of all the others (Hirschi, 1969).

Hirschi (1969) suggested *attachment* is the extent to which we have close ties to others, identify with them, and admire them, causing us to care about their expectations. The greater we care about their expectations, the less likely we are to commit crime – the less we care about expectations, the more likely we are to commit crime. These attachments are primarily to parents, but Hirschi argues that attachment to peers also has a crime reducing effect. Hirschi (1969) argues that things like self-control, internal controls, and consciousness are simply too subjective, cannot be measured, and are often used in tautological ways (his attitude toward self-control would change in his later theory). Further, Hirschi argued that attachment even to delinquent others will still have a crime reducing effect on the individual, as it is the attachment that is crime-reducing rather than to whom one is attached. In other words, attachment to delinquent parents or peers will still result in less deviant behavior.

Hirschi's (1969) second variable in Social Bonding Theory is *commitment*. Commitment is the rational element of the theory that an individual has in conventional society and the risk one takes in deviant behavior (Snipes, et al., 2010). Toby (1957) calls this a "*stake in conformity*" that would be jeopardized or lost by engaging in deviant behavior. By investing in conventional educational and occupational activities, one builds up one's commitment to a conventional life. In other words, a person would not risk years of education being wasted by committing a criminal act. This is the most rational element of the theory (Akers, et al., 2016).

The third of Hirschi's (1969) variables is *involvement* in conventional activities. This operates on the notion that "idle hands are the devil's workshop" (Snipes, et al., 2010, p. 252) and refers to the idea that being busy in conventional activities simply does not leave time for deviant activities. These activities could be studying, spending time with family, participation in a church youth group, or participation in extracurricular activities such as sports teams or clubs.

The final of Hirschi's (1969) variables in Social Bonding Theory is *belief*. This is the concept that is defined by the endorsement of conventional values and norms, especially about laws and society's rules in general. This is not to be confused with "definitions favorable and unfavorable to crime" as conceptualized by Akers but rather "the less a person believes he should obey the rules, the more likely he is to violate them" (Hirschi, 1969, p. 26). These beliefs are different from the Techniques of Neutralization advocated by Sykes and Matza, as they believed that deviants were tied to the conventional moral order and therefore must free or neutralize their beliefs in order to commit crime, while Hirschi assumed that deviant individuals are free from the conventional social order to begin with (Snipes, et al., 2010).

Upon empirical testing, Social Bonding Theory received weak to moderate support (Akers et al., 2016). In fact, one surprising finding that is contrary to the theory is that attachment to delinquent peers is one of the strongest predictors of deviance. This finding is more in line with Social Learning Theory than Social Bonding Theory. Nevertheless, most research on the theory has provided somewhat supportive findings.

## A General Theory of Crime (Self-Control Theory)

In collaboration with Michael Gottfredson, Hirschi moved away from the social bonding tradition of control theories in favor of one specific type of control – self-control (Gottfredson & Hirschi, 1990). Gottfredson and Hirschi framed this theory as the singular theory of all deviant and conforming behavior for all ages and under all circumstances. The theory suggests that individuals with low self-control will be substantially more likely to commit deviant acts compared to individuals with high self-control. The authors suggest that self-control can only lead to crime when opportunities arise to permit deviant behavior – but never specify what those opportunities are. Further, they state that ineffective and incomplete socialization, especially in early childhood, is the primary cause of low self-control. This level of self-control remains stable throughout the life course. Effective parenting, discipline, and socialization of children will raise their self-control out of criminogenic levels.

Empirical tests of Self-Control Theory reveal measurement and tautological issues – mainly, deviant acts are used to determine self-control levels in participants (Akers, et al., 2016). Therefore, deviant acts are being used to predict deviant acts. In a meta-analysis of self-control studies, Pratt and Cullen (2000) found weak to moderate support for the theory, and blatantly refuted the claim that this was the single causal predictor of deviant behavior.

Regardless of the questionable empirical support and the seemingly contradictory nature of the two theories, there is no question that these two theories are the two most popular and tested control theories in the study of criminology and the sociology of deviance. In fact, some have argued that Self-Control Theory has taken over Social Bonding as the principal control theory (Akers, et al., 2016). Either way, there is no question that Hirschi's impact on the field has been immense.

### Profiling the Literature

### Causes of Delinquency (1969)

What began as Hirschi's dissertation turned into a book when his friend Rodney Stark gave a copy of the dissertation to the editor of the University of California Press (Laub, 2011). However, it did not stop there. In what has been described as "an important book" (Phillips, 1972, p. 119) and the "most influential work in twentieth century criminology" (Costello & Laub, 2020, p.22), Hirschi lays out his Social Bonding Theory. However, what is unique to this text is the fact that Hirschi combined "theory construction, conceptualization, operationalization, and empirical testing" all into one text that now "stands as a model" to how criminological theories are published (Akers, et al., 2016, p. 123). This text laid out the assumptions, concepts, and major propositions in a "lucid fashion" while also providing clear measures for each of the four concepts (Akers, et al., 2016, p. 123). No more was the field of deviance research divided between the theorists and the statisticians. Because of Hirschi's influence it is virtually unheard of nowadays to propose a deviance theory without simultaneously providing an empirical test of the theory. Although it is not without its critics, most will still acknowledge that this text "deserves to be a major influence on the theory of delinquency" (Phillips, 1972, p. 121).

### A General Theory of Crime (1990 with Mike Gottfredson)

This work, that even critics admit has a powerful and persuasive argument, is an "important book" that should be "moved ahead of others on your 'to-be-read list'" (Akers, 1991, p. 201). Authors Gottfredson and Hirschi laid out their Self-Control Theory of delinquency, in which the text "presents powerful arguments, turns many neat phrases, shows that much criminology is confused about its purpose or blind to its inconsistencies, demonstrates the profound implications of its argument for criminology, generally, and for the ways it is studied, specifically" (Tittle, 1991, p. 1610). This "provocative, brilliantly argued" (Sampson, 1992, p. 545) text not only lays out the argument for a new theory, but also challenges other theories' assumptions and propositions head on. It is because of this, that this text has become a "must read" (Sampson, 1992, p. 545) for anyone studying deviant behavior.

### Legacy

The legacy of Travis Hirschi cannot be overstated. Not only was he the most cited criminologist of the twentieth century (Cohn & Farrington, 1994), but he was also the intellectual father of a whole theoretical perspective in the study of deviance. Hirschi's work will be studied, examined, and tested for many decades to come. However, as many others in this text, Hirschi was unconcerned about his own legacy. When asked, he replied:

"I am uncomfortable with that. Clearly, if you want to have a legacy in the field the best way is through students…If I could count Michael Gottfredson and John Laub, and Robert Sampson and Chester Britt and Barbara Costello as my students, I'd give myself high marks indeed."

*(Laub, 2011, p. 323)*

## Gresham Sykes (1922–2010) & David Matza (1930–2018)

### Introduction

Gresham Sykes and David Matza are considered two of the most important theoretical predecessors of Travis Hirschi and are considered some of the earliest control theorists – even before that name was well established (Cullen & Agnew, 2011). A hybrid of differential association and control theories, Sykes and Matza's work (1957) defined what Sutherland's did not – deviant definitions – while also suggesting that these deviant definitions allow for the breakdown of controls that lead to deviant behavior. In a clear rejection of the subcultural theories that were popular at the time, these researchers suggested that one could maintain deviant definitions while still maintaining the norms of the larger conventional society. This is why these definitions are referred to as *Techniques of Neutralization* – they are not necessarily pro-deviant definitions, as much as they neutralize the controls that most juveniles are subjected to in school, home, and church (Cullen & Agnew, 2011).

### Biographical Profile

#### Gresham Sykes (1922–2010)

A precocious child with a family motivated to help him succeed, Gresham Sykes attended prestigious schools throughout his life – to include Brooks Academy and Princeton (https://www.asanet.org/obituary-gresham-sykes). However, when the Japanese attacked Pearl Harbor, Sykes found himself an officer in the US Army, helping to liberate Europe from the Nazi regime. Upon retirement after the War, Sykes returned to the academy where he graduated with his BA from Princeton and his Ph.D. from Northwestern University. His passion for sociology was mixed with his passion for art. Sykes took time off from his academic pursuits to occasionally pursue his artistic endeavors – even having his artwork displayed in galleries and private collections across the country and world. After a long battle with Alzheimer's disease, Gresham Sykes passed away in 2010.

#### David Matza (1930–2018)

Growing up in Harlem and the Bronx and playing stickball in the streets, Matza's life did not have an exciting beginning. However, his academic career exploded when he, as a young graduate student, along with Professor Gresham Sykes, wrote an article entitled "Techniques of neutralization: A theory of delinquency" (1957). Over 50 years later, this work is still being studied by sociologists and criminologists alike. After obtaining his Ph.D., Matza went to work at Berkeley, where he never left. Publishing more influential works, such as *Delinquency and Drift* (1964) and *Becoming Deviant* (1969), Matza's impact on the field cannot be overstated. In fact, Travis Hirschi even gave Matza credit for his own foray into control theories and research (Laub, 2011). Matza passed away in 2018 leaving behind a legacy of proud students, a loving family, and a lasting impact on the field of deviance.

## Profiling the Theory

Techniques of neutralization are justifications or excuses for committing deviant behavior (Sykes & Matza, 1957). The authors admit that these techniques are no different from "definitions favorable" to crime as advocated by Sutherland (1937). However, they also rejected subcultural theories that suggested deviant youth were part of a subculture that had widespread delinquent lifestyles. Rather, deviants "appear to recognize the moral validity of the dominant normative system in many instances" (Sykes & Matza, 1957, p. 665). Therefore, the techniques are used to justify or excuse their behavior in light of their deviation from the normative social order. This is evidenced, according to the authors, in the form of the guilt or shame that offenders feel when they commit deviant acts. However, even deviant acts, in certain situations, are acceptable (e.g. killing in war vs. murder). In order to combat these negative feelings, offenders use certain definitional techniques to neutralize their guilt and justify their behavior – hence, "Techniques of Neutralization".

The authors admit that "these techniques make up a crucial component of Sutherland's 'definitions favorable to the violation of law'" (Sykes & Matza, 1957, p. 667). Specifically, the social controls that are present to constrain illegal behavior are rendered ineffective at controlling the deviant, leaving him/her free to engage in delinquency without the feelings of shame or damage to self-image that crime may evince. The five major types of Techniques of Neutralization are as follows:

*Denial of Responsibility* – This technique allows the deviant to define him/herself as lacking the responsibility for their behavior (Sykes & Matza, 1957). This could be that the behavior is accidental, but more often, it is claimed that the deviant acts are due to situations or forces outside of the delinquent's control (e.g., unloving parents, bad neighborhood, etc.). This "billiard ball" self-concept suggests that the deviant is propelled by social forces into the situations in which they find themselves. A common thought process with this technique is "it's not my fault".

*Denial of Injury* – This technique goes to the heart of the deviant act – is the act wrong in and of itself (*mala in se*) or wrong only because those in power say it is wrong but has no moral consequence (*mala prohibita*). To the deviant individual, the question of wrongfulness depends on whther anyone was truly "injured" by the deviant act. While this question is open to interpretation, deviants tend to think there is no true injury in certain deviant acts (e.g., shoplifting, vandalism, etc.). This technique may make use of statements such as "they can afford the loss" or "this was just a prank".

*Denial of the Victim* – This technique is oftentimes confused with denial of injury due to the similarity of the wording – however there is an important distinction between the two. Denial of the victim denies the *status* of the wronged as a victim. Rather, the offender recognizes that their actions are harmful, and even counter to the law, however the "victim" deserved the action against them due to some other, greater offense. The deviance is a form of retaliation or punishment (e.g., Robin Hood is a thief, but he steals from the rich to give to the poor). In property crime, the "victim" may not be present during the vandalism and therefore too far removed to be a true victim. "They had it coming" is a common way this technique is communicated.

*Condemnation of the Condemners* – In this technique, the deviant shifts the attention off him/ herself and onto those who disapprove of the deviant behavior. Those detractors are hypocrites, deviants themselves, or jealous/have personal spite against the deviant. Therefore, their condemnation is no longer valid. The goal is to shift the focus off the deviant and onto those who are reacting to the deviance. Police may be stupid, racist, or classist. Teachers may have their "favorites". This technique is used to virtual perfection in the American political process. We often hear that one side's questionable behavior is okay because at least it is not as bad as the other side. Hearing "you're just as bad" is commonplace in this technique.

*Appeal to Higher Loyalties* – This technique rejects the needs of the larger, law-abiding society in favour of the needs of a more intimate social group (e.g., family, gang members, etc.). In this technique, the deviant admits that the behavior is wrong, but is faced with a dilemma when the pressing needs of the closer group conflict with the law. The need to protect or serve your family, clique, or other group take precedent. Examples of this can be seen in gang/mob culture with ideas like never snitching or refusal to cooperate with law enforcement.

Taken together, these techniques all chip away at the dominant social order, but do not represent a complete subculture of deviance that other theorists have suggested (Sykes & Matza, 1957). These techniques operate in the law-abiding society and act to break down the social controls that help constrain deviant behavior. To reiterate, if an individual is able to redefine their behavior as either not deviant, or excuse the behavior altogether, that behavior is more likely to happen.

Matza (1964) proposed his theory of *drift* that was a direct challenge to most of the theories of the time that suggested deviance happened due to some inherent difference between delinquents and non-delinquents. Matza continued to argue that if that were true, delinquents would commit crime at much higher rates and would not "age out" of delinquency. Since neither of these are true, something else must be causing the delinquency.

According to Matza (1964), the true cause of delinquency was *drift*. Drift occurs when an individual's social controls are loosened, freeing the individual to react to whatever prosocial or antisocial forces he/she happens upon. Rather than identifying a specific cause of delinquency, Matza identifies the *conditions* that make delinquency more likely. Matza did admit that there were some delinquents who were *committed* to a delinquent lifestyle; however, most delinquents were *drifters* who would move into and out of delinquency. When an individual drifts toward delinquency, there is an *episodic release* of moral restraints that allow an individual to become delinquent only temporarily. One form of these episodic releases is the use of Techniques Of Neutralization (Akers, et al., 2016).

### Profiling the Literature

NOTE: Both texts were written by Matza alone, but he relies on his original article with Sykes heavily.

### Delinquency and Drift *(1964)*

In his first major work, Matza "tilts his lance at an interesting assortment of juvenile legal practices, all of which he blames for helping set the juvenile adrift" (Littner & Hazard, 1965, p. 851). This text argues that, in large part, the system is to blame for breaking down the controls in a juvenile's life. If the system neutralizes what seems normal by the use of differing verbiage, the use of mental health professionals to explain the deviance, etc., then it teaches the juvenile that he/she is not responsible for their misdeeds. Worse, the delinquent may view the courts with such skepticism or as being unjust (due to hypocrisy, favoritism, and inconsistencies), that the juvenile feels a sense of injustice from the system and therefore is more willing to ignore the system's prohibitions. In this text, Matza writes in a "flowery manner" that not all readers enjoy (Littner & Hazard, 1965, p. 852). However, when pressed on this, Matza explains that he does write in a literary way because "writing should be taken seriously" (Weis, 1971, p. 36. Nevertheless, Matza's work is regarded as a "thoughtful critique of a legal subsystem that suffers an impoverishment of responsible principle" (Littner & Hazard, 1965, p. 856).

## Becoming Deviant *(1969)*

Viewed as "more significant than his earlier work" (Taylor, 1970, p. 288) and a "watershed in the sociology of deviance" (Beyleveld & Wiles, 1975, p. 338), *Becoming Deviant* is a text that examines a wide range of causes of deviance, but examines the philosophical under-pinnings of those ideas. Matza's (1969) described purpose was to explain how the "process of becoming deviant made little human sense without understanding the philosophical inner life of the subject as he bestows meaning on the events and materials that beset him" (p. 176). This text has been viewed as a "sociological masterpiece" and is just as engaging to new readers in the area as to the seasoned professorate. "There will be many who have been teaching criminology for years without a notion that it was either so interesting or indeed so significant as it becomes in these pages" (Taylor, 1970, p. 291).

## *Legacy*

Sykes and Matza, through their Techniques of Neutralization, were able to accomplish something most unique – they developed a theory that is used by both learning theorists and control theorists; two groups typically at odds with each other (Cullen & Agnew, 2011). The relationship between neutralization and crime has some support, with those who adopt more neutralizations engaging in more crime. Taylor (1970) believed Matza to be "one of the small group of writers who have helped to transform deviancy theory from a developmental trend in academic criminology into a running critique of American sociology" (p. 288). Sykes (who wrote and contributed far more than the scope of this text allows to comment upon) was described by David Toscano as "the rare individual who could combine a keen academic and analytical mind with the eye and skill of an artist" (2010). Whether you view them as learning or control theorists, Sykes and Matza have cemented their place in the deviance literature with a popular explanation to why crime takes place.

## Stanley Cohen (1942–2013)

### *Introduction*

Using a labeling perspective to advance the idea of *moral panics*, Stanley Cohen was influential in our understanding of how society reacts to crime. While the idea of moral panic is not a clearly defined theory as much as it is an abstract idea (Cohen, 1972; Denham, 2008), the concept is used to characterize situations that have been highly exaggerated by the media or politicians based on seemingly obvious facts (Denham, 2008). A harsh critic of most governmental institutions, Cohen (1972) saw these moral panics more as an ability for those in power to maintain their power, rather than as real issues in need of control. Regardless of the theoretical operationalization of the concepts, the idea of moral panic is now common parlance in criminological and sociological circles.

## Biographical Profile

Born in Johannesburg, South Africa in 1942, Stanley Cohen was the son of a Jewish businessman from Lithuania (Pioneers of Social Research Biography). Aware of the discrimination faced by both Jewish and black citizens, Cohen was a Zionist who planned to settle in Israel after graduation. However, while at the University of Witwatersrand, Cohen's focus shifted to the discrimination faced by black people – specifically their exclusion from higher education. Cohen continued his education and graduated with his Ph.D. from the London School of Economics, where he wrote his dissertation on the societal reactions to juvenile delinquency.

Heavily influenced by the conflict between rival youth groups in the United Kingdom (Mods and Rockers), Cohen, with a labelling perspective, began interviewing those involved and examining the media coverage of the events. This led him to develop his concept of *moral panic*. While this was a major area of Cohen's focus, he, along with his family eventually realized his Zionist dream and relocated to Israel to teach in the Criminology Department at Hebrew University. There, he focused his efforts on Israeli/Palestinian relations and denounced torture. This led to another of Cohen's most influential works, *States of Denial: Knowing about Atrocities and Suffering* (2001). Cohen moved back to London where he taught economics at the London School of Economics until 2005 (Taylor, 2005). Cohen died at the age of 70 in 2013 after a battle with Parkinson's Disease.

## Profiling the Theory

Moral panic, while not a true theory of criminal behavior, is still an important component to the study of the sociology of deviance. Drawing on Leslie Wilkins's (1964) work on *deviance amplification*, Cohen suggested that powerful groups target the deviance of smaller groups in order to maintain their power and influence. In this way, a media-driven moral panic will ensue as the exaggerated deviance or deviant becomes a mass communicated truth (Denham, 2008). The more often a story is reported in the media, the truer it becomes. By using this *deviant amplification*, the powerful group reaffirms moral boundaries in what some scholars have referred to as "symbolic moral universes" (Ben-Yehuda, 1990).

One reason moral panics are so successfully adopted by society is because they "often emanate from a key event and involve a familiar issue" (Denham, 2008, pp. 946–947). This allows what psychology calls "the availability heuristic" to take place (Tversky & Kahneman, 1973). In simplified terms, the more easily something is recalled, the more important it becomes. With consistent media coverage, folk devils, or "visual representations of what we should not be" (Cohen, 1972), are more easily accessible in the public's minds.

There are countless examples of moral panics that are easily accessible – e.g. heroin abuse, mugging, or terrorism (Waddington, 1986; Rothe, & Muzzatti, 2004; Denham, 2008). In all of these cases, these actions are not the most common forms of drug abuse or victimization; however, they are all are used to "shed light on profit maximization in media industries, decisions to hold congressional hearings, and resources allocation toward the resolution of social problems" (Denham, 2008, p. 958). In this way, Cohen (1972) argues, the "role of the media in shaping and manipulating popular opinion in a fashion that is coherent with the interests of the state's agents of social control" (Innes, 2005, p. 107) is the cause of these panics.

### *Profiling the Literature*

### Folk Devils and Moral Panic: The Creation of the Mods and Rockers *(1972)*

This text, (which was so popular it justified several editions) examines the concept of *moral panics* that take place within our society. Namely, how we perceive certain phenomena or individuals (crime/criminals) is largely dependent on how these concepts are explained to us by those in power/the media. Arguing that those in power and in the media will use sensationalized verbiage when describing behaviors or groups, the text "traces these reactions, dissecting the rhetoric to show how a set of minor incidents become defined as a major problem" (Best, 1982, p. 120). Although the book was published decades ago, "this classic study has endured over time, has inspired many other studies, and still has contemporary resonance for media scholars" (Boreham, 2007, p. 169).

### States of Denial: Knowing about Atrocities and Suffering *(2001)*

Described as a "a noble tract of our times, written by a modest, honest man" (Morgan, 2002), *States of Denial* details Cohen's strong critique of torture being used by nations. He defines the opposing ideas of denial and acknowledgement, suggesting that to truly acknowledge atrocities of the past, we must first acknowledge truth and reality. This is something that is not often done, as politicians and researchers tend to use post-modern theorizing to suggest "established scientific facts are merely social constructions" (Cohen [1972]2001, p. 282). This denial of truth allows for a necessary gap in the collective acknowledgement that prevents individuals from ever confronting the atrocities and suffering they may have contributed to. Of this text, Tombs (2003) has written, "this is 'not beyond politics' and it is not beyond morality" (p. 115). While this is a challenging book to all who read it, it is "compelling moral sociology" (Olick, 2002, p. 1135), something the field needs.

### *Legacy*

Cohen's influence on the field of sociology of deviance and criminology cannot be overstated. While he may not have developed a true theoretical approach that is widely followed, there can be no doubt that he left his mark on the disciplines. Confronting those in power head on, Cohen was not afraid to take them to task on his perceived abuses of power and manipulation of the public. His "concern with human rights and their violation" (Taylor, 2013) led him into active conflict with a variety of nations and led him to play a central role in the development of the Center for the Study of Human Rights at the London School of Economics. Like many in this text, and as all true academics should strive, Cohen was not as concerned with his own legacy as he was with making a lasting influence on the world – to that end, there is no doubt he was successful.

## References

Akers, R.L. (1991). Self-control as a general theory of crime. *Journal of Quantitative Criminology*, 7(2), 201–211.

Akers, R.L., Sellers, C.D.S., & Jennings, W.G. (2016). *Criminological Theories: Introduction, Evaluation, & Application* (7th ed.). New York: Oxford University Press.

Becker, H.S. (1963). *Outsiders: Studies in the Sociology of Deviance*. New York:Free Press.

Beeley, A.L. (1954). A socio-psychological theory of crime and delinquency: A contribution to etiology. *The Journal of Criminal Law, Criminology, and Police Science*, 45(4), 391–399.

Ben-Yehuda, N. (1990). *The Politics and Morality of Deviance: Moral Panics, Drug Abuse, Deviant Science, and Reversed Stigmatization*. Albany, NY: SUNY Press.

Best, J. (1982). *Folk Devils and Moral Panics: The Creation of the Mods and Rockers* [Book Review]. *Deviant Behavior*, 4(1), 119–120.

Best, J. (1994). *Social Problems*. New York: W.W. Norton & Co.

Best, J. (2017). Joseph Gusfield and social problems theory. *American Sociologist*, 48, 14–22. doi:10.1007/s12108-015-9295-4.

Beyleveld, D., & Wiles, P. (1975). Man and method in David Matza's *Becoming Deviant*. *British Journal of Criminology*, 15(2), 337–338.

Boreham, D. (2007). *Folk Devils and Moral Panics*, 3rd ed. [Book Review]. *Media International Australia, Incorporating Culture & Policy*, 123, 168–169.

Cohen, S. ([1972]2001). *Folk Devils and Moral Panics: The Creation of the Mods and Rockers*. London: Routledge.

Cohen, S. (2013). *States of Denial: Knowing about Atrocities and Suffering*. Hoboken, NJ: John Wiley & Sons.

Cohn, E.G., & Farrington, D.P. (1994). Who are the most influential criminologists in the English-speaking world?. *The British Journal of Criminology*, 34(2), 204–225.

Conrad, P. (2017). Reflections on Joseph R. Gusfield. *American Sociologist*, 48(1), 4–7. doi:10.1007/s12108-016-9327-8.

Costello, B.J., & Laub, J.H. (2020). Social control theory: The legacy of Travis Hirschi's causes of delinquency. *Annual Review of Criminology*, 3, 21–41.

Cullen, F.T., & Agnew, R. (2011). *Criminological Theory: Past to Present. Essential Readings*. New York: Oxford University Press.

Denham, B.E. (2008). Folk devils, news icons and the construction of moral panics: Heroin chic and the amplification of drug threats in contemporary society. *Journalism Studies*, 9(6), 945–961.

Fine, G.A. (1995). *A Second Chicago School? The Development of a Postwar American Sociology*. Chicago: University of Chicago Press.

Goffman, E. (1963). *Stigma: Notes of the Management of Spoiled Identity*. New York: Simon & Schuster.

Gottfredson, M.R., & Hirschi, T. (1990). *A General Theory of Crime*. Palo Alto, CA: Stanford University Press.

Gusfield, J.R. (1963). *Symbolic Crusade: Status Politics and the American Temperance Movement*. Urbana: University of Illinois Press.

Gusfield, J.R. (1967). Moral passage: The moral process in public designations of deviance. *Social Problems*, 15(2), 175–188.

Gusfield, J.R. (1968). On legislating morals: The symbolic process of designating deviance. *California Law Review*, 56(1), 54–73. doi:10.2307/3479496.

Gusfield, J.R. (1981) *The Culture of Public Problems: Drink-driving and the Symbolic Order*. Chicago: University of Chicago Press.

Gusfield, J.R. (1990). My life and soft times. In B.M. Berger, *Authors of their Lives: Intellectual Autobiographies of Twenty American Sociologists*. Berkeley: University of California Press (pp. 104–129).

Hirschi, T. (1969). *Causes of Delinquency*. Berkeley, CA: University of California Press.

Hirschi, T. (2004). Self-control and crime. In R.F. Baumeister & K.D. Vohs (Eds.), *Handbook of Self-regulation*. New York: Guilford Press (pp. 537–552).

Innes, M. (2005). A short history of the idea of moral panic. A Review of the book *Folk Devils and Moral Panics (3rd)* by Stanley Cohen. *Crime, Media, Culture*, 1(1), 106–111.

Laub, J.H. (2011). Control theory: The life and work of Travis Hirschi.In F.T. Cullen, C.L. Jonson, A. J. Myer & F. Adler, *The Origins of American Criminology: Advances in Criminological Theory*. London and New York: Routledge (pp. 277–331).

Littner, N., & Hazard Jr, G.C. (1965). Review of *Delinquency and Drift* by David Matza. *University of Chicago Law Review*, 32(4), 850–856.

Matza, D. (1964). *Delinquency and Drift*. New Brunswick, NJ: Transaction Publishers.

Matza, D. (1969). *Becoming Deviant*. New Brunswick, NJ: Transaction Publishers.

Morgan, R. (2002). *States of Denial: Knowing about Atrocities and Suffering. British Journal of Criminology*, 42 (4), 807–809.

Olick, J.K. (2002). Review of the book States *of Denial:* Knowing *about Atrocities and Suffering* by S. Cohen. *American Journal of Sociology*, 107(4), 1134–1135.

Phillips, L. (1972). Review of the book Causes of Delinquency by Travis Hirschi. *Journal of Human Resources*, 8(1), 119–121.

Pioneers of Social Research. Stan Cohen. UK Data Service, funded by the ESRC, Economic and Social Data Service, undated. https://www.ukdataservice.ac.uk/teaching-resources/pioneers/pioneer-detail?id=pioneer_people_cohen

Pratt, T.C., & Cullen, F.T. (2000). The empirical status of Gottfredson and Hirschi's general theory of crime: A meta-analysis. *Criminology*, 38(3), 931–964.

Reiss, A.J. (1951). Delinquency as the failure of personal and social controls. *American Sociological Review*, 16(2), 196–207.

Roizen, R. (2016). Joseph R. Gusfield, 1923–2015. *Addiction*, 111(2), 371–373.

Rothe, D., & Muzzatti, S.L. (2004). Enemies everywhere: Terrorism, moral panic, and US civil society. *Critical Criminology*, 12(3), 327–350.

Sampson, R.J. (1992). Review of the book A General Theory of Crime by M. Gottfredson & M. Hirschi. *Social Forces*, 71(2), 545–546.

Snipes, J.B., Bernard, T.J., & Gerould, A.L. (2010). *Vold's Theoretical Criminology*. New York: Oxford University Press.

Srole, L. (1956). Social integration and certain corollaries: An exploratory study. *American Sociological Review*, 21(6), 709–716.

Sutherland, E.H. (1937). The professional thief. *Journal of Criminal Law and Criminology (1931–1951)*, 161–163.

Sykes, G.M., & Matza, D. (1957). Techniques of neutralization: A theory of delinquency. *American Sociological Review*, 22(6), 664–670.

Taylor, L. (1970). Review of Becoming Deviant. *The British Journal of Criminology*, 10(3), 288–291.

Taylor, L. (23 January 2013). Stanley Cohen obituary. *The Guardian*. London.

Tittle, C.R. (1991). Review of the book A General Theory of Crime by M. Gottfredson and T. Hirschi. *American Journal of Sociology*, 96(6), 1609–1611.

Toby, J. (1957). Social disorganization and stake in conformity: Complementary factors in the predatory behavior of hoodlums. *Journal of Criminal Law, Criminology, & Police Science, 48(1)*, 12–17.

Tombs, J. (2003). Review of the book States of Denial: Knowing about Atrocities and Suffering by S. Cohen. *Punishment & Society*, 5(1), 113–115.

Tversky, A., & Kahneman, D. (1973). Availability: A heuristic for judging frequency and probability. *Cognitive Psychology*, 5(2), 207–232.

Waddington, P.A. (1986). Mugging as a moral panic: A question of proportion. *British Journal of Sociology*, 37(2), 245–259.

Weis, J.G. (1971). Dialogue with David Matza: An interview conducted and prepared for *Issues in Criminology*. *Issues in Criminology*, 6(1), 33–54.

Wilkins, L.T. (1964). *Social Deviance*. London: Tavistock.

# 5

# LEARNING THEORIES

## Tarde, Sutherland, Akers

## Introduction

This is the second major sociological explanation in the study of crime and deviant behavior. This group of theories suggests that criminal behavior is not substantially different from any other behavior in an individual's life. Individuals simply learn how to be deviant from those around them. While this is a simplistic idea, the effects of this research are wide-reaching as learning theorists suggest that their theoretical views explain both conforming and deviant behavior.

Ideas of imitating those around you (Tarde), how individuals define certain acts (Sutherland), and who one associates with (Akers) are all discussed in this chapter. This type of learning is not substantively different from any other kind of learning that happens in people and therefore some of the theorists below argue these theories could be used to explain behavior outside of deviant contexts. Taken together, these theories cover both the content of what is learned and the process that takes place when one learns a new behavior.

## Gabriel Tarde (1843–1904)

### Introduction

A contemporary of Émile Durkheim and a fierce critic of Cesare Lombroso, Gabriel Tarde was a French sociologist, magistrate, and lawyer who established himself as an intellectual in France while he was alive, but whose influence on the larger field of criminology waxes and wanes (King, 2016; Renneville, 2018). Like other sociologists of that time (e.g. Durkheim), Tarde influenced a lot more than just the study of crime and the sociology of deviance, however, this chapter will be focused mostly on the influence of Tarde on the field of criminology.

### Biographical Profile

Born in 1843, Tarde came of age during the Third Republic of France that saw tumultuous times marked by economic recession mixed with a heightened debate about crime and

DOI: 10.4324/9781003036609-5

criminal justice (Renneville, 2018). Having been born into a minor professional family in 1843, Tarde was always a studious child (King, 2016; Renneville, 2018). With expectations that he would enter some scientific discipline, Tarde travelled to Paris to attend university where he studied law. His career saw him work as a magistrate, lawyer, professor, and director of criminal statistics for the Ministry of Justice in Paris (King, 2016). Never satisfied with his work, Tarde continued to engage in academic research and publishing. This helped him to be known as one of the major criminological figures in nineteenth-century France (Renneville, 2018).

As a statistician and researcher, Tarde recognized serious flaws in the popular Lombrosian theory of crime and the Positivist School (Wilson, 1954). Using data and statistics from the criminal anthropologists themselves, Tarde showed the lack of support for the idea of a born criminal, shattering the theory. Lombroso was not the only criminologist with whom Tarde found himself in conflict. Tarde and Durkheim also fiercely debated sociology and criminology, with history declaring Durkheim as the winner (Thomassen, 2012). Tarde was an established figure in French life, 15 years Durkheim's senior, with a more storied educational reputation. It was therefore unsurprising when Tarde was named chair of modern philosophy at Collège de France, much to Durkheim's anger (Thomassen, 2012). However, their disagreements were more than just professional. Durkheim felt that Tarde's sociology and criminology was nothing more than restated philosophy, while Durkheim wanted to establish sociology as a new, independent scientific discipline. This was the foundation of all their debates. Tarde sought to combine sociology with other disciplines and form a subfield, Durkheim sought to start a new field altogether. In the end, Durkheim won the debate, as sociology is clearly now its own academic, scientific discipline. In fact, criminology, as its own scientific discipline, has its roots clearly held in the sociological tradition, in large part thanks to the conflict between Durkheim and Tarde.

### Profiling the Theory

The major theoretical idea proposed by Tarde was the idea of *imitation* (Tarde, 1890). Defining imitation as the "powerful, generally unconscious, always partly mysterious, action by means of which we account for all the phenomena of society" (1890, p. 322), Tarde viewed crime as a social phenomenon like any other in our society. Beginning with the urban, wealthy, and powerful, and traveling downward to the rural and poorest members, society is bound together by the fancies and fashions of the upper class (Beirne, 1987). Imitation affects all aspects of life, not just crime. It causes individuals to be both good and evil; to make prosocial choices as well as antisocial. Most crimes, including drunkenness, smoking, adultery, assassinations, arson, etc. all began in the feudal nobility and were transmitted through this imitative power to the masses.

A devoutly religious man, Tarde viewed crime as a shift in devotion from religious (or traditional) morality to the worship of gold as part of the imitative process that caused crime (Beirne, 1987). Still, Tarde valued the "social" aspects of imitation such that in a letter to an interested writer on reform schools, Tarde penned, "where there is high morality among the parents whose children attend the school, it can do much good; where the immorality of the families is notorious, it can only produce more or less bad efforts" (Tarde, 1897, p. 263). He also differentiated individual deviance from *mob* deviance such that a mob is a "gathering of heterogeneous elements, unknown to one another; but as soon as a spark of passion, having flashed out from one of these elements, electrifies this confused mass, there takes place a sort of sudden organization, a spontaneous generation" (Tarde, 1890, p. 323). This form of *mental contagion* is what Tarde used to explain the seeming abnormality of mob formation and behavior during his time.

While Tarde also discussed prison reform, philosophies of science, and recidivism, those are outside the scope of this text. Further, not all who study Tarde's work are of the opinion that his theoretical ideas were ever fully refined or fleshed out (King, 2016; Renneville, 2018). "Tarde's system seems to offer contemporary social theory very little substantively in terms of concepts or empirical evidence" (King, 2016 p. 58). Other have argued that many of his written works "makes it difficult for the reader to gain a clear picture of the author's theoretical stance" (Renneville, 2018, p. 15).

## Profiling the Literature

### La Criminalité Comparée *(1886)*

This work of comparative criminology was published when Tarde was still working as a magistrate on the bench (Renneville, 2018). This was the first time readers were exposed to the serious flaws of *L'uomo delinquente* (*The Criminal Man*) written by Lombroso. This was also the text that launched Tarde onto the scene as "one of the leading specialists in the field" (Renneville, 2018). A text of previously published essays of unequal length all addressed the issue of crime and deviance. In the first chapter, Tarde made an extended critical review of Lombroso's work. The second chapter was dedicated to criminal statistics and the issue of recidivism. Recidivism was evidence of *contagious imitation* indicating that the born criminal was not the real issue in criminal causality. The third and fourth chapters covered problems in criminal law and the *criminal geography*. (While interesting from a larger criminological stance, they are also outside the scope of this text). The text was widely discussed in scholarly circles with reviews being overwhelmingly positive (Renneville, 2018). Even Durkheim, a critic of Tarde's, praised the text as introducing the new science of criminology (Durkheim, 1886).

### La Philosophie Pénale *(1890)*

Tarde used this text to develop his theory of *criminal responsibility*, viewing crime as a mix between the free-will of the classical school and the determinism of positivists (Renneville, 2018). The second largest debate of his time, after Lombrosoian *crime type*, was that of responsibility. Specifically, Tarde was interested in the legal conundrum of multiple offenders. If there can be multiple offenders, all equally responsible, could there be crimes committed by a whole nation?

## Legacy

Tarde was more than just an academic and legal scholar. A "writer and poet" (Thomassen, 2012, p. 248), Tarde died as one of the most famous sociologists in nineteenth-century France (Kinnunen, 1996). While his work and influence have been "regularly forgotten, rediscovered, and then forgotten again", there is no question that Tarde deserves his rightful place in the history of criminological thought that so dominates our academic discipline today. Tarde has also been recognized as the first theorist to recognize Social Learning, even in its nascent stages, as a cause of deviant behavior (Hinduja & Ingram, 2009). While clearly influential in his time, Tarde's lack of a secure position in a university setting, with no strong allies and no trained disciples, all but guaranteed his intellectual work would die with him

(Beirne, 1987). To put it succinctly, "there would be no 'Tardian School' of criminology" (Renneville, 2018, p. 16). However, not all share the opinion of Tarde's insignificance. "He was an independent thinker as well as an original one who left an indelible mark on criminology" (Wilson, 1954, p. 11).

## Edwin H. Sutherland (1883–1950)

### Introduction

Edwin H. Sutherland is arguably the leading criminologist of the twentieth century (Vold, 1951). His major contributions are not limited to just his theory of Differential Association – he is also credited with developing the idea of white-collar crime. Sutherland is said to have been "sincere, objective, soft spoken, gentle, and respectful" (Martin, Mutchnick, & Austin, 1990, p. 139), however, his work was anything but soft spoken and gentle. Sutherland's work has made some of the loudest splashes and invigorated some of the liveliest debates in American criminological circles. Both his theoretical proposals and his critique of corporate America made him worth profiling in criminology.

### Biographical Profile

Little is known about Sutherland's upbringing (Martin, et al., 1990). He was born one of eight childrens to George and Lizzie Sutherland; all were raised to respect education and religious pursuits (Schuessler, 1973). While it seems that Sutherland eventually broke with the church, the ideas of moral right and wrong, as opposed to legal right and wrong, are clear in his work on white-collar crime.

Sutherland's higher education career is atypical to what one would think of a giant in any field. His Ph.D. was granted in Sociology and Political Economy with most of his course work being in Political Economy (Geis & Goff, 1983). Sutherland found the discipline of sociology to be too far removed from the problems that the theories were supposed to be addressing and found the methods used to research such theories wanting (Gaylord & Galliher, 1983). Also, the majority of his major contributions to the field came later in his career. In fact, the first six years of his career, he only published one article (Geis & Goff, 1983).

Sutherland's career was marked by numerous moves to colleges primarily throughout the Midwest. Unlike many other prominent researchers and theorists, Sutherland was not an efficient researcher. However, he was compulsively thorough (Snodgrass, 1972). The amount that he published seems modest, but there is no question that the impact of what he published is quite large.

### Profiling the Theory

Sutherland's contributions began when he was the pioneering researcher into professional theft and white-collar crime (Sutherland 1937; 1940; 1949). Sutherland's basic suggestion in white-collar crime is that just because something is not a violation of a criminal statute does not mean it is not a crime.

Sutherland is best known for his theory of Differential Association (1947). Sutherland laid out the theory of Differential Association in his textbook, *Principles of Criminology* – which was the leading text in the field for over 30 years (Akers, Sellers, & Jennings, 2016).

Differential Association Theory has nine major propositions:

1.  Criminal behavior is learned.
2.  Criminal behavior is learned in interaction with other persons in a process of communication.
3.  The principal part of the learning of criminal behavior occurs within intimate personal groups.
4.  When criminal behavior is learned, the learning includes (a) techniques of committing the crime, which are sometimes very complicated, sometimes simple; (b) the specific direction of motives, drives, rationalizations, and attitudes.
5.  The specific direction of motives and drives is learned from definitions of the legal codes as favorable or unfavorable.
6.  A person becomes delinquent because of an excess of definitions favorable to violation of law over definitions unfavorable to violation of the law.
7.  Differential associations may vary in frequency, duration, priority, and intensity.
8.  The process of learning criminal behavior by association with criminal and anti-criminal patterns involves all of the mechanisms that are involved in any other learning.
9.  While criminal behavior is an expression of general needs and values, it is not explained by those needs and values, since non-criminal behavior is an expression of the same needs and values.

Differential Association Theory, simply put, posits that criminal behavior, like any other behavior, is learned. This learning takes place through a process of symbolic interaction with others. These others are typically members of an individual's primary or intimate groups. While all nine propositions make up the theory, the sixth proposition is viewed as the principle of differential association (Akers, et al., 2016). More specifically, "a person becomes delinquent because of an excess of definitions favorable to violations of the law over definitions unfavorable to violations of the law" (Sutherland, 1947, p. 6). The process of acquiring these deviant or conforming definitions is what Sutherland called *differential association*.

Differential Association Theory explains deviant behavior by exposure to others' definitions as either favorable or unfavorable to crime (Sutherland, 1947). If an excess of definitions favorable to crime is present, criminal behavior is more likely to take place. However, it is not simple association with antisocial individuals that makes one deviant. Modalities of association are also important. That is, if people are exposed to deviant definitions first (priority), more frequently, for a longer period of time (duration), and with greater intensity (importance), they are more likely to be deviant. In the same way, if people are exposed to conforming definitions first (priority), more frequently, for a longer period of time (duration), and with greater intensity (importance), they are more likely to be conforming.

Sutherland's Differential Association Theory suggested that criminal behavior was a closed system in that differential association was both a necessary and sufficient cause of crime. Differential association is a necessary cause of crime because no one would initiate criminal behavior without association with criminal behavior patterns. Differential association is a sufficient cause of crime because all individuals who have such associations with deviant behavioral patterns participate in deviant behavior, unless inhibited by stronger associations with pro-social patterns of behavior.

Sutherland, with the help of Donald Cressey (1968), suggested that cultural or normative conflict also plays a role in deviant behavior such that certain cultures or norms for behavior are acceptable in certain groups, but more broadly rejected or illegal in the broader society. For example, underage drinking is illegal in broader society, but permissible during certain religious ceremonies like communion and Sabbath celebrations. The differential association of

Christian or Jewish individuals (in this example) allows and encourages the consumption of alcohol, whereas broader society would probably reject the notion that teenagers should be drinking.

## White-Collar Crime

Differential Association Theory is not the only way that Sutherland made an impact on the fields of sociology and criminology. Sutherland also introduced the idea of white-collar or corporate crime. In 1939, at the age of 56, Sutherland delivered his presidential address to the American Sociological Society entitled "The White Collar Criminal". He later published his address and wrote a book in 1949 called *White Collar Crime* detailing the concept. This thought-provoking text defines white-collar crime as "a violation of criminal law by a person of the upper socioeconomic class in the course of his occupational activities" (Sutherland, 1949, p. 112). Basically, Sutherland challenged the view that poor, lower class individuals committed crime. Instead, respectable people, during their careers, commit crime by using their positions to enrich themselves.

Sutherland tested the hypothesis that crime is more evenly distributed across class structure by analyzing the 70 largest corporations in America in 1929 for criminal violations. While there is some debate as to the inclusion criteria of the violations (Sutherland used a more liberal definition of crime, to include federal administrative regulation violations, than some felt was appropriate), Sutherland found that the corporations were convicted of 14 offenses on average. He viewed these corporate criminals as a greater danger to society than street crime because corporate offenders were damaging social relations, public morale, and the structure of society and its organization. In Sutherland's mind, these damages were significantly more destructive than ordinary street crime (Reckless, 1973; Martin, et al., 1990).

## Profiling the Literature

### Principles of Criminology (1947)

This is the work for which Sutherland is most widely known (Vold, 1951). In this text, Sutherland lays out the basic propositions for this theory of Differential Association and advocates approaching criminal behavior from a more sociological perspective than other theorists at the time. "Criminal behavior is part of human behavior, has much in common with non-criminal behavior, and must be explained within the same general framework as any other human behavior" (Sutherland, 1947, pp. 4–5). This was a revolutionary idea at the time.

### White Collar Crime (1949)

Sutherland's first formal discussion of *White-Collar Crime* came as his presidential address at the American Society of Sociology's annual meeting. Sutherland proceeded to write up his major ideas of white-collar deviance in this text. Sutherland stated

> The thesis of this book, stated positively, is that persons of the upper socio-economic class engage in much criminal behavior; that this criminal behavior differs from the criminal behavior of the lower socio-economic class principally in the administrative procedures which are used in dealing with the offenders; and that variations in administrative procedures are not significant from the point of view of causation of crime....

White collar crime may be defined approximately as a crime committed by a person of respectability and high social status in the course of his occupation.

*(1949, p. 9)*

### Legacy

When profiling the legacy of Edwin Sutherland, it is difficult to assess which area of his professional life has had more influence. In his theoretical work on Differential Association Theory, Sutherland leaves behind a legacy upon which several other leaders in criminology are standing – to include Ronald Akers, Gresham Sykes, and David Matza. Differential Association Theory is the foundational theory that Akers used when developing Social Learning Theory (Burgess & Akers, 1966), which has become one of the most widely accepted theories of crime to ever be empirically validated. Also, Sykes and Matza's (1957) Techniques Of Neutralization were originally developed to be types of definitions favorable to crime as originally stated by Sutherland (Akers et al., 2016).

In terms of his other legacy, white-collar crime, Sutherland quite literally developed a new type of deviance that was not otherwise discussed in sociological circles. In fact, Sutherland was able to support and validate his theory of Differential Association by using white-collar offending as the form of deviance that no other theory of crime at the time could explain. This is one of the main reasons there was so much hostility to the idea of white-collar offending as a type of crime. Theoretical orientations like strain, labeling, and control, lacked the face validity needed to explain corporate deviance. Regardless of his contemporaries' acceptance of his definition of white-collar crime or their support for his theory, there is no doubt that Sutherland left a mark on the field of criminology that can still be felt today. In eulogizing Sutherland, Vold accurately prognosticated,

> It is not just empty eulogy to say that the stimulating challenge of his ideas coupled with the effect on others of his sensitive, kind, and generous personality have influenced profoundly an entire generation of criminologists, both in America and in other countries. It seems likely that for a long time to come criminologists will continue to concern themselves with the further exploration of problems brought into sharp focus by his work. A modest man in everything, he probably would not ask for more.
>
> *(1951, p. 7)*

## Ronald L. Akers (1939–)

### Introduction

Ronald Akers is an American criminologist most well-known for his development of Social Learning Theory – one of the core theoretical perspectives in criminology today (Pratt, et al., 2010). A contemporary of Travis Hirschi, Albert Cohen, Richard Cloward and Lloyd Ohlin, Howard Becker and Richard Quinney as well as many other prominent theorists, Akers came of age in a time when the development and testing of theories was commonplace, and the field was ripe with competing ideas (Akers, 2011). However, the theorist that Akers believed offered the best explanation to deviant behavior was Edwin Sutherland (Akers, 2011). Akers, with the help of Robert Burgess (Burgess and Akers, 1966), modified Sutherland's original theory into what we know today as Social Learning Theory.

### Biographical Profile

Ronald Akers was born on January 7, 1939 and raised in New Albany, Indiana (Akers, 2011). The son of "lower blue-collar working class" parents (Akers, 2011, p. 348), Akers was raised in a religious home that was grounded by love, strict rules, and discipline. While his parents had no formal higher education, Akers recognized that they were bright people who worked hard to support their family. Akers was also bright and hard-working, receiving high grades in virtually all his classes, but he also had discipline problems which would often lead to fights. Luckily, he was never in any serious trouble and had no run-ins with law enforcement during this time.

Akers developed a desire to be a schoolteacher upon entering college and believes this was largely due to his own teachers being the only model of educated people he had (Akers, 2011). To that end, he decided that his specialty topic would be social studies which is where he received his first in-depth exposure to sociology – a subject area which dominated his elective list. As graduation approached, Akers's fraternity faculty advisor suggested he pursue graduate education, and was able to get him admission to Kent State University for his master's degree – all without Akers having to take the Graduate Record Examinations (GRE) nor having to secure letters of recommendation. Upon receiving his master's degree, Akers became a full-time instructor at Kent State. His department chair thought he should pursue a Ph.D., but Akers was worried about money. Akers was accepted to the Ph.D. program at the University of Kentucky the following year – a condition of his instructorship was applying to doctoral programs. Without strong mentors, Akers may not ever have ended up in graduate school at all, let alone become one of the most influential figures in criminology.

Akers Christian faith plays a big role in his life, but that did not attract him to sociology per se (Akers, 2011). In fact, Akers stated that "Sociology was less secularized than it is now and at that time stressed building a value-free science of society" (2011, p. 351). To support this notion, Akers states that he has always taken a positivist, value-free approach to his research. So, it stands to reason that he denies that his faith played a role in his development of Social Learning Theory, however, he does acknowledge that it played a role in his policy preferences and recommendations.

### Profiling the Theory

Together with Robert Burgess, Akers authored Social Learning Theory – then referred to as "Differential Association-Reinforcement Theory" (Burgess & Akers, 1966). The theory was an extension of Sutherland's Differential Association Theory; however, Sutherland never specified how learning takes place (Akers, et al., 2016; Snipes, et al., 2010). Burgess and Akers (1966), quite successfully, attempted to fill the void in the theoretical development of Differential Association by specifying how learning takes place. While Burgess's career took him in a different direction, Akers dedicated his career to developing, testing, and evaluating what would eventually become known as Social Learning Theory (Akers, 1973; Akers, Krohn, Lanza-Kaduce, & Radosevich, 1979). Specifically, Akers (1985; 1988) developed four variables that together make up Social Learning Theory – Differential Association, Differential Reinforcement, Definitions Favorable and Unfavorable to Crime, and Imitation.

Beginning with Differential Association, Akers suggested the group with which one associates provides the social context in which learning operates. These associations could be prosocial or antisocial (e.g. church youth group vs. youth gang affiliation), but they provide the normative and interactional dimensions in which behavior is learned. An individual's

Differential Association with either prosocial or antisocial peers and family also provides the social environment in which they are reinforced, where they learn definitions favorable or unfavorable to crime, and where imitation takes place (Akers, 1973; 1977; 1985).

Differential Reinforcement refers to the balance of anticipated or actual rewards or punishments an individual receives as a consequence of their behavior (Akers, 1985; 1988). Whether a deviant behavior will continue or desist is a direct result of the rewards or punishments the behavior elicits. The probability that an act will be committed or repeated is increased by a rewarding outcome and decreased by a punishing outcome. It is important to note that the rewarding outcome can be social, nonsocial, or even self-reinforcing. For example, the approval of family and friends would be social reinforcement. Non-social reinforcement could be feelings of pride, satisfaction, or even the effects of drugs or alcohol. Self-reinforcement involves an element of self-control over one's own rewards or punishments, even when alone.

Definitions favorable or unfavorable to crime (for sake of space, "Definitions") are one's own attitudes or meanings that one attaches to specific behavior (Akers, 1985; 1988). In other words, these are one's own rationalizations as to why committing certain crimes are either good or bad. For example, some people argue that they would never do drugs, but smoke marijuana or drink alcohol underage. This may be because they do not define those as drugs, while others abstain from those behaviors due to negative definitions of those behaviors.

Imitation is the idea that one engages in behavior after the observation of similar behavior in others (Akers, 1985; 1988). This initiation of behavior typically takes place due to vicarious reinforcement (Bandura, 1977) – or the observation of positive rewards for the same behavior in others. It is argued that imitation is more important in behavior acquisition than it is in behavioral maintenance because *how* the behavior is reinforced becomes more important (Akers, et al., 2016).

While this theory has four variables, it also operates as a process of sequence and feedback effects such that a change in any one variable influences the other remaining variables (Akers, et al., 2016). For example, a change in the associations one spends time with may affect the definitions, reinforcement, and imitation that one experiences. Similarly, a change in reinforcement may cause one to seek out a different group to associate with, adopt different definitions, or cause one to imitate the novel, reinforced behavior. These reciprocal effects are why this theory is not simply one of cultural deviance but a general theory of crime (Akers, et al., 2016).

Extending the model, Akers (1998) proposed Social Structure and Social Learning in which he added social structural factors that were hypothesized to indirectly effect an individual's deviant behavior. These factors are a) differential social organization, b) differential location in the social structure, c) theoretically defined structural variables, and d) differential social location. Differential social organization suggests there are structural correlates of crime in society that affect the rates of crime to include age composition, population density, and other characteristics that lean society toward or away from crime (Akers, 1998; Akers, et al., 2016). Differential location in the social structure refers to sociodemographic characteristics of individuals which indicate their niches in the larger societal structure (i.e. class, gender, race, ethnicity, marital status and age). Theoretically defined structural variables refer to the variables, such as anomie, social disorganization, etc. that have been used in other theories to identify criminogenic conditions of societies or groups. Finally, differential social location refers to individuals' membership in their primary, secondary, and reference groups such as family, classroom, or employment groups (Akers, 1998; Akers, et al., 2016). These variables all affect social learning variables, which affect crime. For example, a city with a high degree of racial tension may have a higher-than-average number of juveniles living within its borders. This could lead to gangs of ethnically similar people forming. In these gangs, an individual will associate with other gang members, learn definitions of the gang, imitate older gang members, and be reinforced for behavior viewed as positive to the gang. In this way, the social structural variables are affecting the social learning variables, which are then predicting criminal or conforming behavior. (See Figure 5.1.)

## Profiling the Literature

### Deviant Behavior *(1973)*

Akers's first text, in a similar fashion as Sutherland's text *Principles of Criminology* (1947), was written as a textbook (Welch, 1976). This "solid, well-presented" text integrates "coverage of the field without diluting its substance" while also providing the groundwork and overview of Social Learning Theory (Roncek, 1987, p. 215). While this text primarily covers a range of traditional topics from a social learning approach, Akers does not ignore other theoretical orientations (or even criticism of social learning theory) in this text. In his preface, Akers even states that he wrote the book "with the student in mind" (1973, p. xx). His goal was to make the text "understandable without being intellectually condescending" – a goal that Welch (1976, p. 213) believes Akers accomplished. In fact, Roncek believes that the text is so "thorough, well-rounded, [and] comprehensive" that "There is no reason that it could not be used by sociologists from any theoretical perspective, regardless of its social learning approach" (1987, p. 217).

### Social Learning and Social Structure: A General Theory of Crime and Deviance *(1998)*

Akers's second major text has been described as "required reading for the profession" and has been called "a model of how good sociology is done" (Simpson, 2000, p. 1172). This text is where Akers expands Social Learning Theory to include the social structural variables that make up Social Structure Social Learning Theory. Much like his first, this text is "attractive" and "accessible" (Simpson, 2000, p. 1172) to a wide audience. Taking a "sensible view" Akers uses data to support the claim that his theory better explains deviance than other, notable theoretical orientations (e.g. control and anomie theories) while avoiding "fundamentalist" claims about his own work.

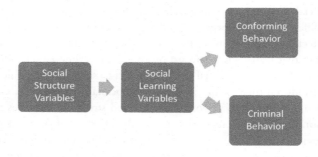

**FIGURE 5.1**

## Legacy

The extension of Differential Association Theory and the writings of Akers have "universalize[d] the study of deviance and crime" (Simpson, 2000, p. 1173). Social Learning Theory has become one of the "major contemporary theories of crime" (Pratt, et al., 2010, p. 768; Agnew & Brezina, 2012; Cullen, Agnew, & Wilcox, 2006). In fact, differential association – a major variable in the social learning tradition – "emerges as the strongest correlation of delinquency in most studies" (Cullen et al., 2006, p. 120). Therefore, it almost goes without saying that Akers's legacy in the field of criminology will be felt for generations of criminologists still to come.

In truth, the first author (Joshua D. Behl) of this text is a direct legacy of Akers, being one of his former Ph.D. students – so in effect, this very text is a part of Akers's legacy. However, in knowing Akers personally, it is safe to say that his legacy is not important to him. Akers is much more devoted to his family and his faith than he is to his legacy. In closing out his autobiographical chapter of his life and the development of Social Learning Theory, Akers (2011) makes that very clear by stating:

> "It goes without saying that I love my family. I love my wife and cleave only to her. She belongs only to me, and I only to her. I am committed without reservation to my Christian faith. That is not my relationship to social learning theory. I certainly have invested enormous amounts of time, effort, and professional reputation on the theory, but I am not married to it, and I do not hold to it as a faith. It does not belong to me and I do not belong to it. It belongs to the body of ideas about crime and deviance open to anyone."
>
> *(p. 364)*

## References

Agnew, R., & Brezina, T. (2012). *Juvenile Delinquency: Causes and Control*. New York: Oxford University Press.

Akers, R.L. (1973). *Deviant Behavior: A Social Learning Approach*. Belmont, CA: Wadsworth Pub Company.

Akers, R.L. (1998). *Social Learning and Social Structure: A General Theory of Crime and Deviance*. Piscataway, NJ: Transaction Publishers.

Akers R.L. (2011). The origins of me and of social learning theory. In F.T. Cullen, C.L. Jonson, A.J. Myer, & F. Adler, (Eds.) *The Origins of American Criminology: Advances in Criminological Theory* (Vol. 16). Piscataway, NJ: Transaction Publishers.

Akers, R.L., Krohn, M.D., Lanza-Kaduce, L., & Radosevich, M. (1979). Social learning and deviant behavior: A specific test of a general theory. *American Sociological Review*, 44(4), 636–655.

Akers, R.L., Sellers, C.D.S., & Jennings, W.G. (2016). *Criminological Theories: Introduction, Evaluation, & Application* (7th ed.). New York, NY: Oxford University Press.

Bandura, A. (1977). *Social Learning Theory*. Englewood Cliffs, NJ: Prentice Hall.

Beirne, P. (1987). Between classicism and positivism: Crime and penalty in the writings of Gabriel Tarde. *Criminology*, 25(4), 785–820.

Burgess, R.L., & Akers, R.L. (1966). A differential association-reinforcement theory of criminal behavior. *Social problems*, 14(2), 128–147.

Cullen, F.T., Agnew, R., & Wilcox, P. (2006). *Criminological Theory: Past to Present: Essential Readings*. New York: Oxford University Press.

Durkheim, É. (1886). Les études de science sociale. *Revue Philosophique de la France et de l'Étranger*, 22, 61–80.

Gaylord, M.S., & Galliher, J.F. (1983). *The Criminology of Edwin Sutherland*. New York: Routledge.

Geis, G. & Goff, C.H. (1983). Introduction. In *White Collar Crime: The Uncut Version*, E.H. Sutherland. New Haven: Yale University Press.

Hinduja, S., & Ingram, J.R. (2009). Social learning theory and music piracy: The differential role of online and offline peer influences. *Criminal Justice Studies*, 22(4), 405–420.

King, A. (2016). Gabriel Tarde and contemporary social theory. *Sociological Theory*, 34(1), 45–61.

Kinnunen, J. (1996). Gabriel Tarde as a founding father of innovation diffusion research. *Acta sociologica*, 39(4), 431–442.

Martin, R., Mutchnick, R.J., & Austin, W.T. (1990). *Criminological Thought: Pioneers Past and Present*. New York: Macmillan Publishing Company.

Pratt, T.C., Cullen, F.T., Sellers, C.S., Winfree Jr, L.T., Madensen, T.D., Daigle, L.E., Fearn, N.E., & Gau, J.M. (2010). The empirical status of social learning theory: A meta-analysis. *Justice Quarterly*, 27(6), 765–802.

Reckless, W.C. (1973). *American Criminology; New Directions*. New York: Appleton-Century-Crofts.

Renneville, M. (2018). *Gabriel Tarde, the Swallow of French Criminology. The Anthem Companion to Gabriel Tarde*. Anthem Press.

Roncek D. W. (1987) Review of the book Deviant Behavior by R. Akers. *Deviant Behavior*, 8(2), 205–219.

Schuessler, Karl. 1973. *Edwin H. Sutherland on Analyzing Crime*. Chicago: University of Chicago Press.

Simpson, J. (2000). Social learning and social structure: A general theory of crime and deviance. *Social Forces*, 78(3), 1171–1173.

Snipes, J.B., Bernard, T.J., & Gerould, A.L. (2010). *Vold's Theoretical Criminology*. New York: Oxford University Press.

Snodgrass, J.D. (1972). *The American Criminological Tradition: Portraits of the Men and Ideology in a Discipline*. [Unpublished doctoral dissertation]. University of Pennsylvania.

Sutherland, E.H. (1937). The professional thief. *Journal of Criminal Law and Criminology (1931–1951)*, 161–163.

Sutherland, E.H. (1940). White-Collar Criminality. *American Sociological Review*, 5(1), 1–12.

Sutherland, E.H. (1947). *Principles of Criminology*. Philadelphia: Lippencott.

Sutherland, E.H., & Cressey, D.R. (1968). *Principles of Criminology*. Philadelphia: Lippencott.

Sutherland, E. (1949). *White Collar Crime*. New York: The Dryden Press.

Sykes, G.M., & Matza, D. (1957). Techniques of neutralization: A theory of delinquency. *American Sociological Review*, 22(6), 664–670.

Tarde, G. (1886). *La criminalité comparée* [Criminality Compared]. Paris: Flix Alcan.

Tarde, G. (1890). *The Laws of Imitation*. New York: Henry Holt.

Tarde, G. (1897). La jeunesse criminelle. Trans. H.C. Warren. *Revue pédagogique*, 15, 255–273.

Thomassen, B. (2012). Émile Durkheim between Gabriel Tarde and Arnold van Gennep: Founding moments of sociology and anthropology. *Social Anthropology*, 20(3), 231–249.

Vold, G.B. (1951). Edwin Hardin Sutherland: Sociological criminologist. *American Sociological Review*, 16(1), 2–9.

Welch, M. (1976). Deviant behavior. *Teaching Sociology*, 3(2), 212–213.

Wilson, M.S. (1954). Pioneers in Criminology I: Gabriel Tarde (1843–1904). *Journal of Criminal Law, Criminology, & Police Science*, 45(1), 3–11.

# 6

# ANOMIE AND STRAIN THEORIES

## Durkheim, Merton, Agnew

## Introduction

Anomie and strain theories are the third of the three major sociological explanations of deviant and criminal behavior. Anomie and strain approaches to deviant behavior are different from other theoretical ideas in that they suggest that crime or deviance happens as a response to some form of anomic situation or strain. That strain could be financial (see Merton) or psychological (see Agnew). Anomie theorists suggest that malintegration and disorder are the necessary societal conditions to cause individuals to feel strain in their lives. However, individuals will not commit crime unless the social structure coupled with the lack of access to resources, or economic goals, is also blocked.

What is unique about these anomie or strain approaches to deviance is the focus on societies as a whole – not just the individual. It is the society that places a particular emphasis on certain accomplishments or goals. It is, therefore, societal expectations that cause the anomic structure, or normlessness, that one feels when they do not reach those goals. Theorists in this area will point to societies, like the United States of America, as the unit of analysis compared to other societies with different crime rates, like Great Britain or Japan. This chapter traces the idea of anomie from its first intellectual development (Durkheim), to its application in American society (Merton), to its modern-day usage (Agnew).

## Émile Durkheim (1858–1917)

### Introduction

Émile David Durkheim, along with Max Weber and Karl Marx, is considered one of the founders of the discipline of sociology, and is a key figure in other academic disciplines, including criminology and anthropology. His primary concern, reflected in all his work, is the maintenance of social order (Timasheff & Theodorson, 1976). He also made contributions to religion, government, suicide, education, and the family, however, this description of Durkheim will be confined mostly to his contributions to crime and deviance.

### Biographical profile

Durkheim was born in Épinal, France in the mid-twentieth century, descending from a long line of rabbis. It was anticipated that young Émile would follow suit, however, he eventually

DOI: 10.4324/9781003036609-6

changed this path. He was a very good student at one of France's great high schools and later attended the prestigious École Normale Supérieure. The first French sociologist began teaching philosophy in France and Germany, as sociology was not a discipline at the time. While teaching at the University of Bordeaux, he married, and he and his wife had two children. His doctoral dissertation was published as *The Division of Labor in Society* in 1893; two more groundbreaking works quickly followed, *The Rules of Sociological Method* and *Suicide*, firmly establishing sociology as a scientific discipline (Coser, 1971).

Durkheim was a major Paris intellectual and played a role in reorganizing the university system. In 1915, Durkheim's son, also expected by his father to be a major force in the new discipline, died of wounds suffered in World War I. Émile Durkheim never fully emotionally recovered from this loss and died in 1917 at 59 years of age (Coser, 1971).

## Profiling the Theory

As noted earlier, this section will focus on Durkheim's contributions in the areas of crime and deviance. However, there needs to be a general overview of his sociological theorizing to provide a backdrop for this analysis. Durkheim was concerned about how excessive individualism could serve to disrupt society in the form of anomie, or a state where norms are absent or ambiguous. He believed sociology should focus on social facts, things that exist in society that are independent of individual activity.

Durkheim's focus on cohesion and social order would come to be further developed as a major theoretical paradigm known as *structural functionalism*. Deviance and crime were important areas of study for Durkheim as he believed the unifying effects of conformity to norms could most easily be observed. In his famous work *Suicide* (1951), Durkheim used empirical data to determine possible causes of the act of suicide, suggesting the act was determined more by society than individual factors; in this way, Durkheim furthered his fledgling discipline, especially as a contrast to the more established psychology. In *Suicide*, Durkheim found that social cohesion and levels of integration to society were a protective barrier to taking one's life (Collins & Makowsky, 1998). By extension, this focus toward sociological influences and away from psychological determinism extends to other acts considered deviant as well. The concept of anomie was developed in this work as describing a type of suicide caused by excessive individualism: if many people are detached from their society, the collective consciousness (sometimes called the collective conscience) becomes unstable and society's bonds become weakened, allowing increased levels and types of deviance and crime. Concerns over a breakdown of the normative structure would later find influence in strain theory and theories of social disorganization.

Although Durkheim is concerned with the anomic conditions that create the potential for crime and deviance, he also noted that deviant behavior is a normal process in society. This might sound strange at first blush since so many resources are committed to controlling it, but Durkheim's point was this: all societies past and present have actions that are labeled deviant and criminal – since all societies have crime, how can it be abnormal? Also, if the current criminal acts were all expunged from the legal system, they would be replaced with a new set immediately, as there will always be norms and ways to break them. Crime will not go away; it will simply change. The relationship of deviance is represented in the fact that some actions currently considered deviant were not so considered in the past, and some from the past are no longer considered deviant today. In fact, Durkheim claimed that both major crimes and minor infractions of "good taste" have the same effect – insulting the "collective-sentiments" of society, and each deserving of punishment (though very different types). Durkheim's contention that crime is normal drastically repudiates theories (e.g., Lombroso's atavism) that focus on some personal abnormal and undesirable traits (Zeitlin, 1990).

Durkheim takes an interest in punishment as it was a way to analyze the collective consciousness at work. Understanding the types and extent of punishment provides a window into the moral framework of society, especially regarding its social cohesion. Durkheim takes an evolutionary approach and observes how earlier, primitive societies used more barbaric means of punishment due to fears of society collapsing if extreme actions were not taken, while modern societies use a more measured, reflective approach due to a more secular understanding of the world. While most early penal theorists focused on two groups – the punished and the punishers – Durkheim's sociological approach also includes those who are observing the punishment. It also observes the emotions provoked by the offensive actions as a gauge of moral sentiments in society (Garland, 1990).

Durkheim's functionalism is evident in the fact that crime and its punishment have a positive value to society. Through laws and norms, individuals make clear what behaviors are acceptable and which ones are not, thereby reinforcing the collective consciousness. Punishment is symbolic and the rituals associated with the formal systems of justice, as well as the informal systems of collective action, augment the solidarity which will protect society from *excessive* deviant behavior (after all, deviance is normal).

## *Profiling the Literature*

### The Rules of Sociological Method *(1895)*

In this work, Durkheim starts at the beginning, by describing his most basic concept – *social facts*, which refer to "types of behavior and thinking external to individuals, but they are endued with a compelling and coercive power by virtue of which, whether he (sic) wishes it or not, they imposed themselves on him (sic)" (Durkheim, 1982, p. 51). Activity involving crime, and certainly measures taken to control it, then, are social facts. In *Division of Labor in Society* (1893), Durkheim describes social facts as the seemingly internal experiences and actions that are, however, induced by external factors, independent of the person. Originally, he used the term *moral facts* but later changed it to social facts in *Rules* (Turner, Beeghley, & Powers, 2002).

### The Division of Labor in Society *(1893)*

Considered by some scholars to be Durkheim's masterpiece, this work sets up the analysis of basic social problems that Durkheim addressed his entire career (Garland, 1990). Durkheim is concerned with the glue that holds society together; thus, solidarity comes from the collective consciousness which refers not to a "group mind" but rather a situation where "people have feelings of belonging to a group" (Collins & Makowsky, 1998, p. 105). Early societies possessed *mechanical solidarity* and low levels of division of labor (specialization), while modern industrial society is characterized by *organic solidarity*. Different types of legal systems developed due to the level of solidarity they possess: in preindustrial societies, the system was based on criminal law, which came with demands for retribution, through the infliction of pain, discomfort, or even death. Modern industrial societies are more likely to be characterized by civil-administrative and restitutive systems, those based on restoration of normative behavior (Collins & Makowsky, 1998).

## Suicide: A Study in Sociology *(1897)*

In this work, Durkheim uses statistical data from different countries to identify types of suicide that are related to "extra social factors" rather than individualist motivations. The main point of the work is how environmental factors can influence a seemingly psychological act. While the study seems to provide empirical data on a narrow social act, the work attempts to explain social organization generally (Turner, et al., 2002). More specifically, the level of connection to a moral society has very strong implications for the study of deviance and crime.

If sociology as a discipline is seen as beginning with Durkheim's *Rules of Sociological Method*, *Suicide* can be considered the first empirical work in the modern sense (Inkeles, 1959). Often criticized for questionable methodology by today's standards, it should be remembered *Suicide* was an early attempt at research in a new discipline. Decades after its publication, the work was considered the "paradigm of sociological studies of deviance in the United States and the rest of the world" (Douglas, 1971: 67).

## Moral Education: A Study in the Theory and Application of the Sociology of Education *(1925)*

Although it might not seem that a book about the sociology of education would contribute to understandings of crime and deviance, Durkheim links the issue of education to punishment. The educational system, according to the author, helps establish a collective consciousness and reflects the importance of this social institution to maintaining normative standards. School instruction should reflect social norms that will contribute to social morality and cohesion. When this does not occur, punishment in educational institutions is acquired in a manner that mirrors punishment by legal authorities in the greater society; however, in school systems as in society, the punishment must be appropriate to the offense committed. In his discussion on school-based punishment, Durkheim's analogy provides proscriptions for deviance and crime.

### Legacy

Durkheim's theories reached into many areas of social life, as did the work of many early social theorists seeking to understand the relationship of individuals to society. Durkheim's investigations into government, religion, the economy, education, and deviance were foundational to the new discipline of sociology, which he helped found. As some scholars note (Turner, et al., 2002), Durkheim's greatest contribution to the sociology of deviance and crime is that the cause of deviance reflects the same social facts that create the degree to which people are connected, or disconnected, to society. Merton, for example, used anomie theory as a basis for his strain theory. The Chicago School disorganization theorists such as Ernest Burgess, Clifford Shaw and Henry McKay used anomie as a way of seeing disorder. Even micro sociologist Erving Goffman used Durkheim's focus on ritual to form his interaction-based theory. Durkheim's views on deviance as being a normal state of societies was a departure from other conceptions of deviance as being a pathological state, but his conception influenced those who saw crime as a social construction, apart from biological factors such as race and ethnicity, sex and gender, and sexual identity.

## Robert King Merton (1910–2003)

### Introduction

Robert Merton is considered to be one of the intellectual leaders of modern-day sociology (Calhoun, 2010). However, when most people think of the Harvard alumnus and eventual University Professor Emeritus at Columbia, they hardly think of a former gang member and practicing magician. Merton's work on strain and anomie theory along with his larger ideas of unintended consequences of law creation are some of what warrants his profile for inclusion in this text. Merton's contributions to sociology and criminology are vast. For the purposes of this text, we will only be discussing his influence as it relates to deviance and crime. However, Merton as a theorist is widely influential outside this limited scope.

### Biographical Profile

Born to Jewish immigrants in 1910, Robert Merton was originally named Meyer R. Schkolnick (Calhoun, 2003). However, in an attempt to create a more American stage name for his magic act, Schkolnick renamed himself Robert Merton – a name he kept when going off to Temple University for college (Lilly, Cullen, & Ball, 2015). While Merton's family was quite poor, Merton suggested that every opportunity was available to him, except financial opportunity.

At Temple University, Merton developed a close friendship with George E. Simpson, a sociologist (Martin, Mutchnick, & Austin, 1990). Merton fell in love with sociology less because of Simpson's influence and more because Merton enjoyed being able to examine human behavior without the "loaded moral preconceptions" (Hunt, 1961, p. 57) of other fields. Temple, along with Merton's precocious intellectual interest as a child, growing up in a city filled with museums and opportunity, provided Merton with knowledge and experience in such socially dignified activities as classical music, dancing the foxtrot, and tennis (Martin, et al., 1990). This helped Harvard view Merton as a "comer", or someone who would probably be a successful graduate.

Harvard was correct and Merton went on to graduate with a Ph.D. in sociology in 1936. Merton remained on staff at Harvard for a number of years as a tutor and instructor, but the Great Depression did not allow for new faculty lines to be issued at Harvard. To that end, Merton accepted an Associate Professorship at Tulane University in 1939. For the two years Merton was at Tulane, he was made department Chair of sociology and promoted to Full Professor. In 1941, Merton accepted a position as an Assistant Professor at Columbia University where he would retire after being promoted to Associate Professor in 1944 and Full Professor in 1947.

Merton's professional accomplishments begot many rewards, as he received over 20 honorary degrees and awards from numerous professional organizations. In his personal life, Merton married Suzanne M. Carhart and they had three children together. He has published heavily in his career, writing over ten books and countless articles. In fact, after a visit to Merton's office, Morton Hunt stated that Merton's works covered bookshelves and would be enough to make a nice bibliography if Merton could ever be "persuaded to release them" (1961, p. 61).

### Profiling the Theory

Merton's intellectual ideas, like all theorists, cannot be separated from the time period in which the theorist lived. Merton's coming of age was during the Great Depression and the reformulation of society through The New Deal. This meant that Merton, as a sociologist, was interested in topics ranging from social stratification to mass media, from the sociology of science and religion to reference group theory. However, his most important theoretical work in the topic of deviance and criminological thought was in anomie (Martin et al., 1990).

Merton's work on reference group theory is not what he is most well-known for – but it has had a profound effect on other theories, namely labeling theory and conflict theory (Martin et al., 1990). Reference group theory basically states that individuals will evaluate members of their reference groups and out groups to form a reference of their own values, attitudes, and behaviors.

Merton's work on *self-fulfilling prophecy* is also of considerable mention – especially as it relates to deviance. The idea of a *self-fulfilling prophecy* is basically "a false definition of the situation evoking a new behavior which makes the originally false conception come true" (Merton, 1957, p. 423). An example of this which may be relevant to readers is the idea of a student who is having difficulty in a class. The student spends so much time worrying about passing an exam that the student spends virtually none of their time studying. What is likely to happen to that student? They will fail the exam. This idea's connection to labeling theory is somewhat straightforward. If someone perceives society viewing them as a criminal, they will interpret everything through this lens and then commit deviance.

Merton's most popular deviance work is in the area of anomie. Anomie is also famously credited to Émile Durkheim, but the two men use this term differently. Durkheim used anomie to discuss an abnormal form of the division of labor and as a form of suicide that is caused by a sudden and unexpected change in the norms of society. Merton has different ideas.

In "Social structure and anomie" (1938), Merton defines anomie as "a breakdown in the cultural structure, occurring particularly when there is an acute disjunction between the cultural norms and goals and the socially structured capacities of members of the group to act in accord with them" (Merton, 1957, p. 162). This is the first in a larger theoretical group known as "strain" theories (Martin, et al., 1990). Merton believed that in order for a society to enter into an anomic state, several things must be present. First, there needs to be an agreed upon goal that everyone is culturally expected to desire and obtain. Second, there needs to be an imbalance in the emphasis placed on the goal such that the *ends* of achieving the goal is more important than the *means*, or way you achieved the goal. Finally, there need to exist structural impediments to achieving this goal through legitimate means. The disjuncture of legitimate means to achieve the agreed upon goals is what creates anomie (Martin, et al., 1990; Akers, Sellers, & Jennings, 2016). Take, for example, Italian immigrants around the turn of the twentieth century. Presumably, they came to America in order to have a better life for themselves and their families. However, due to blocked access to good jobs and good schools, they did not have legitimate means to achieve the agreed upon goals of American society. This disjuncture caused strain.

Merton believed that the responses to strain varied based on one's position within the social strata as well (Clinard, 1964). Children learned the appropriate response to strain from their parents such that parents provide children with values and goals specific to their social class or the class they identify with (Merton, 1957). The responses can be generally grouped into two different categories: the first group places greater emphasis on the goals and the second group places greater emphasis on the means to achieve these goals. In the first category of responses to strain, the emphasis on the goal is so great that any means necessary, legitimate or not, is accepted as long as the goal is achieved. In the second set of responses, the emphasis on the means to achieve the goals are so great that individuals are prevented from violating the rules, even if that means failure to achieve the goals.

Within these two broader categories of responses to anomie, there are five adaptations that individuals engage in depending on how they perceive their goals, the availability of means to achieve their goals, and the emphasis they place on each. Merton states that "these categories refer to behavior, not personality, and the same person may use different modes of adaptation in different circumstances" (Bierstedt, 1981, p. 463).

The five adaptations are as follows:

1.  Conformity – this is the most common response to anomie (Akers, et al., 2016; Martin et al., 1990). Basically, individuals accept the goals and the means to achieve those goals in the social system. The individual accepts the state of affairs as it is currently structured and strives for success within the prosocial means available to them. This response is the only response that is not deviant.

2.  Innovation – This is the most common deviant response to anomie or strain (Akers, et al., 2016; Martin et al., 1990). Individuals accept the goals, especially the goals of success or wealth, but accept any means to achieve these goals, regardless of the legality of those means. Merton believes that the "greatest pressures toward deviation are exerted upon the lower strata" (Merton, 1957, p. 144). This is largely because a lot of conventional means to achieve success have not, historically, been available to lower class groups – things like college and familiar connections/wealth. Due to this disjuncture between the goals and the means to attain these goals, individuals will feel pressure to attain these goals at almost any cost – including deviance. Examples of this are street gangs or the Italian mafia who felt they have been systematically blocked from the prosocial ways of obtaining wealth. They create new ways to obtain wealth that are typically less than legal.

3.  Ritualism – This response to anomie accepts the means to achieve the goals with the realization that the goal is unattainable (Akers, et al., 2016; Martin et al., 1990). In American society especially, status is determined by achievement and competition. This pressure to compete causes anxiety for individuals who do not feel they can actually achieve the goals society has established. "One device for allaying these anxieties is to lower one's level of aspirations – permanently" (Merton, 1957, p. 150). Whether this is a deviant response is up for debate as most ritualist individuals are not necessarily criminally deviant. However, Merton (1957) argues that this behavior is deviant in the sense that it goes against what is socially and culturally acceptable.

4.  Retreatism – This is an escapist response (Akers, et al., 2016). While this is the least frequently used adaptation to anomie, these individuals accept both the goals and the means to achieve these goals – but feel the institutional mechanisms are not actually available to them. Merton suggests these individuals are "in the society, but not part of it" (1957, p. 153) and include alcoholics, drug addicts, vagrants, and the mentally ill. While these individuals do not have any of the rewards of society, they also have very little of society's frustrations as they have effectively removed themselves from society. Individuals who accept a retreatist response to anomie typically get "excessive amounts of sleep and develop no real discernable respectable pattern of behavior" (Martin et al., 1990). In extreme cases, individuals in this category will aim to annihilate the world by taking their own lives in a final act of retreat.

5.  Rebellion – This adaptation to anomie is when the individual rejects the means and ends in society all together and advocates for a new system – or at least a significantly modified system – even if that means a violent overthrow of the entire system (Akers, et al., 2016; Martin et al., 1990). An example of this could be the Bolshevik Revolution of 1917. A complete economic and societal system was overthrown in favor of a perceived new, better system.

The sociological community embraced Merton's theory of deviance as the "quintessential sociological theory of crime" (Akers, et al., 2016, p. 175). In fact, Shaw and McKay (1972), in developing Social Disorganization Theory, adopted the concept of anomie in their theory formation. By the 1950s Merton's theory of crime was widely accepted and applied to many different areas of criminological thought – most prominently subcultural delinquency (Akers, et al., 2016).

### Profiling the Literature

### On Theoretical Sociology: Five Essays Old and New *(1967)*

What has been described as a "collection that might well be required reading for a graduate, or perhaps an upper-level undergraduate theory course" (Kutner, 1968, p. 91), Merton's collection of five important theoretical works, some of which are reprinted for the next text, describe Merton's views on the history, semantics, and beliefs of sociological theory. Specifically, Merton was quite concerned with the "clarification of continuities in sociological theory" (Kutner, 1968, p. 91) – an overarching goal of this text as well. While Merton's style of writing is susceptible to rereading, Kutner (1968) argues that it serves the latent function of drawing readers into the nuance of sociological theories in which Merton was most concerned.

### Social Theory and Social Structure *(1938; 1957)*

Described as an "invaluable reference work" (Stone, 1958, p. 557), this text of Merton's essays lay out his theoretical ideas in the form of a "magnificent and demanding book" (Naegele, 1957, p. 759). One of Merton's "strong points" (Stone, 1958, p. 560) in this text is his desire of "operational specification and the clarification of concepts" for there to be better continuity of social research. The influence of such an idea did, in fact, "usher in a fundamental change in socio-psychological research design" (Stone, 1958, p. 562) as was prognosticated in an early review of this text.

### Legacy

Merton has been viewed as one of the most influential sociologists of the twentieth century (Cullen & Wilcox, 2010). He made contributions far beyond the criminological literature, to include the sociology of science and developed a paradigm of social analysis. However, his contributions to the criminological literature should not be understated. The idea of strain as a cause of criminal and deviant behavior helped propel another dominant theoretical orientation – General Strain Theory. Merton's introduction of the ideas of manifest and latent functions are still common discussions in Sociology of Law and Sociology of Deviance courses today.

## Robert Agnew (1953–)

### Introduction

While most viewed the shortcomings of Merton's Strain Theory as evidence that strain was not a strong predictor of deviance, Robert Agnew, saw the potential and pursued it. As the intellectual father of General Strain Theory, Agnew built on the ideas that Merton began, but transformed them into his own. Never intending to be a criminologist, Agnew has left a lasting impact on the field as one of its most well-known modern-day theorists.

## Biographical Profile

Robert Agnew grew up in Atlantic City before the excitement of big hotels and casinos made it a tourist destination (Agnew, 2011). Born to parents who did not finish high school, Agnew still credits his father with his academic prowess, teaching him to question the world around him. Falling in love with sociology after taking an Introduction course at Rutgers, Agnew pursued his Ph.D. in sociology at University of North Carolina at Chapel Hill intent on becoming a social psychologist. In fact, Agnew (2011) admits that he never took a class in criminology as an undergraduate or graduate student.

Agnew began his dissertation process intent on studying the relationship between social factors and creativity, but soon found that there was a dearth of data available on this topic (Agnew, 2011). A fellow graduate student pointed him to a relatively untapped data source – the Youth in Transition survey. This survey did not directly measure creativity, but did have variables such as independence, autonomy, and delinquency. Agnew began reading various works in an effort to select a new dissertation topic and became attracted to the strong theoretical and empirical works of such criminal theorists as Merton (1938), Cohen (1955), and Hirschi (1969) – all profiled in this text.

After selecting a deviance dissertation topic, Agnew got hired as the sole criminology professor at Emory University – a job he felt he was unqualified for (Agnew, 2011). While some in this situation might have viewed it as a career hinderance, Agnew appreciated his freedom to explore the topic that was most interesting to him – his revision of Merton's Strain Theory. It is here that Agnew transformed the theory from "Revised Strain Theory to General Strain Theory" (Agnew, 2011, p. 142). Agnew retired from Emory after a long career, being honored as the President of the American Society of Criminology and an Edwin H. Sutherland award recipient – viewed as the highest honor for any criminologist, for his contributions to the field of criminology and the sociology of deviance.

## Profiling the Theory

Building on the work of Merton's (1938) Strain Theory, Agnew proposed a General Strain Theory (GST) of crime, a micro-level theory that integrates the fields of sociology, criminology, and social psychology. The major propositions of the theory are that crime takes place as a reaction to stress but does not limit that stress to the purely financial, as does Merton (1938). Agnew, in fact, states that crime is a result of stress, whatever the cause (Akers, et al., 2016). Specifically, Agnew identified three major sources of strain: failure to achieve positively valued goals, removal of positively valued stimuli, and confrontation with negative stimuli.

Failure to achieve positively valued goals is the basic idea of the disjuncture between expectations and achievements, as well as the disjuncture between one's perceived outcomes compared to actual outcomes (Agnew, 1985; Snipes, Bernard, & Gerould, 2010; Akers, et al., 2016). For example, someone who dreamed of being a college athlete may experience strain when he/she does not make the team – or the disjuncture between expectations and achievements. However, another may experience strain if they have perceived themselves to be the most talented player at tryouts and still did not make the team due to returning team members getting priority. Both examples are causes of strain, but for different reasons.

The removal of positively valued stimuli can also be a source of strain (Agnew, 1985; Snipes, et al., 2019; Akers, et al., 2016). This form of strain can be the removal of anything an individual finds important. For example, the death of a close relative, a breakup or divorce, or the loss of a job can all be viewed as the removal of a positively valued stimulus. In the same way, the presence of a negative stimulus can also cause strain (Agnew, 1985; Snipes, et al., 2019; Akers, et al., 2016). Negative stimuli can be anything the individual finds unpleasant or *noxious* in their lives. For example, abuse from a relative or friend, or failing grades at school are introducing negative stimuli into one's life.

Agnew (1985; 1992) makes the point that previous iterations of strain theory focused on the disjuncture between positively valued goals and outcomes, such as monetary success or status. In his iteration of strain theory, Agnew focuses on relationships which the individual finds unpleasant and cannot escape. Specifically, Agnew focuses quite a bit of his attention on juvenile delinquency, where adolescents cannot escape from strain at home or school (Agnew, 1985; Snipes, et al., 2019). In fact, even attempting to escape from these strain-inducing situations can cause problems as they are typically illegal (running away or truancy).

There are several ways that one responds to strain, according to Agnew (1985; 1992) – cognitive, behavioral, and emotional coping mechanisms. Cognitive strategies include such things as minimizing the adversity or accepting the adversity as part of life (e.g. It isn't important, or I deserve it). Behavioral strategies involve escaping the strain in various ways (e. g. transferring schools) or revenge (either conventional or deviant methods). Emotional responses can be healthy (e.g. prayer, meditation, or exercise) or unhealthy (e.g. drugs/alcohol). While most who experience strain opt for conventional methods of coping, GST focuses on the deviant or illicit responses.

Empirical support for GST is mixed (Akers, et al., 2016; Kubrin, Stucky, & Krohn, 2009; Agnew & White, 1992; Botchkovar, Tittle, & Antonaccio, 2009; Snipes, et al., 2010). While several authors have found general support for GST's proposition that negative relationships and life events are associated with delinquent behavior (see Snipes et al., 2010 for a review), others have found weak to moderate support for the theory, arguing that the inadequate tests of GST do not accurately account for other, theoretically significant, variables, (see Akers, et al., 2016; Kubrin, et al., 2009). In cross-cultural tests of the theory (e.g. Botchkovar, et al., 2009), GST's validity seems to be weak, suggesting a culture-specific scope. This may be because strain is felt in varying degrees by different societies, and how strain is defined varies by society as well.

### *Profiling the Literature*

### Pressured into Crime: An Overview of General Strain Theory *(2006)*

This text was Agnew's attempt at simplifying what has been defined as "one of the most sophisticated – and complicated – areas of criminological theory" (De Angelis, 2007, p. 296). This "straightforward introduction to one contemporary version of strain theory" (De Angelis, 2007, p. 296) gives the most complete review of General Strain Theory to date. Agnew's goal of this text was not to advance the formulation of the theory, as other criminologists before him, rather he was attempting to provide an overview of GST in a format that made it accessible to students. This clearly written, well organized text has received acclaim for the sociologist turned criminologist author and has helped cement his place in the annals of deviance literature.

### Juvenile Delinquency: Causes and Consequences *(2001)*

Recognizing that the field of juvenile delinquency was of popular interest to students, Agnew also concluded that any texts on the topic were too cumbersome. Enter *Juvenile Delinquency: Causes and Consequences*. The stated goals of this text were to: a) be shorter and cheaper than most texts on juvenile delinquency, b) provide more synthesis of theory and research, c) be more student focused, and d) promote applied learning of the material being written (Desmond, 2003). Agnew achieved all of these goals. This book is not only shorter than most texts on juvenile delinquency, but Agnew also structured the text to be a question/answer format rather than studying topics like traditional texts. Instead of chapters on "Causes of Delinquency" Agnew had sections on "Are teenage mothers more likely to have delinquent children". By offering questions as opposed to topics, Agnew found "students [become] more actively involved in the learning process" (2001, p. xxi). The book has received such critical acclaim as one of "the best written texts, regardless of subject matter" and is written in a "quality that is hard to find" (Desmond, 2003, p.121).

### *Legacy*

Robert Agnew remains one of the modern-day theorists who is widely respected as a true colossus of criminological and sociological thought. His expansion of Merton and the recognition of various types of emotional reactions to strain have helped integrate the social sciences (specifically sociology, criminology, and psychology) to help better understand the phenomenon of deviance. While the empirical support for his theory may leave something to be desired, there is no question that Agnew's impact on the field will be everlasting. As a current professor emeritus at Emory, Professor Agnew's legacy has not even really begun.

### References

Agnew, R. (1985). A revised strain theory of delinquency. *Social Forces*, 64(1), 151–167.

Agnew, R. (1992). Foundation for a general strain theory of crime and delinquency. *Criminology*, 30(1), 47–88.

Agnew, R. (2001). *Juvenile Delinquency: Causes and Control*. Los Angeles, CA: Roxbury Publishing Company.

Agnew, R. (2006). *Pressured into Crime: An Overview of General Strain Theory*. New York: Oxford University Press.

Agnew, R. (2011). Revitalizing Merton: General strain theory. *The Origins of American Criminology*, 16, 137–158.

Agnew, R., & White, H.R. (1992). An empirical test of general strain theory. *Criminology*, 30(4), 475–500.

Akers, R.L., Sellers, C.D.S., & Jennings, W.G. (2016). *Criminological Theories: Introduction, Evaluation, & Application* (7th ed.). New York, NY: Oxford University Press.

Bierstedt, R. (1981). Robert K. Merton. In *American Sociological Theory: A Critical History*. New York: Academic Press (pp. 443–489).

Botchkovar, E.V., Tittle, C.R., & Antonaccio, O. (2009). General strain theory: Additional evidence using cross-cultural data. *Criminology*, 47(1), 131–176.

Calhoun, C. (Ed.). (2010). *Robert K. Merton: Sociology of Science and Sociology as Science*. New York: Columbia University Press.

Clinard, M.B. (1964). *Anomie and Deviant Behavior*, Glencoe, IL: Free Press.

Cohen, A.K. (1955). *Delinquent Boys: The Culture of the Gang*. Glencoe, IL: Free Press.

Collins, R., & Makowsky, M. (1998). *Discovery of Society*, 6th ed. Boston, MA: McGraw-Hill.

Coser, L.A. (1971). *Masters of Sociological Thought: Ideas in Historical and Social Context*. New York: Harcourt Brace Jovanovich.

Cullen, F.T., & Wilcox, P. (Eds.). (2010). *Encyclopedia of Criminological Theory* (Vol. 1). Sage.

De Angelis, J. (2007). Review of the book Pressured into Crime: An Overview of General Strain Theory. *Teaching Sociology*, 35(3), 295–297.

Desmond, S.A. (2003). Juvenile delinquency: Causes and control. *Teaching Sociology*, 31(1), 120–121.

Douglas, J.D. (1971). *American Social Order: Social Rules in a Pluralistic Society*. New York: Free Press.

Durkheim, E. (1951). *Suicide: A Study in Sociology*. Trans. J.A. Spaulding and G. Simpson. New York: Free Press. (Original work published 1897.)

Durkheim, E. (1961). *Moral Education: A Study in the Theory and Application of the Sociology of Education*. Trans. E.K. Wilson and H. Schnurer. New York: Free Press. (Original work published 1925.)

Durkheim, E. (1965). *The Division of Labor in Society*. Trans. G. Simpson. New York: Free Press. (Original work published 1893.)

Durkheim, E. (1982) *The Rules of Sociological Method*. Ed. with an introduction by S. Lukes, trans. W.D. Halls. New York: Free Press. (Original work published 1895.)

Garland, D. (1990). *Punishment in Modern Society: A Study in Social Theory*. Chicago, IL: University of Chicago Press.

Hirschi, T. (1969). *Causes of Delinquency*. Berkeley, CA: University of California Press.

Hunt, M.M. (1961). How does it come to be so? Profile of Robert K. Merton. *New Yorker*, 36(28), 39–63.

Inkeles, A. (1959). Psychoanalysis and sociology. In S. Hooks (Ed.). *Psychoanalysis, Scientific Method, and Philosophy*. New York University Press, pp. 117–132.

Kubrin, C.E., Stucky, T.D., & Krohn, M.D. (2009). *Researching Theories of Crime and Deviance*. New York: Oxford University Press.

Kutner, N. (1968). Book Review: *Theoretical Sociology–Five Essays, Old And New*. *Social Forces*, 47(1), 91. doi:10.2307/2574724.

Lilly, J.R., Cullen, F.T., & Ball, R.A. (2015). *Criminological Theory: Context and Consequences*. Los Angelas, CA: Sage.

Martin, R., Mutchnick, R.J., & Austin, W.T. (1990). *Criminological Thought: Pioneers Past and Present*. New York: Macmillan Publishing Company.

Merton, R.K. (1938). Social structure and anomie. *American sociological review*, 3(5), 672–682.

Merton, R.K. (1957). *Social Theory and Social Structure*. Rev. and enlarged ed. New York: Free Press.

Merton, R.K. (1967). *On Theoretical Sociology: Five Essays, Old and New*. New York: Free Press.

Merton, R.K. (1968). *Social Theory and Social Structure*. New York: Simon and Schuster.

Naegele, K.D. (1957). Social Theory and Social Structure (Book). *American Sociological Review*, 22(6), 759–760.

Shaw, C.R., & McKay, H.D. (1972). *Juvenile Delinquency and Urban Areas*. Rev. ed. Chicago: University of Chicago Press.

Snipes, J.B., Bernard, T.J., & Gerould, A.L. (2010). *Vold's Theoretical Criminology*. New York: Oxford University Press.

Stone, G.P. (1958). Social Theory and Social Structure. *Administrative Science Quarterly*, 2(4), 556–562.

Timasheff, N.S., & Theodorson, G.A. (1976). *Sociological Theory: Its Nature and Growth*, 4th ed. New York: Random House.

Turner, J.H., Beeghley, L., & Power, C.H. (2002). *The Emergence Of Sociological Theory*, 5th ed. Belmont, CA: Wadsworth.

Zeitlin, I.M. (1990). *Ideology and the Development of Sociological Theory*, 4th ed. Englewood Cliffs, NJ: Prentice-Hall.

# 7

# SOCIAL DISORGANIZATION

## Park & Burgess, Thrasher, Shaw & McKay

### Introduction

Adopting a similar macro level focus to deviance as anomie and strain theories, Social Disorganization theorists are focused on the structure of society to help explain crime and deviant behavior. Also called *structural theories*, these theories focus on the structural characteristics of different communities. Most of these theories were developed out of the University of Chicago and used the city of Chicago as their research focal point. Because of this, these theories are usually called "The Chicago School".

All of these theories focus on ideas of urban ecology whereby individuals in an urban environment are no different than an animal struggling to survive in nature. The survival of the fittest ideas of Darwin are no different to city dwellers than they are to animals in the jungle. These theorists focus on breaking the city down into concentric zones (Parks and Burgess), focusing on gangs living in a complex urban social environment (Thrasher), and crime mapping to predict socially disorganized neighborhoods (Shaw and McKay).

### Robert E. Park (1864–1944) & Ernest Burgess (1886–1986)

#### Introduction

Robert Park and Ernest Burgess were faculty members of the famed Chicago School of Sociology that developed a unique theoretical and methodological approach to sociology and criminology. Graduate students at the university were sent out into the streets of Chicago to understand the problems of a rapidly increasing city. Park, Burgess, and others at the university developed the *ecological model* of studying the phenomenon of urban life, e.g., crime, delinquency, poverty, homelessness, and suicide. Analogizing the urban environment to animal and plant environments, Burgess' expansion of the ecology model, known as the concentric circle schema, has offered an understanding of the environmental effects, especially in urban areas, to the study of criminology and the sociology of deviance.

DOI: 10.4324/9781003036609-7

## Biographical Profiles

### Robert E. Park (1864–1944)

Robert Ezra Park was born at the end of the American Civil War in rural Pennsylvania and his family moved to rustic Red Wing, Minnesota. He had an interest in writing in high school and edited the school newspaper, a path he would follow in the future. He enrolled at the University of Michigan in 1883 and graduated with an undergraduate degree in philosophy. After a brief stint teaching, he began a career as a news reporter in several large cities, including Chicago. His immersion in the details of urban life would help energize sociology in the United States. Park, in his thirties, pursued graduate education at Harvard, graduating with a master's degree in philosophy at the turn of the twentieth century. He continued his studies in Germany, receiving his Ph.D. in 1904 from the University of Heidelberg (Matthews, 1977; Mutchnick, Martin, and Austin, 2009).

Park continued his study of urban life and race relations, working for a time with African American leader Booker T. Washington. After meeting with renowned sociologist W.I. Thomas, he was convinced to take a faculty position at the University of Chicago in 1914, where he remained until his retirement in 1933. When Thomas left the program, Park became the new leader of the Chicago School of Sociology, with assistance from a younger colleague named Ernest Burgess. Park retired from the university in 1933 and accepted a visiting professorship at Fisk University, a historically black institution in Tennessee. In 1944, he died of a stroke at age 79 (Matthews, 1977; Mutchnick, et al., 2009).

### Ernest Burgess (1886–1986)

Canadian by birth and the son of a minister, Ernest W. Burgess was educated in the United States and received a Ph.D. in 1913 from the University of Chicago with a specialization in the sociology of the family. Burgess never married and preferred to live with his sister and father. He was brought to the university where he became an academic collaborator to Robert Park. Thin, meticulous in his appearance, and exceptionally organized, Burgess presented a contrast to the older, large, and disheveled Park. However, Burgess provided the coherence and consistency to the Chicago School's theoretical work and their research mentorship to the institution's students. Burgess was an effective project manager and maintained close ties to community leaders such as Jane Addams and other progressives of the era. Park was more charismatic and attracted students to the various projects underway, many of which addressed crime and delinquency. Burgess was a dedicated mentor, though he could be blunt when he believed students' projects were unsatisfactory (Matthews, 1977; Mutchnick, et al., 2009). He died in 1966 at age 80.

## Profiling the Theory

Being from a rural area, Park, with his unusual curiosity perhaps saw the city, with all its problems and promise, as a mystery to be solved (and reported on). Unmoored by informal social controls that characterize rural life, urbanity exposed deviance and criminal behavior. Park and the Chicago School theorists saw the city as a laboratory with which to study these conditions. By envisioning human communities in a similar fashion to plant and animal communities, the idea of the city as an ecological system took hold with the Chicago School theorists.

Burgess augmented the model in his well-known conceptualization involving the ways in which cities expand outward in their growth activity (Park, Burgess, & McKenzie, 1925). In this model, often called concentric zone theory or the Burgess model, cities are conceptualized as developing from a central business region, known as Zone I, which will eventually replace the homes with businesses in Zone II. Zone III is inhabited by workers and families that were able to afford a better environment than Zone II. The more expansive urban residential areas exist in Zone IV and beyond those areas are the residences away from the city – the suburbs and commuter regions constitute Zone V.

The ecological model has presented a rich area of exploration into the specific phenomena of the criminogenic conditions of urban life as well as the promotion of innovative forms of research methodology. However, the model has some flaws as shown in later research projects. For example, the model assumes people are born into the corrupting influences of disorganized communities rather than having a criminal orientation before moving into these areas. Also, the theory focuses primarily on low-income areas, as if deviance and crime do not exist in financially prosperous areas. In that regard it suffers from the ecological fallacy that focuses on the conceptions of the participants under study from the standpoint of the criminogenic areas in which they reside. In addition, the theory failed to create clarity in the sociological concepts of stratification, power, and political process (Collins & Makowsky, 1998).

### *Profiling the Literature*

### Introduction to the Science of Sociology *(Park & Burgess) (1921)*

Referred to affectionately by students in the sociology department at the University of Chicago as the "Green Bible", this early sociology textbook was significant in both content and breadth (at over a thousand pages). It contains information mostly contributed by Park although Burgess obviously collaborated in the effort (probably using his project management skills). This book brings forth the ecological model that had been developed by Park. Although the text does not focus specifically on crime and deviance, the ecological model underpinning the work throughout the book provided the groundwork for later work in criminology.

### *"The Study of the Delinquent as a Person" (Burgess) (1923)*

Burgess describes how the general European theories of delinquency by Cesare Lombroso, Gabriel Tarde, Willem Bonger, and Enrico Ferri (although quite different) are ineffective in addressing delinquency. Burgess contrasts these general theories with those of American psychiatrist William Healy, who in his case studies in *The Individual Delinquent* (1915), posits that delinquency should be studied at the individual level and that young offenders are not born criminal or reflecting specific social types. Burgess, however, questions the idea of delinquency as being represented at an *individual* level and replaces it with delinquency as represented at a *personal* level, using Park's distinction of *person* as a social, rather than individual, being. However, Burgess believes these two levels of analysis are complementary in explaining delinquency. This line from the article is insightful of Burgess' approach, "the criminal...is first of all a person, and second a criminal" (1923, p. 680).

## The City *(Park, Burgess, & McKenzie)* *(1925)*

This short collection of essays that represent Chicago School philosophy was primarily composed by Park and Burgess, however one chapter was penned by R.D. McKenzie. The book provides a general version of the ecological system and includes a bibliography provided by Louis Wirth. The work introduced the concept of *natural areas*, a key concept in Chicago School theory. One essay is especially germane to crime and deviance – an essay entitled "Community Organization and Juvenile Delinquency". In this chapter, Park describes juvenile delinquency as resulting from rapid social change, primarily from the transition to urban and industrialized society, as evidenced by the introduction of automobiles, movie theaters and news outlets, and changes in immigration. Park suggests that delinquency formed not in the individual, but in social groups; however, he makes the naïve assumption that community playgrounds, which in early developmental stages create a sense of social cohesion, later contribute to delinquency (this idea can also be found in the work of Frederick Thrasher, see p. 00).

## *"Protecting the Public by Parole and by Parole Prediction"* *(Burgess) (1936)*

In this article, Burgess argues for parole as a strategy in American correctional policy (this was written in 1936). He notes that the public is often concerned about parolees victimizing citizens while residing in the community under parole supervision. His observations are that extreme correctional policy positions that are too strict or too lenient are ineffective, but parole strategies provide both protection to the community and rehabilitation to the offender, especially where appropriate classification and prediction plans are used. The article expresses Burgess' interest by in the practical and scientific application of criminology.

### *Legacy*

The Chicago School's legacy on criminology and the study of deviance is undeniable. The Chicago School scholars used the city as a laboratory to train many young graduate school students on methods for studying urbanization. Park and Burgess directly trained numerous students, many of whom went into the connected field of criminology. Frederic Thrasher and Clifford Shaw went on to write seminal works on gangs and juvenile delinquency; Nels Anderson produced works on homelessness and unemployment, and Donald Cressey completed important works on organized crime. Others, though not directly trained by Park and Burgess, were trained in the Chicago School tradition, and are described in this book – Erving Goffman, Howard Becker, and Edwin Lemert are examples. The theoretical approach developed by Park and Burgess (and others of the Chicago School) influenced other theoretical perspectives including symbolic interactionism, labeling theory, and crime-place theories such as environmental criminology.

The Chicago School scholars, certainly including Park and Burgess, were interested in the practical nature and progressive promise of sociology to intervene in the problems that existed in the areas they studied. Burgess, in his early writings, suggested the utility of the new field of social work as it was being developed by Jane Addams and others, and although in the later years he seemed to dissociate himself from the field (Shaw, 2010), the field of social work was enhanced by its connections with the Chicago School.

## Frederic M. Thrasher (1892–1962)

### Introduction

Frederic Thrasher was a Chicago School trained scholar, most noted for his study of gangs in Chicago. His interest in studying gangs and their environments made him a major contributor to the Social Disorganization Theory. In addition to being a pioneer in social disorganization and urbanization studies, he was a founder of educational sociology and was associate editor of the *Journal of Educational Sociology* (Dimitriadis, 2006); this is notable in his studies of gangs and the institutions with which they are engaged.

### Biographical Profile

Thrasher was born in Shelbyville, Indiana. He attended DePauw University in his home state and graduated with an undergraduate degree in social psychology. He then attended graduate school at the University of Chicago where he obtained a master's degree in 1918, completing his master's thesis on the Boy Scout movement. He received his Ph.D. from Chicago in 1926. Thrasher taught at Ohio State University, the University of Chicago, and Illinois Wesleyan University, before arriving at New York University in 1923, where he remained until 1937 (American National Biography, 2021). His interest in youth programs would be later extended to an interest in the prevention of gang activity. In addition to his work in delinquency and gangs, Thrasher was also interested in the sociology of education and published several journal articles dedicated to this subfield.

### Profiling the Theory

Not only does Thrasher provide a sound theoretical basis for understanding gangs, but he also introduces readers to an underground world of urban deviance, which he vividly describes in his work. He describes gang activity as resulting from a restless boredom and the subsequent engagement in spontaneous play groups from which emerge "gangs in embryo" (Thrasher, 1963, p. 233). Children are bored, find gangs, and then crave increased levels of excitement. The gangs have their own character, defined primarily by the geographic areas they inhabit.

A typology of gangs appears in his major work (Thrasher, 1963) in which he describes these five groupings: 1) the diffuse type which lacks organization and solidarity; 2) the solidified type which is well-defined, cohesive, and organized; 3) the conventionalized type which consists of athletic, dance, social, or other entertainment activities and that seeks to express legitimacy; 4) the criminal type that commits petty crimes and deviant acts (such as truancy) and progresses to habitual crime and delinquency; and 5) the secret society that has cabalistic rituals and a mysterious aura.

A key concept in Thrasher's work is the *situation complex* which details how the social institutions in the gang members' lives affect and are acted upon by their gang memberships and activity. The situation complex is made up of the members' families, religious institutions, educational programs, and recreational outlets; these often are inadequate or maladaptive. The institutions in the situation complex are interrelated – as systems of institutions which reformers must address in their totality (Dimitriadis, 2006).

Thrasher observes that gang members of the period were drawn to movies and comic books, however he does not buy into the popular idea that gang members are induced to commit crimes by popular culture outlets; instead, he argues that many factors converge to create delinquency (we can refer here to his concept of the situation complex; Dimitriadis, 2006). Thrasher asserts comic book violence was simply used as a scapegoat when other factors should be considered (Thrasher, 1949).

### Profiling the Literature

### The Gang: A Study of 1313 Gangs in Chicago *(1927)*

This is Thrasher's landmark study of gangs in Chicago in the 1920s. In the editor's preface, mentor Robert Park states the title *The Gang* is inadequate – the work, he states, is a study of *gangland*, or a study of gangs in their urban habitats. This is indeed the case as Thrasher vividly describes the lives of urban gangs of various ethnic and racial backgrounds with names like the Black Hand, the Dirty Dozen, and the Night Riders, operating in places known as the North Side Jungles, the South Side Badlands, and the West Side Wilderness. In the work he notes the etiology of gangs, the typology mentioned earlier. Thrasher describes the gang's *playgrounds*, geographic hangouts such as certain downtown areas, areas along waterways, alleys, and parks and forest preserves, noting the importance of place. He also describes the activities with which they become involved such as feuds, sexual behavior (immoral gang activity between gangs with members of both sexes), and organization patterns.

### *"Social Backgrounds and School Problems"* (1927)

This represents a study of school children in *Town X*, a small urban area described as a "wicked community" teeming with vice activity such as gambling, bootlegging, and prostitution. Different *intimate* adolescent groups are identified: the play-group, the gang, the orgiastic (or expressive) group, the clique (or set), the club, the sports team, the followers, and the ill-defined *secret societies*. Thrasher describes these groups as "vital groups" from which youth develop an identity (an idea similar to the concept of "master status", later developed by the University of Chicago faculty). Thrasher follows with a discussion of the gang activity in the school under study and the strategies developed by school officials to control unruly activity, mostly by the gangs. Interestingly, the reporting to the police for intervention was recommended only for "extreme cases" (although these were not described).

### *"How to Study Boys' Gangs in the Open"* (1928)

Thrasher returns to the common theme of adolescent gangs in the school system, referred to as "one of the most vital social backgrounds of certain types of boys" (p. 244). Thrasher presents a how-to guide in the study of gangs from the perspective of an outsider (without a social service agency affiliation). He describes an ethnographic study in Greenwich Village (chosen for its proximity to his home and its reputation for housing a large amount of gang activity) as an example of how to get access to, become familiar with, gain rapport, collectively interview, continue meeting, and address minor acts of mischief or as he calls them "incidents of a disconcerting sort" (p. 242). He recommends the collective interview method as an adjunct to reports from other sources, such as teachers and social workers, to complete the case histories on the gang members. The author paints a very rosy image of interviewing gang members that would appear dubious today, but it provides a window into doing ethnographic research in the Chicago School tradition during the late 1920s.

### "The Boys' Club and Juvenile Delinquency" (1936)

This is a study of the effectiveness of a Boys' Club organization in the prevention of juvenile delinquency – today this type of study is called evaluation research, as it seeks to determine if an organization or agency is meeting its goals. It only studied one Boys' Club in New York City from the years 1927–1931. The findings of the research suggest the organization was not an effective deterrent to juvenile crime in the era, but it did ascertain that it provides other community functions and could be useful in overall crime prevention in communities. This study shows more of an advancement in technical research proficiency than some of Thrasher's work in the previous decade.

### "The Comics and Delinquency: Cause or Scapegoat?" (1949)

Many current themes of the cause of juvenile delinquency have a history in early social discourse. For example, in this article, Thrasher takes to task current positions in vogue that comic book crime is a contributor to delinquency. He especially targets the assumptions of Fredric Wertham, a psychiatrist who promoted this idea in several articles in the late 1940s. Thrasher refutes the use of *monistic* theories (those that reduce explanations to a single cause, such as Lombroso's theory of atavism), and points out the flaws in Wertham's two-year study that Thrasher claims is "more forensic than scientific". Among those claims is that the study was not as meticulous as those conducted by fellow Chicago School sociologist Clifford Shaw. Thrasher's claims are that comic books are used as a "whipping boy" in lieu of more complex explanations. Arguments of crime causation have likewise been attributed to movies, television, music, and, more recently, violent videos games and internet content.

### Legacy

Thrasher's *The Gang* is considered a founding text on the subject and as such is cited in almost all comprehensive work regarding gangs; it has generated many questions on the topics about the makeup of gangs, their locations, their organization patterns, their activities, their relationship to the communities in which they live, and the ultimate question – what communities should do about them (Dimitriadis, 2006). Its influence can be found in later works such as Cohen's highly influential study *Delinquent Boys* (Madge, 1962) and is often mentioned today in current studies on gangs.

The study of gang activity is still very germane to modern social life, especially in school settings. The often-discussed concept of the school-to-prison pipeline is also a current concern and refers to the practice by some educational institutions of doling out excessive discipline to certain students, encouraging them to drop out of school and leaving them vulnerable to end up incarcerated in the prison system.

## Clifford R. Shaw (1895–1957) & Henry D. McKay (1899–1980)

### Introduction

Clifford Shaw and Henry McKay were two of the delinquency scholars most associated with the Chicago School tradition. Both were trained in the school's methodology and exemplified some of the tradition's best work. Both were raised on farms but went to study delinquency in the big city. Inspired by their mentors, notably Robert Park and Ernest Burgess, the two applied the concentric zone theory to the study of crime and delinquency.

## Biographical Profiles

### Clifford R. Shaw (1895–1957)

Clifford Shaw was born on a farm in a small town near Muncie, Indiana, where his father was a farmer and store owner. He was the middle child of ten children and sporadically attended school before dropping out at age 14 to work on the farm. In an early brush with delinquency himself, he stole some bolts from a blacksmith who later picked him up by the ankles and turned him upside down, shaking the bolts from his pockets. Shaw longed to leave the farm and spent hours educating himself before his minister encouraged him to study for the clergy at Adrian College, which he did, but left disillusioned with religion. He enrolled in the US Navy in 1917, but when the war ended, he decided to study sociology at the University of Chicago. He lived in a settlement in a big city slum (like Edwin Sutherland in his introduction to this new urban environment). He worked part time from 1921–1923 during his graduate studies but did not complete his Ph.D. He worked for a few years as a probation officer before getting married and becoming a professor at McGill University in Canada. He continued to conduct research at the juvenile institute while teaching criminology at different colleges, including later, the University of Chicago (Snodgrass, 1976).

### Henry D. McKay (1899–1980)

Henry McKay was born on a sizable farm in South Dakota, the grandson of immigrants from Scotland, which probably influenced his later ideas on race and immigration status. Like Shaw, he was from a large family – he was the fifth child of seven – but from a slightly less religious environment. He attended and graduated from Dakota Wesleyan University and spent some time in graduate school at the University of Chicago, before leaving to teach classes at the University of Illinois. There, he met (though did not study under) Edwin Sutherland; this was the beginning of a long friendship with this eminent criminologist. He also got married during this period and had a daughter. He returned to the University of Chicago to do graduate work but, like Shaw, did not complete his Ph.D. He was a major contributor to two major national crime commission reports, reflecting his high level of regard by criminologists and practitioners.

## Profiling the Theory

As noted in the introduction, Shaw and McKay drew on the work of the Chicago School and especially benefitted from the tutelage of Park and Burgess. While their mentors created the concentric zone theory to better understand social patterns and disorganization in the expansion of urbanization, it was Shaw and McKay who focused on the specific patterns of crime and delinquency. As with other researchers of their era who lacked the sophistication of modern statistical analysis, the two plotted delinquency rates on maps and made assumptions about the larger social, historical, and economic effects on local areas, based on these data (Kubrin & Weitzer, 2003).

Shaw and McKay posited that prevention measures taken when offenders were still juveniles provided the best promise of slowing adult criminality. In their research, they used qualitative data from *life histories*, or detailed narratives of the juveniles' experiences and living conditions, along with the quantitative data received from maps and court records (Curran & Renzetti, 2001).

In 1932, Shaw started the Chicago Area Project (CAP) in which attempts at crime control were decentralized to communities where leaders and members organized social programs such as athletic activities and summer camps for youth – this long-lasting project has produced many positive outcomes that aid in the prevention of delinquency, when it is used as part of a larger crime control campaign (Curran and Renzetti, 2001).

## Profiling the Literature

### The Jack-Roller *(1930) (Shaw)*

A classic in Chicago School sociology and criminology, this work tells the story of a 17-year-old boy named Stanley who was involved in a delinquent lifestyle in Chicago from an early age. The work is a life history, interpreted by the researcher Shaw. A *jack-roller*, as referenced in the title, refers to a person, often a youthful offender, who attacks and robs vulnerable people, often alcoholics. By using the life history method, Shaw depicts the everyday life of Stanley and the life on the Chicago streets. Shaw took copious notes in his conversations with the teenager and consulted official records to ensure the veracity of his claims. The attempt to provide the story in Stanley's voice reflected the influence of the symbolic interactionism of George H. Mead, W.I. Thomas, and others of the Chicago School (Shaw, 2009).

Shaw ended the book with the pronouncement that Stanley had given up his delinquent lifestyle, however a chance encounter with Stanley by another sociologist 50 years later provided a different story – one that revealed a life of adult crime and unfortunate life events since his youth (Snodgrass, 1982).

### The Natural History of a Delinquent Career *(1931) (Shaw)*

This book follows the same pattern as *The Jack-Roller* and provides a case history of a boy from the ages of 7 to 16. His delinquent career involved a series of crimes that increased in frequency and severity until a rape charge placed him in a penal institution. This view of the youngster's case history involved autobiographical information to augment the reports from others with whom he was engaged. In his review of the work, Edwin Sutherland (1932) expresses some concerns over the reliability of the autobiography (due to recall or the veracity of the claims), however he also sees how the method can work if several biographies of offenders can be compared for consistency. He also describes concerns regarding the potential for bias in the investigator's selection or omission of details from the autobiography. On the positive, Sutherland notes the utility in using the method to better understand conditions (and therefore motives) when the delinquent's career is truncated.

### Juvenile Delinquency in Urban Areas *(1942) (Shaw & McKay)*

This work provides an overview of 20 years of research in 21 American cities and examines the consequences of social disorganization in the different ecological zones and their relationship to juvenile delinquency. The data confirms that most of the social disorganization can be found in the central zones of cities, moderate disorganization can be found in the intermediate areas, and much less in the other areas. Delinquency is correlated with 1) population changes, 2) housing problems, 3) poverty, 4) presence of racial and immigrant populations, 5) tuberculosis, 6) mental problems, and 7) adult criminality. The book is replete with the urban maps for which Shaw and McKay are famous, and the last chapter involves some information on the Chicago Area Project (CAP).

## Legacy

The newer "crime place" theories owe a debt to Shaw and McKay. Technological advancements have made crime mapping more beneficial to criminologists than the primitive methods used in the early to mid-twentieth century. Neighborhood watch programs and more recent attempts to alter physical environments, such as crime prevention through environmental design and broken windows approaches, are all "descendants" of the Chicago School disorganization theory (Curran and Renzetti, 2001).

Shaw's work with the Chicago Area Project began in 1932 and has been another legacy of Shaw and McKay's approach. Although at Shaw's death in 1957 the program was turned over to the state of Illinois, the remnants of the program remain, providing beneficial effects for young people (Curran and Renzetti, 2001). The program's projects, as well as its heritage, events, news, and other information can be found on its website (Chicago Area Project n.d.).

## References

American National Biography (2021). *Thrasher, Milton Frederic*. Oxford, England: Oxford University Press.

Burgess, E.W. (1923). The study of the delinquent as a person. *American Journal of Sociology*, 28(6), 657–680.

Burgess, E.W. (1936). Protecting the public by parole and parole prediction. *Journal of Criminal Law and Criminology*, 24(4), 491–502. doi:10.2307/1137495.

Chicago Area Project (n.d.). Retrieved on February 1, 2021 at http://www.chicagoareaproject.org/.

Collins, R., & Makowsky, M. (1998). *Discovery of Society*, 6th ed. Boston, MA: McGraw-Hill.

Curran, D.J., & Renzetti, C.M. (2001). *Theories of Crime*, 2nd ed. Boston: Allyn & Bacon.

Dimitriadis, G. (2006). The situation complex: Revisiting Frederic Thrasher's *The Gang: A Study of 1,313 Gangs in Chicago*. *Cultural Studies: Critical Methodologies*, 6(3), 335–353.

Healy, W. (1915). *The Individual Delinquent: A Text-book of Diagnosis and Prognosis for all Concerned in Understanding Offenders*. Boston, MA: Little, Brown.

Kubrin, C.E., & Weitzer, R. (2003). New directions in social disorganization theory. *Journal of Research in Crime*, 40(4), 374–412.

Madge, J. (1962). *The Origins of Scientific Sociology*. New York: Free Press.

Matthews, F.H. (1977). *Quest for an American Sociology. Robert E. Park and the Chicago School*. Montreal and London: McGill-Queen University Press.

Mutchnick, R.J., Martin, R., & Austin, W.T. (2009). *Criminological Thought: Pioneers Past and Present*. Upper Saddle River, New Jersey: Prentice-Hall.

Park, R.E., & Burgess, E.W. (1921) *Introduction to the Science of Sociology*. Chicago: University of Chicago Press.

Park, R.E., Burgess, E., & McKenzie, R.D. (1925). *The City*. Chicago: University of Chicago Press.

Shaw, C.R. (1930). *The Jack-roller: A Delinquent Boy's Own Story*. Chicago: University of Chicago Press.

Shaw, C.R. (1931). *The Natural History of a Delinquent Career*. Chicago: University of Chicago Press.

Shaw, C.R., & McKay, H.D. (1972). *Juvenile Delinquency and Urban Areas*, revised ed. Chicago: University of Chicago Press. (Original published 1942.)

Shaw, I. (2009). Re-reading The Jack-Roller: Hidden histories in sociology and social work. *Qualitative Inquiry*, 15(7), 1241–1264.

Shaw, I. (2010). Sociology and social work: An unresolved legacy of the Chicago School. In C. Hart (Ed.), *Legacy of the Chicago School: A Collection of Original Essays in Honor of the Chicago Schools of Sociology during the First Half of the Twentieth Century*. Cheshire, England: Midrash Publications.

Snodgrass. J. (1976) Clifford R. Shaw and Henry D. McKay: Chicago Criminologists. *British Journal of Criminology*, 16(1), 1–19.

Snodgrass, J. (1982). *The Jackroller at Seventy: A Fifty-year Follow-up*. Lexington, MA: Lexington Books.

Sutherland, E.H. (1932). Reviewed work: The natural history of a delinquent career. *American Journal of Sociology*, 38(1), 135–146.

Thrasher, F.M. (1927) Social backgrounds and school problems. *Journal of Educational Sociology*, 1(3), 121–130.

Thrasher, F.M. (1928). How to study boys' gangs in the open. *Journal of Educational Sociology*, 1(5), 244–254.

Thrasher, F.M. (1936). The boys' club and juvenile delinquency. *American Journal of Sociology*, 42, 66–80.

Thrasher, F.M. (1949). The comics and delinquency: Cause or scapegoat? *Journal of Educational Sociology* 23(4), 195–205.

Thrasher, F.M. (1963). *The Gang: A Study of 1313 Gangs in Chicago*. Chicago: University of Chicago Press. (Originally published 1927.)

# 8

# SOCIETAL REACTIONS AND LABELING OF DEVIANCE

## Tannenbaum, Lemert, Goffman, Becker, Braithwaite

## Introduction

In this chapter, the idea of societal reactions to crime and labeling of a criminal are discussed. The main theories discussed use the basic idea of symbolic interaction, or the idea that we all act and react toward things based on the meaning we ascribe to those things. For example, the term *criminal* conjures up all sorts of ideas in our minds. We all act, or believe we should act, a certain way toward people whom we deem as deviant or criminal. This chapter examines how theorists use this symbolic interaction in a deviance or crime enhancing way.

The chapter begins with the idea of the dramatization of evil (Tannenbaum), discusses ideas like secondary deviance (Lemert), stigma (Goffman), labeling (Becker), and restorative justice (Braithwaite). All of these deal with how an offender is treated by society and questions whether the role of society in causing this deviance outweighs the contributions of the individual.

## Frank Tannenbaum (1983–1969)

### Introduction

Frank Tannenbaum was a criminologist best known for his conception of the *dramatization of evil*, an early notion of what would become labeling theory in the sociology of deviance and criminology. He was also instrumental in the production of criminological knowledge of delinquency and professional crime. Tannenbaum was also involved in research and activism in what has come to be called *convict criminology*. He became an academic and moved away from his critical roots in criminology to focus on other interests involving Latin American issues (Yeager, 2011). Though his views and interests changed dramatically at that point, he made a substantial contribution to early criminology.

### Biographical Profile

Born in Galicia in what is now Poland, Tannenbaum's parents moved him and his two siblings to a Massachusetts farm, not far from Great Barrington, the small town where W.E.B.

DOI: 10.4324/9781003036609-8

Du Bois was raised. Tannenbaum worked on the farm until moving (against his father's wishes) to New York City to pursue his education. In New York he lived with relatives, occasionally returning to the farm when necessary, however, he preferred life in the city (Whitfield, 2013).

He became a naturalized citizen in New York and began spending time with famous anarchist Emma Goldman. He joined the Marxist-influenced International Workers of the World (IWW) and worked with the city's poor and unemployed to obtain food and shelter for them. In his relief work, he was arrested on charges of unlawful assembly and sentenced to a year's incarceration at a faculty known as Blackwell's Island. He became a spokesperson for a riot at the facility, causing him to end up in solitary confinement for two months. After his release, he provided an exposé on the prison's abuses, which included unhealthy conditions and violence against the inmates, that resulted in official investigations and a warden's resignation, as well as a book on his experiences (Tannenbaum, 1922).

In 1916, Tannenbaum decided to continue his education at Columbia University, but a short stint in the military delayed his graduation until 1921 (Yeager, 2011). At Columbia, he studied under famed education scholar and activist John Dewey (Winn, 2010). Tannenbaum was active in penal reform even in college and toured prisons and published articles on the subject while a student. He published his first book on the labor movement in 1921 and contributed articles on prisons and prison reform, including governmental reports on abuses in prison that angered some of those working in the system (Yeager, 2011).

In the early 1930s, he began to change his radical activist views, rejecting leftist approaches to penology and to criminology generally. He began teaching at Columbia University in 1935 and focused on Latin American history and politics. He retired from this position in 1961. Five years later, he was robbed and knifed by two assailants but survived the attack; however, cancer would claim his life in 1969 (Yeager, 2011).

## Profiling the Theory

The dramatization of evil concept refers to how criminal conduct committed by a person, often a young person, results in that person becoming an exemplar of the act itself. Tannenbaum sees the juvenile as being *tagged* when a deviant label is applied, which then separates them from their social group. From this tagging comes a process in which the person *becomes* the deviant act in the disapproving eyes of society. The agents of society charged with controlling the evil – parents, older siblings, the police, the probation officer, the juvenile court system – in their enthusiasm make the deviance worse. The labeled child is then ostracized and finds refuge with other youngsters so labeled, creating situations where gangs can flourish; as Tannenbaum (1938) states, "we are dealing not with an individual, but with a group" (p. 20).

Barmaki (2019) claims the labeling process developed by Tannenbaum was in fact a product of the Chicago School theorists and other early symbolic interactionists, and better formulated by these groups. He also states the conceptualization of labeling theory is markedly different from those proposed by Lemert and Becker, however, it can certainly be said there are distinct differences in all forms of labeling theory.

Another contribution to crime and criminology is Tannenbaum's theorizing on what is known as *convict criminology*. Building on penology, the scientific study of prisons and incarceration, convict criminology is a newer subfield that seeks to understand the worlds of inmates based on real-life observations from inside correctional institutions, that has a social justice focus, and seeks a series of remedies to alleviate injustices (Richards & Ross, 2001). As an inmate, Tannenbaum received an inside view of prisons, which he was later to describe to others.

## Profiling the Literature

### Wall Shadows: A Study in American Prisons *(1922)*

This is an account of Tannenbaum's one year of imprisonment at Blackwell's Island Penitentiary where he provides a typology of criminal inmates: 1) casual (non-recidivist); 2) economic (financially motivated); 3) derelict (impoverished); 4) accidental (crime of passion); 5) sick or disabled; and 6) professional (career criminal). The emphasis is on the professional criminal whose recidivist tendencies (which can be traced to poverty, family dysfunction, gang involvement, and poor educational services) have led to incarceration so frequently that he has become institutionalized. In the process he obtains a criminal record that *brands* or *marks* him. It was this branding process that formed his version of labeling theory, which was developed more fully in his essay on "The Professional Criminal" (1925).

### Darker Phases of the South *(1924)*

In this interesting but concise analysis of the Southern United States during the early twentieth century, Tannenbaum discusses diverse subjects such as the origins of the Ku Klux Klan; life in mill villages; the consequences of a single crop (cotton) economy to socio-economic status; race relations and prejudice; and conditions in Southern prisons. Regarding the chapter on prisons, Tannenbaum begins by expressing the inhuman treatment of the prisoner – "a figure in gray with a black number painted on him" (1924, pp. 75–76). He also gives an unflattering depiction of the correctional officer (prison guard), whom he describes as poorly educated and sadistic toward inmates. Tannenbaum describes prison farms, tent camps, *chain gangs* (inmates who are chained together or caged during periods of their incarceration), and the general unsanitary and neglectful treatment of both male and female inmates. Tannenbaum focused on the penalties inmates received, often very severe, but surmised that correctional officers did not fully understand their actions. He also describes attempts at some prisons for improvement, but due to the low standards of prisons in the region generally, he offers a call for a national program for reform.

### Crime and the Community *(1938)*

This work has been cited by some scholars as the beginning of the criminological perspective known as labeling theory, and the concept of the *dramatization of evil* became known to the study of crime and deviance. Tannenbaum's focus on how the labeling process affects those so labeled is found in this statement from his book *Crime and Community*, published in 1938: "the person becomes the thing is he described as being" (pp. 19–20); this is certainly suggestive of the concept of the self-fulfilling prophesy as proposed by Merton (1948) or the concept of secondary deviance proffered by Lemert (1951). The process of making criminals itself is also vividly described in this famous description by Tannenbaum in the same work: "tagging, defining, identifying, segregating, describing, emphasizing, making conscious and self-conscious: it becomes a way of stimulating, suggesting, emphasizing, and evoking the very traits that are complained of" (pp. 19–20). There is an intriguing intellectual exercise in breaking down and analyzing all the concepts presented in this stimulating passage, however that is beyond the scope of this chapter (hopefully readers can discuss this in class).

## Legacy

As we have noted, there is some controversy over the origins of labeling theory; some scholars consider Tannenbaum as the originator while others doubt that claim. However, without uncertainty, he contributed greatly to the labeling and societal response perspectives which started early in the twentieth century and became prominent in the 1960s. His concept of the dramatization of evil has endured and found its way to other social psychology theories that focus on stigma.

Tannenbaum also contributed to the study of penology and the newer focus on convict criminology which emphasizes, from personal knowledge, the lived experiences of inmates, and which also proposes social justice initiatives; as we remember, Tannenbaum himself reported the abuses he experienced as an inmate and called for institutional reforms. Convict criminology is growing in reputation, and as of 2020 became a division of the American Society of Criminology (American Criminological Society, 2020).

## Edwin M. Lemert (1912–1996)

### Introduction

Lemert is one of the primary theorists of the societal reaction approach, which states that emphasis should not only be placed on the offender, but also on the social control system and how it can contribute to deviance. Of special concern to Lemert was what he called *secondary deviance*, the internal reaction to the labeling process which has significant consequences for continuing deviant behavior. Reflecting his Chicago School training, Lemert posits that deviance is a process which only becomes significant when it is experienced subjectively, results in action considered by society as deviant, and which meets criteria by which a deviant status is assigned.

### Biographical Profile

Edwin Lemert was born in 1912 to a middle-class family in Cincinnati, Ohio. His father, like Bonger's, was an insurance agent. He attended Miami University of Ohio and took up the study of sociology, much to the chagrin of his father who hoped young Edwin and his brother would study law and medicine. Sociology was not Lemert's first choice but a social problems course by Professor William F. Cottrell (who would always be an influence on his work), convinced him to choose this course of study. After graduation, he worked a year as a social case worker and took a course at the University of Cincinnati before entering graduate school at Ohio State University in 1935. His Ph.D., awarded in 1939, was a dual concentration in both sociology and anthropology, and his dissertation was a study of social control measures in Russia (Winter, 2000).

Lemert taught at Kent State University in Ohio and Western Michigan University before beginning a fruitful career at the University of California at Los Angeles in 1944, which ended in 1953. During this time, he published *Social Pathology: Systematic Approaches to the Study of Sociopathic Behavior* (1951), his major work. At the time, UCLA was still a young school and although it had a robust anthropology program, it had a small and undeveloped sociology program. He decided to take a teaching position at University of California at Davis and became chair of the department; he worked there from 1953 to 1993. He published books and many articles in sociological criminology but a major backlash against labeling theory in the early 1970s caused Lemert to differentiate his societal reaction theory, which was intricately connected to the labeling perspective. His focus turned strictly to the study of criminal behavior and he provided a major contribution on juvenile justice for President Lyndon Johnson's National Commission on Law Enforcement and the Administration of Justice that became widely cited (Winter, 2000).

Lemert assumed the presidency of the Society for the Study of Social Problems and the Pacific Sociological Society and was awarded the American Criminological Association's E.H. Sutherland lifetime award (Winter, 2000). Described by his nephew Charles Lemert as a "cowboy sociologist" (Lemert, 2000, p. 15), his uncle shunned city life, preferring to live among local Californians and on his ranch. His image was reinforced by his choice of cowboy boots and bolo ties as he presented his work on secondary deviance (described on p. 00). He was a complex and influential scholar in the study of criminology and the sociology of deviance.

## Profiling the Theory

Lemert reversed the order of traditional sociology of deviance and criminology by stating that rather than deviance and criminal activity leading to social control, types of social control can lead to deviance and crime. As described by Sumner (1994), there are six major elements in Lemert's labeling theory:

1.   There is a repudiation of binary categorization of normal and pathological.
2.   Deviance is normal and not pathological.
3.   Rule-breaking normally results in the adoption of a new deviant ideology.
4.   Social control measures often contribute to the deviant behavior.
5.   The labeling process is normally not linked to a specific act but generates programs for broad moral reform.
6.   These elements can be better explained as a beneficial orientation for understanding deviance than a formalized theory of deviance and criminality.

The key to understanding deviance lies in the secondary processes that take place. If the initial action of violating norms is the primary deviation, the acceptance of the label provided by others constitutes a core part of one's selfhood and reflects secondary deviance. Secondary deviance is defined by Lemert as "deviant behavior...which becomes (a) means of defence, attack, or adaptation to the overt and covert problems created by the societal reaction to primary deviation" (Lemert, 1967, p. 17).

There are eight steps that lead to secondary deviance (Lemert, 1951):

1.   The act of breaking of an established rule (primary deviance).
2.   Penalties to the norm breaker because of the act.
3.   A continuation of the primary deviance by the offender.
4.   Increased punitive responses by social control agents.
5.   Continued deviance by the wrongdoer, often with increasing resentment over the penalties.
6.   The acquisition of a "tolerance quotient" in which the community stigmatizes the offender.
7.   An amplification of the deviant behavior as a reaction to the stigmatization.
8.   Full acceptance of the status of deviant.

When one fully accepts a rule-breaking status, the result is continued deviant activity. The result is akin to what Robert K. Merton (1948) called a *self-fulfilling prophecy*, in which a person follows the expectations of society. It also reflects what sociologist Charles H. Cooley (1902) referred to as the *looking glass self* in which people use the responses of others to create their identity (a deviant) and influence their subsequent behavior (deviant activity). The person's identity is wrapped up in the deviant status, which becomes a master status, the most prominent status a person holds (Cullen & Agnew, 1999).

### *Profiling the Literature*

### Social Pathology: Systematic Approaches to the Study of Sociopathic Behavior *(1951)*

Social pathology is addressed in Lemert's detailed work on the construction of a sociological theory of deviance. He begins with the ineffectiveness of prior efforts of explaining social pathology and issues a call for a new approach, one that is an updated sociological theory rather than a psychological or psychiatric theory. The idea of social (as opposed to individual) pathology was prominent in the nineteenth century and expressed, as we recall, in Durkheim's thesis on the normality (as opposed to the pathology) of crime. The examples of behavior include the actions expected in a work from the mid-twentieth century, e.g., crime, prostitution, and drunkenness, but he also mentions disability issues such as blindness, speech defects, and mental illness (reminiscent of Goffman's inclusion of physical *marks*). Moving in more of a social movement direction, he also addresses behavior related to radicalism, represented in the red scare of communism during the period (Lemert, 2000). Lemert's focus is on the societal reaction to behavior that deviates from the norm, e.g., awe, envy, fear, disgust, repulsion, and the process that develops from the reactions. When secondary deviance develops, as noted earlier, continued deviation (recidivism) is a possible outcome. The book seeks to develop Lemert's theory in a clear and detailed manner and has clear and noticeable elements of the work of Durkheim, Goffman, and others.

### Human Deviance: Social Problems and Social Control *(1967)*

This is a volume of essays on a variety of topics regarding deviance, including the crimes of forgery and alcohol abuse, along with non-crime related issues such as stuttering. The structure of the book – using both criminal and non-criminal behaviors – resembles Becker's *The Other Side: Perspectives on Deviance* (1964), though all the essays in this volume were penned by Lemert. There are also themes on deviance, social problems, and social control, along with his theoretical elaboration of secondary deviation (often referred to as secondary deviance). In this book's preface, the author states that in "older sociology", there is the notion that deviance leads to social control, however, Lemert supports the inverse – that "social control leads to deviance" (1967, p. v.). In one of the chapters, he clearly defines the societal reaction approach to deviance and crime as a process that includes "both the expressive reactions to others (moral indignation) toward deviation and action directed to its control" (p. 42). The topic of check forgery is a common one throughout the work and reflects as one of Lemert's major research interests.

### *"Beyond Mead: The Societal Reaction to Deviance" (1974)*

This article, Lemert's 1973 presidential address to the Study of Social Problems professional organization, begins with a response to other scholars' dire prediction of the demise of deviance sociology. He proceeds to discuss his societal reaction theory, especially later versions that focus on how "deviance is shaped and stabilized by efforts to eliminate or ameliorate it" (1974, p. 458) – a crux of his theory. The theories of George Herbert Mead, founder of what would be developed by others as symbolic interactionism and a prominent theory in sociology, are examined in the labeling context and found to be lacking. For instance, values (which result in laws and rules) are formed in the complex interaction of competing groups, who often must renegotiate their roles; as an example, he uses his research on the various players in the legislative changes to the California juvenile court system to make his points. Complex theories, he concludes, are less than useful tools in understanding actual deviance policies, therefore he proposes a middle ground between theory and practice. Interestingly, Lemert mentions the concept of total institutions without an attribution to Erving Goffman, the person most connected to the concept.

### Legacy

Lemert paved the way for many other labeling theorists through his influential work in this area. While he did not formulate the elements that would become labeling theory – the roots can be found in nineteeth-century Britain – but his work paved the way for the explosion in interest in the theoretical perspective in the 1960s. Labeling theory has had many critics, in fact, many scholars see it as more of a perspective than a theory. However, the change in focus from offenders to the social apparatus that controls their behavior has made the sociology of deviance and criminology more complete. His concept of what he terms secondary deviance places the social psychology of the offenders at center stage and continues to inspire both labeling and critical perspectives of crime and deviance. His perspective focused on diverting offenders, especially younger ones, into less punitive programs, a proposal that has not always been accepted by criminal justice practitioners (Winter 2000). The consequences of labeling offenders continue to be debated and assessed, depending on the changing political tides in the American justice system.

## Erving Goffman (1922–1982)

### Introduction

Erving Goffman was a sociologist who studied the micro level interactions that often are missed by more macro level analyses of social behavior. His examinations of social life were broad and, though not totally focused on crime per se, he produced many theoretical insights that are extremely useful to the study of deviance and crime; for example, he developed theoretical perspectives on how the creation and maintenance of a devalued self-identity, or *stigma*, is involved in deviant behavior. Goffman brought a needed perspective to understanding not only large level interactions (such as those found in criminal enterprises) within the *how* framework, but also the *why* explanations (Manning, 1992).

Well known for his sardonic writing and easy to read style, Goffman's work has been so familiar and applicable to theorists of different types, even though no formal *Goffman School* exists (Manning, 1992). For a theorist whose work deals with labels and labeling, Goffman had a great disdain for having his work pigeonholed into a specific category. He is not normally considered a criminologist, as crime specifically was not his focus, in fact he considered the study of crime something unworthy of his attention (Mutchnick, Martin, & Austin, 2009). However, his influence on the field of deviance and crime are great, especially as it relates to the effects of labeling and stigma on those who violate social norms. His development of the concept of total institutions has significantly contributed to our understanding of the social control of deviance.

## Biographical Profile

Goffman was born in Manville, Alberta, Canada, the child of Jewish parents who emigrated from Ukraine. Goffman's father, an established tailor, moved his family to Manitoba and after high school Erving attended the University of Manitoba but dropped out to work in the film industry. After a brief foray into the film industry, he returned to school at the University of Toronto, majoring in sociology and anthropology. He received his undergraduate degree in 1945 and entered graduate school at the famed University of Chicago's sociology department, which had a major impact on his subsequent theorizing. He again studied both sociology and social anthropology and adopted the school's focus on conducting ethnographic research by observing subjects in their natural environments. His Ph.D. dissertation (not published but mentioned in his other works) was an ethnographic study of people living on the Shetland Islands in Scotland, completed in 1953 (Burns, 1992). The dissertation was unique in that the geography of the Shetlands had few obstructions, allowing Goffman to get a better view of how people's expressions were modified in interaction patterns (Manning, 1992).

He worked as a visiting scientist with the National Institute of Mental Health in Maryland prior to beginning a very productive career with the University of California at Berkeley in 1957, quickly rising to a full professor in a few years. He moved to the University of Pennsylvania in 1968 to work at the school of sociolinguistics where he taught and researched, until his death from cancer in 1982 (Burns, 1992).

## Profiling the Theory

Goffman taught courses in the sociology of deviance at the University of California at Berkeley in the 1960s though he was skeptical of the subfield's ability to develop a general theory that would distinguish it from the related sociological subfield of social problems. The concept of deviance is not easy to describe and although theories of deviance all involve some form of rule-breaking, to assume all forms of deviance are similar enough to the classified and scientifically investigated is a mistake, according to Goffman. However, he was able to develop a theory of deviance based on two factors involving rule breaking – mental illness and stigma (Manning, 1992). In his investigations of the mental health system, he studied the mental institutions that were at the time known as asylums (Goffman, 1961). Goffman conceived of mental illness as being a consequence of the disobedience to social norms rather than a medical condition, this placing him in direct conflict with the psychiatric establishment.

Goffman created the concept of *total institutions* to describe controlled environments in which people are placed to go through a resocialization process. In total institutions, authority is maintained by a single entity, all those institutionalized are treated the same, and there is a focus on the time management of activities, all of which promote the program's mission. His classic study on mental institutions was an in-depth exploration of all people involved in the program, including the mental health professionals and staff as well as the residents; it also described the interactions between these groups. The concept of total institutions has been applied to environments that involve other forms of rule-breaking such as various institutions of incarceration.

Another concept that has made contributions to the study of deviance and crime is *stigma*. Goffman (1964) describes stigma as a discrediting *mark* that is promoted by society to control behavior and maintain order. The effect on the individual is significant, however, and serves to damage the selves and identities of those disgraced. The avoidance of powerful stigmatizing marks can result in different impression management techniques that are used to protect or mitigate the damage to the self. People attempt to hide the damaging effects of stigma through three means: 1) *concealment*, when people simply hide the mark; 2) *cover* or *covering*, where people use deceptive behaviors so the mark will not be revealed; and 3) *disclosure*, in which the person openly admits, or even flaunts, their difference, thereby changing the situation from "a person who is discreditable" to "one who is discredited" (Manning 1992, p. 99).

Goffman's work contradicted the structural functionalist emphasis on rule maintenance by focusing on the internal mechanisms and micro level interactions regarding the violation of norms (Manning, 1992). However, his observation that deviance is supported by a vast bureaucratic network of institutions staffed by professionals whose job it is to protect society (Sumner, 1994) requires an understanding of the larger level motivation for controlling crime and other forms of deviant behavior. Goffman (1963) describes four types of deviants: 1) social deviants, who are stigmatized by the outside society; 2) in-group deviants, who are shunned but tolerated by the group in which they identify; 3) racial and ethnic minorities; and 4) lower income persons.

Goffman (1963) also describes the concept of *role misalignment* in which people maintain a persona that is more *normal* (in appearance) than that possessed by other people. For this concept, he provides the examples of a minister and a police officer, as they must maintain an impression of being more pious, and more law-abiding, respectively. For this idea, Goffman credits Howard Becker's work *Outsiders* (1963) as an inspiration.

### *Profiling the Literature*

### *"On Cooling the Mark Out: Some Aspects of Adaptation to Failure" (1952)*

This essay was written while Goffman was a graduate student at the University of Chicago. It was published in the 1950s and is filled with crime argot of that era. In colorful terms it describes how confident people (often still referred to as *con men*) exploited their victims (the *mark*); note that this is a different usage of the word mark than in his conceptualization of stigma. The mark is set up for some type of loss (usually financial) and Goffman notes the social psychological process that occurs when this person realizes they have been duped. In this interaction there is often a second person (the *outside man*) whose job is to redefine the situation in a way to soften the blow to the mark's self-esteem and decrease the chances the mark will *blow his top* (become aggressive) or report the con to the authorities (*raise a squawk*). This process not only applies to those deceived but to others who must adapt to the stigma of being taken advantage of.

### Asylums: Essays on the Social Situation of Mental Patients and Other Inmates *(1961)*

In this work based on a study conducted of a mental institution in the mid- to late 1950s, Goffman introduces the concept of total institutions, or places where social needs are met through bureaucratic institutions. Goffman identifies five groups of these institutions: 1) those that offer care for people with disabilities, are lacking in family resources, or the poor; 2) those that remove people deemed a threat (although unintentional) from society; 3) those that house people who represent an intentional danger; 4) those that house people that have a specific task; and 5) those that provide a respite for designated people. The second type, which includes mental institutions, is the focus of the book. The third type, however, is of importance to scholars of deviance and criminology, and includes jails and prison. Goffman provides a detailed observation of both the inmates and those who supervise them, as well as their relationships in the institutional setting.

## Stigma: Notes on the Management of Spoiled Identity *(1963)*

Goffman defines stigma as a deeply discrediting characteristic, however, he also adds "it should be seen as a language of relationships, not attributes" (1963, p. 3); in other words, it is only through connections with other people that a *mark* (a visible sign) exists, as identified by both the person with the mark, at least those who cannot conceal it, and the others that observe it and make distinctions based on it. A hypothetical example follows this distinction in the book in which a middle-class youth will have no problem with being seen at a library while a professional criminal will look around to see if anyone sees him. Goffman refers to many groups in his analysis other than just criminal offenders, including the disabled, addicted persons, racial minorities, sex workers, people in the LGBTQ community, and other "shamed groups", but the relevance to criminal offenders and the results of shaming, as found in many punishments throughout history to the present, is notable. In addition, the effect of labeling based on stigmatic responses, especially as it relates to the formation and maintenance of a criminal identity, is understanding the world of this population. Interestingly, Goffman, who claims to promote a "language of relationships instead of personal attributes" (as we recall), uses the labels "cripples", "village idiots", and "gypsies" in this work, revealing that the terms for stigmatized people are relative and are deemed acceptable or unacceptable at various times and places.

### Legacy

Goffman's development of the concept of total institutions certainly has benefitted the study of crime and deviance. Focusing on certain criminal acts and forms of deviance that are socially controlled through placement in the total institutions of prison or juvenile detention programs suggests American society values the idea that people can be resocialized (or reformed or corrected). In many cases, however, the institutions often serve to punish or warehouse offenders rather than correct them, but the ideal is there (covering, perhaps) as evidenced by the name provided to *correctional facilities* or in the antiquated name of juvenile *reform* programs.

The concept of stigma has been useful in the development of labeling theories of deviance in that it demonstrates the effects to selfhood created by the labels of deviants or criminal as well as the strategies employed by those labeled. His differentiation of the different types of stigmatized groups also provides a more comprehensive understanding of stigma and its effects.

In addition, Erving Goffman left behind a legacy on a more personal note. His daughter, Alice Goffman, is also an established scholar having achieved renown, and some degree of controversy, with her 2014 book *On the Run: Fugitive Life in an American City*, a six-year ethnographic study of the activities of inner-city residents with outstanding warrants.

## Howard Becker (1928–)

### Introduction

Howard S. Becker is best known for his work in a book titled *Outsiders: Studies in the Sociology of Deviance*, one of the best-selling and most often cited books in criminology (Muller, 2014). Becker is a major figure in criminology and the sociology of deviance, most notably in labeling theory. Though he reportedly never read the works of earlier labeling theorists such as Frank Tannenbaum and Edwin Lemert, Goode (2016) claims if Tannenbaum was the labeling theory's grandfather and Lemert the godfather, Becker should be considered the field's father, even if he refuses to accept that status.

### Biographical Profile

Raised in a comfortable, middle-class neighborhood in Chicago, Howard Becker was very independent as a youth and freely wandered around Chicago, observing the different aspects of freedom offered by the city. He had a love of music from an early age and his experiences as a musician in the jazz world provided him a window into the illicit activity connected with the music scene, such as prostitution, white-collar crime, and violence (Muller, 2014).

Academically, Becker was ahead of his time and attended classes at the University of Chicago while still in high school. Since there were very few schools in which to study jazz (his passion), he planned to study literature or anthropology, but eventually decided on sociology, without a true understanding of what the discipline entailed. The University of Chicago was an exciting academic environment in the 1940s with excellent faculty, including Ernest Burgess. He was in graduate school with another major contributor to the sociology of deviance, Erving Goffman (Mutchnick, et al., 2009).

After receiving his master's degree, Becker got married and at age 23 completed his doctorate at the University of Chicago. After graduation, Becker, due to his youthful appearance, was considered unqualified for an academic appointment, therefore he decided to embrace some small research projects, basically acting as a "research bum" for 14 years (Goode, 2016; Molotch, 2012). Research funding was available at the time and he began studying different groups such as drug users and medical students (Goode, 2016; Mutchnick, et al., 2009)

### Profiling the Theory

Mirroring the work of Chicago School sociologist Everett Hughes, Becker (1964) describes a career path to deviance and criminality, one which begins with a person possessing a motivation for deviance, which is often created through the establishment of a learning process. The person then commits an act defined by society as rule-breaking, and gets caught and publicly labeled, or *branded*, as a deviant. The offender then personally accepts the label of deviant and identifies as such (reflecting the concept of Lemert's secondary deviance), and then obtains membership in a group that is defined as an *out-group*.

Becker's theory redirects the focus from the behavior of norm (or rule) violators to the actors that determine normative and non-normative behavior. He describes three major issues: 1) how the phenomenon of deviance is defined and sanctioned; 2) how the offender commits unconventional acts; and 3) the consequences of rule violations (Goode, 2016). He classifies those who foster rules and obedience to them, *moral entrepreneurs*, and the activities they use to widely promote them, *moral crusades* (Becker, 1964). Two key players, *rule creators* and *rule enforcers* seek to stamp out the rule breaking behavior and to punish the deviants who fail to conform. Becker focuses on this larger process rather than just the motivations of those actors who break the rules.

Becker (1963) provides an interesting scheme that describes four types of deviance. To do this, he created a cross classification model with two types of behavior – obedient and rule-breaking – and two ways others view people regarding this behavior. If a person is obedient but perceived as deviant, they are *falsely accused*. If a person is not perceived by others as deviant and are indeed obedient, they are *conforming*. If a person is a rule-breaker and perceived as deviant, they are considered a *pure deviant*. If a person who is not perceived as deviant commits rule-breaking behavior, they are deemed a *secret deviant*. While this model introduces the perceptions of others in the formation of a deviant identity, it is easily notable that the falsely accused and obedient categories are not actually deviants. It is also obvious that the category of secret deviant ignores the fact that if the deviance is secret, it cannot elicit a response from others, which is the crux of the social reaction approach.

### Profiling the Literature

### "Becoming a Marijuana User" (1953)

This classic essay (which used the spelling "marihuana") involves interviews with many marijuana smokers. Becker describes the process in which recreational use is maintained and, rather than focus solely on the internal processes, he describes three steps through which users progress if they are to continue use of the drug: 1) a novice must initially learn the technique of using marijuana to provide the state of intoxication; 2) the user must link the feelings produced to the drug itself; and 3) the user learns to enjoy the sensations of intoxication. If any of these stages are not successfully completed, the smoking will likely be discontinued; however, if the novice is guided through the process by a more experienced person, use will likely continue. This developmental approach, Becker claims, can be applied to other behaviors to explain why they persist or cease. Becker borrows from George Herbert Mead the importance of how meaning and interpretation of experience affect human behavior, and directly from Alfred Lindesmith on how users experience opiate use. Later the use of LSD would also find a home in Becker's work, as the hallucinogenic effects experienced by the drug should follow a guided interpretation to avoid a bad trip (Muller, 2014). Becker (1974) later expounded on the process involved in the drug experience.

### Outsiders: Studies in the Sociology of Deviance *(1963)*

Becker's major work in the sociology of deviance outlined his theory of deviance early in his career. In this book, he explored the world of marijuana using jazz musicians, a category which he also occupied. By focusing on the learning process derived through the interaction between members of this subculture, he borrowed from Edwin Sutherland's theory of differential association; however, in Becker's work, there was no predatory activity against others – if the musicians were deviants, they were *cool* and presented a different image from other stereotypical criminals (Goode, 2016). *Outsiders* did not consist of one study – seven chapters were part of the jazz study, but two others were taken from his master's thesis on marijuana use, making the work a bit disjointed, which Becker acknowledges. As mentioned earlier, this was a best-seller, primarily because it was an easy read at a time when sociology books were not very comprehensible to non-academic audiences.

## The Other Side: Perspectives on Deviance *(1964)*

This is a volume edited by Becker that consists of papers featured in the journal *Social Problems* in 1962. The authors consisted of some of the biggest names in the sociology of deviance and included the topics of drug addiction, forgery, gambling, and the "dirty work" of carrying out genocide, although the book also included some topics that related to non-crime related acts. In the introduction to his work, Becker explains that interest in deviance, once a key area of sociological focus, waned for a time but was revived by the inclusion of topics other than young people described as delinquents and those addicted to drugs. The book therefore includes other types of stigmatized identities, such as those resulting from disability, sexual identity, and others. In this manner, he further develops the process of labeling as a process of deviance definition.

## *"Whose Side Are We On?" (1967)*

In this classic essay, which was his presidential address at the 1966 Society for the Study of Social Problems annual meeting, Becker grapples with a dilemma that social science researchers face: whether to approach their projects from a value free perspective or one that is committed to a value position. He contends that consequential topics, and he mentions deviance specifically, are "seen by society as morality plays and we shall find ourselves, willy nilly, taking part in those plays on one side or the other" (1967, p. 245). Becker contends that research cannot be value free and that researchers should: 1) "take sides as their personal and political commitments may dictate" (p. 247), 2) recognize that a "hierarchy of credibility" exists in which situations are defined by those in power, and 3) take measures to reduce or eliminate methodological distortions, and 4) accept the criticisms that follow.

## *Legacy*

Becker has the honor of being declared the true creator of the labeling perspective; this honor was bestowed by esteemed labeling theorist Edwin Lemert (Laub, 1983). Becker shunned the *label* of labeling theorist, or even a sociologist of deviance or criminologist, however his influence on these fields is highly significant. His contributions to understanding drug use is also important as his research on marijuana use is foundational to addiction studies.

   Becker considered himself a sociologist of professions, as he sought to understand the social lives of people in their occupations (musicians, medical students, teachers); however, this was what gave his work on deviance a different approach than labeling theory's predecessors (Muller, 2014). His writing style makes his work accessible to a wide audience, providing more exposure of this theory to people interested in understanding the labeling process and the experiences of those so labeling. The labeling perspective will remain in the fields of sociology and criminology, and criminology will change as new understandings of deviant behavior appear, but Becker's seminal work will remain as a solid base of knowledge upon which to build.

## John Braithwaite (1951—)

### *Introduction*

John Braithwaite's theoretical perspective is based on a broad model of punishment known as restorative justice. A major focus of his theory regards shaming penalties and how currently criminal offenders are chastened using *disintegrative* measures, meaning they are labeled as criminals and ex-cons. Western society tends to focus on punishment based on a *just deserts* philosophy in which offenders must be forced to feel some discomfort for the pain they cause the community. Instead of this traditional approach, he introduces a *reintegrative shaming* model that allows the offenders to make reparations then be reintegrated back into the community (Lilly, Cullen, & Ball, 2002).

## Biographical Profile

Born and raised in Queensland, Australia, Braithwaite was a successful rugby player in his youth. At the University of Queensland, he studied sociology, psychology, anthropology, and he obtained his Ph.D. in sociology in 1977. He taught the institution's first criminology course as a graduate student completing his doctorate. For a year after completing his degree, he became a lecturer at the University of Queensland, followed by a post-doctoral fellowship at the University of California at Irvine. He returned to Australia and worked as a criminologist for a few years before joining the faculty at Australian National University in 1984. He has many publications and awards for his work in criminology (Piquero & Clipper, 2014).

## Profiling the Theory

Braithwaite notes that societies with high levels of urbanization and industrialization, such as those in the West, also have high levels of individualism. Therefore, they have correspondingly low levels of communitarianism, i.e., cohesion developed through interdependence. Due to this, crime rates are high and the means for dealing with offenders involve a highly punitive approach based on strategies that seek to have the offender pay back victims (and society) through their punishment methods. These methods, however, involve shaming practices that are disintegrative in that the system excludes, demoralizes, and stigmatizes. The result is that offenders will seek out other stigmatized people and form their own deviant subcultures.

Braithwaite suggests there should be an alternative to this process – one that involves reintegrative shaming. In this approach, the offense committed, rather than the person committing it, is shamed. Braithwaite recommends a restorative process where conferences between offender, victim, and others affected by the crime are utilized rather than a formal court process, which is adversarial in nature. Offenders are expected to show remorse and to fully understand the consequences of their actions, and to engage in some activity, such as community service, that restores them back into the community, and at the same time provides some degree of comfort and satisfaction to the aggrieved. Of course, not all types of criminal behavior or offenders will be appropriate for these conferences, but many would benefit, according to Braithwaite and advocates of the program; these advocates often include religious organizations and victim rights advocates, as well as peacemaking and feminist criminologists.

The interest in restorative justice seemed to be a new approach in the 1990s, however, its roots can be traced back decades earlier. Interest arose due to four factors: 1) growing dissatisfaction with the criminal justice system; 2) concerns over the costs of correctional practices; 3) increased social interest in the use of informal means of punishment; and 4) renewed interest in metaphors of healing, restoration, and reconciliation rather than traditional processes of punishment. Due to a greater understanding of indigenous justice practices, interest sprang up in the Midwestern United States and Canada. Initially carried out in moderated conferences with offenders and victims, later other parties were included, e.g., family members, friends, advocates, and professional justice and service practitioners. Other components and derivations such as sentencing circles (adopted from indigenous tribes), conflict resolution and mediation programs, inmate rights activism, victim rights activism, and victim impact panels were also involved (Immarigeon & Daly 1997).

## *Profiling the Literature*

### Crime, Shame, and Reintegration *(1989)*

In this often-cited book, Braithwaite introduces his theory of reintegrative shaming and adopts the contention by labeling theorists that labeling offenders worsens the original infraction: he states this is both right and wrong and introduces the concept of shaming to explain this contradiction. Traditional shaming techniques, as a correctional strategy, are disintegrative, meaning offenders are cast out of society; or they can be reintegrative, which means offenders are punished through a focus on the act rather that the person, and accepted back into the community once they admit the pain they caused and take steps to right the wrong. When offenders are shamed in a disintegrative manner, they often become involved in subcultural deviant activity.

### *"Restorative Justice and a New Criminal Law of Substance Abuse" (2001)*

In this article, Braithwaite illustrates his enthusiastic advocacy of restorative justice programs and their utility in various behaviors, in this case, substance abuse. Substance abuse itself is not a crime (although it is often linked to criminal conduct), but it does have the potential to inflict harm on the user, the user's family, significant others, and others who might be victimized by substance abusing behavior. A lack of motivation to change is key to maintaining the substance addiction, therefore there should be significant demotivating strategies to control the problematic actions. As with other restorative justice schemes, it is the behavior itself – the addiction – that is the problem, not the addicted person. Since it is easy to *drift* away from control on drug use, Braithwaite offers hope in "ritual impact that might shake a substance abuse out of drift" (2001, p. 231). Using programs in a Native American community as a guide, he believes that: 1) the abuse of substances and people constitute a *vicious circle*; 2) the concern and comfort of a community creates a *virtuous circle*; and 3) the abuses should be openly discussed and confronted. Some recommendations are made involving practices that divert substance abuse programs from the courts to local communities. It is easy to relate this to the technique in addiction treatment known as the intervention process, where members and other people in an addicted person's life directly confront them about the addiction and the effects it has on others. The description offered in this article is similar but on a more macro level.

### Restorative Justice and Responsive Regulation *(2002)*

Braithwaite provides a wide-ranging description of restorative justice beginning with a history of the practice's underpinnings. He defines restorative justice as a process whereby the mission is the restoration of victims, offenders, and their communities. He outlines several aspects of the concept including comparative data on its effectiveness, its potential benefits, common misconceptions, and concerns, and its relationship with other current initiatives such as world-wide peacemaking strategies and sustainable development. He introduces the concept of *response regulation* to this discussion, which refers to the responsible oversight of justice practices as opposed to *regulatory formalism*, the strict adherence to official prescriptions for offending behavior. Responsible regulation seeks the reasons and motivations for the behavior, followed by some potential diversionary strategies, e.g., persuasion tactics and warnings, if appropriate. Although this perspective lacks the consistency of traditional justice approaches currently in use, Braithwaite believes it will result in a more humane and benevolent system.

He explains restorative justice's current appeal to people of both major political persuasions as people on the political left appreciate a move from the current punitive-based justice system into a more human approach (the welfare model), and those on the right support justice through the empowerment of individuals rather than dictated by the government and for a desire for fiscal responsibility (the justice model).

### "Redeeming the 'F' Word in Restorative Justice" (2016)

As suggestive as the title sounds, the "f word" referenced is "forgiveness" and Braithwaite claims genuine forgiveness is normally not given in restorative justice practices and as such should not be demanded. In Western society, earlier ideals of justice were derived from Christian values; however over time justice has become commodified. The increasing professionalism of the police, the courts, (and though not mentioned, one would assume corrections) has obvious advantages in an ever-modernizing society, but it also moves societies away from the basic element of seeking restoration instead of retribution and has "set back the civilizing journey of forgiveness" (2016, p. 93). Restorative justice, to be effective, requires a return to doctrines that emphasize its benefits, whether they involve Christian, Muslim, or other religious ideology, or even secular or scientific ideals.

### Legacy

Braithwaite is a major contributor of the theory, research, and practice of restorative justice, an ideology whose programs have been instituted worldwide and are far too numerous to mention here. In addition, his theory of reintegrative shaming in the broader context of restorative justice has had significant policy implications in the criminal justice field. In a commendation for Braithwaite prior to his acceptance of an honorary doctorate, Braithwaite is described as having earned a reputation as the "new Durkheim", one of the most influential and cited criminologists in the world, an intellectual giant who belongs to the absolute world top and " continues to shape this very world top from day to day" (Parmentier, 2011, p. 7).

### References

American Criminological Society. (2020). *Division of Convict Criminology*. Retrieved on December 27, 2020 from https://www.concrim.org/.

Barmaki, R. (2019). On the origin of "labeling" theory in criminology: Frank Tannenbaum and the Chicago School of sociology. *Deviant Behavior*, 40(2), 256–271.

Becker, H.S. (1953). Becoming a marihuana user. *American Journal of Sociology*, 59(3), 235–242.

Becker, H.S. (1963). *Outsiders: Studies in the Sociology of Deviance*. New York: Free Press.

Becker, H.S. (Ed.) (1964). *The Other Side: Perspectives on Deviance*. New York: Free Press.

Becker. H.S. (1967). Whose side are we on? *Social Problems*, 14(3), 239–247.

Becker, H.S. (1974). Consciousness, power and drug effects, *Journal of Psychedelic Drugs*, 6(1), 67–76.

Braithwaite, J. (1989). *Crime, Shame, and Reintegration.* Cambridge, UK: Cambridge University Press.

Braithwaite, J. (2001). Restorative justice and a new criminal law of substance abuse. *Youth and Society,* 33(2), 227–248.

Braithwaite, J. (2002). *Restorative Justice and Responsive Regulation.* Oxford, England: Oxford University Press.

Braithwaite, J. (2016). Redeeming the "f" word in restorative justice. *Oxford Journal of Law* 5(1), 79–93.

Burns, T. (1992). *Erving Goffman.* London and New York: Routledge.

Cooley, C.H. (1902). *Human Nature and the Social Order.* New York: Scribner's.

Cullen, F.T., & Agnew, R. (1999). *Criminological Theory: Past to Present, Essential Readings.* Los Angeles: Roxbury.

Goffman, A. (2014). *On the Run: Life in an American City.* Chicago, IL: University of Chicago Press.

Goffman, E. (1952). On cooling the mark out: Some aspects of adaptation to failure. *Psychiatry,* 15(4), 451–463.

Goffman, E. (1961). *Asylums: Essays on the Social Situation of Mental Patients and Other Inmates.* New York: Anchor Books.

Goffman, E. (1963). *Stigma: Notes on the Management of Spoiled Identity.* Englewood Cliffs, NJ: Prentice-Hall.

Goode, E. (2016). The paradox of Howard Becker's intellectual identity. *Deviant Behavior,* 37(12), 1443–1448.

Immarigeon, R., & Daly, K. (1997). Restorative justice: Origins, practices, concepts, and challenges. *ICCA Journal of Community Corrections.*

Laub, J.H. (1983). *Criminology in the Making: An Oral History.* Boston: Northeastern University Press.

Lemert, C.C. (2000). Whatever happened to the criminal? Edwin Lemert's Societal Reaction. In C.M. Lemert & M.F. Winter (Eds.). *Crime and Deviance: Essays and Innovations of Edwin M. Lemert.* Lanham, MD: Rowman & Littlefield, pp. 1–15.

Lemert, E.M. (1951). *Social Pathology: Systematic Approaches to the Study of Sociopathic Behavior.* New York: McGraw-Hill.

Lemert, E.M. (1967). *Human Deviance: Social Problems and Social Control.* Englewood Cliffs, NJ: Prentice-Hall.

Lemert, E.M. (1974). Beyond Mead: The societal reaction to deviance. *Social Problems,* 21(4), 457–468.

Lemert. E. (2000). *Crime and Deviance: Essays and Innovations of Edwin M. Lemert.* Lanham, MD: Rowman and Littlefield.

Lilly, J.R., Cullen, F.T., & Ball, R.A. (2002). *Criminological Theory: Contexts and Consequences,* 3rd ed. Thousand Oaks, CA: Sage.

Manning, P. (1992). *Erving Goffman and Modern Sociology.* Palo Alto, CA: Stanford University Press.

Merton, R.K. (1948). The self-fulfilling prophecy. *Antioch Review,* 8(2), 193–210.

Molotch, H. (2012). Howard S. Becker interviewed by Harvey Molotch. *Public Culture,* 24(2), 421–443.

Muller, T. (2014). Chicago, jazz, and marijuana: Howard Becker on Outsiders. *Symbolic Interaction,* 37(4), 576–594.

Mutchnick, R.J., Martin, R., & Austin, W.T. (2009). *Criminological Thought: Pioneers Past and Present.* Upper Saddle River, NJ: Prentice-Hall.

Parmentier, S. (2011). Laudatio for John Brathwaite. In *The Sparking Discipline of Criminology: John Braithwaite and the Construction of Critical Social Science and Social Justice.* Belgium: Leuven University Press, pp. 6–10.

Piquero, N.L., & Clipper, S. (2014). Braithwaite, John. *The Encyclopedia of Crime and Criminal Justice.* Wiley Online Library. Received on December 27, 2020 from https://doi.org/10.1002/9781118517383.wbeccj483.

Richards, S.C., & Ross, J.I. (2001). Introducing the new school of convict criminology. *Social Justice,* 28(1), 177–190.

Sumner, C. (1994). *The Sociology of Deviance: An Obituary.* Buckingham: Open University Press.

Tannenbaum, F. (1922). *Wall Shadows: A Study in American Prisons.* New York: G.P. Putnam Sons.

Tannenbaum, F. (1924). *Darker Phases of the South.* New York & London: G.P. Putnam Sons.

Tannenbaum, F. (1925). The professional criminal: An inquiry into the making of criminals. *Century Magazine*, 110, 577–588.

Tannenbaum, F. (1938). *Crime and the Community*. Boston, MA: Ginn.

Whitfield, S.J. (2013). Out of anarchism and into the academy: The many lives of Frank Tannenbaum. *Journal for the Study of Radicalism*, 7(2), 93–124.

Winn, P. (2010). Frank Tannenbaum reconsidered: Introduction. *International Labor and Working-Class History*, 77, 109–114.

Winter, M.F. (2000). Edwin M. Lemert: An intellectual portrait. In C.C. Lemert & M.F. Winter (Eds.) *Crime and Deviance: Essays and Innovations of Edwin M. Lemert*. Lanham, MD: Rowman & Littlefield, pp. 273–294.

Yeager, M.G. (2011). Frank Tannenbaum: The making of a convict criminologist. *The Prison Journal*, 91 (2), 177–197.

# 9

# CONFLICT THEORIES

## Bonger, Chambliss, Quinney, Taylor, Walton, & Young, Black

## Introduction

Most theories of crime and deviance assume a level of consensus amongst individual members of society in order to function. For example, it may not be in my own personal interest to stop for a red light, but I have agreed to do so in a social contract with other citizens so that when I have a green light, I can drive through an intersection safely. Conflict theorists take a different approach to this view – they view society, and therefore law, as created by the ruling class for their own interests. That means the values of the ruling class are the impetus behind the passage of any laws.

In this chapter, different forms of conflict theories, to include Marxist (Bonger), legal realism (Chambliss), peacemaking (Quinney), radical/*new* criminology (Taylor, Walton & Young), and the behavior of law (Black) are all discussed. While these theories are all somewhat different, they all use a conflict approach to power as the backdrop for their explanations of deviant behavior.

## Willem Adriaan Bonger (1876–1940)

### Introduction

Though he would be followed by several others, Willem Bonger was one of the early criminologists to develop a Marxist criminology and is considered by many to be the father of critical criminology. Eschewing other theories of crime that focused on the individual, especially rational choice theories, Bonger focused on how economic conditions contribute to crime and thus turned to the work of Karl Marx and Friedrich Engels to formulate his theory (Stichman, 2010). He also rejected positivist theories of the era that theorized the roots of criminality can be found in the genetic makeup of individuals (Birmingham, 1970). Therefore, Bonger was the first criminologist to develop a large body of work with a Marxist foundation (Taylor, 1971).

### Biographical Profile

Bonger grew up in a liberal home, the youngest of ten children, one of whom became the sister-in-law of famed painter Vincent van Gogh. His father was active in the insurance

DOI: 10.4324/9781003036609-9

industry and both parents were religious, an interest that did not characterize Bonger. One scholar (Bemmelen, 1955) presumes his rejection of religion and subsequent interest in socialism stems from the contrasts he saw in his family's religiosity. Willem was a sensitive young man who developed a sympathy for marginalized groups, a temperament that would later be revealed in his later work. He married Marie Hendrika van Heteren in 1905. Bonger became interested in the study of social problems and saw socialism as the most appropriate means of remedying them (Bemmelen, 1955).

Studying at the University of Amsterdam, Bonger sought to understand deviance and crime and became involved with a group at the university that viewed criminal behavior from both sociological and anthropological perspectives. He came to believe that economic and social factors rather than heredity were the primary contributions to crime. His doctoral thesis was transformed into his first book, *Criminality and Economic Conditions*, in 1905 and translated into English in 1916; this became a groundbreaking work in criminology which influenced scholars in other academic fields such as psychology and psychiatry to pay attention to sociological factors in human behavior (Bemmelen, 1955).

Bonger became a professor of sociology and criminology at the University of Amsterdam in 1922, and retained this position until his death in 1940, leaving a large body of work in Marxist criminology. He was the founder of the Netherlands Sociological Association, editor of the journal *Men and Society*, and an active member of several national councils and boards (Wigmore, 1941). A staunch and openly defiant opponent of Nazism, he refused to flee the Netherlands when the country was invaded by Hitler's army and died by suicide in 1940 (Bemmelen, 1955).

## Profiling the Theory

Bonger observes the world of criminality from his vantage point in the late nineteenth and early twentieth century as it was becoming increasingly shaped by capitalism. As noted earlier, Bonger was heavily influenced by Marxist ideology, which is a critique of the capitalist system and a focus on the ways inequality is maintained in society. Karl Marx, and his cowriter, financial supporter, and friend Friedrich Engels, sought to reveal the oppression of workers by the owners of the modes of production (at that time, the factories); the workers (the proletariat) were involved in a constant struggle with the wealthy and powerful elites (the bourgeoisie) to obtain some degree of economic fairness, better working conditions, and positive relations with others. Marx and Engels were primarily focused on the divisions of wealth and class resulting from capitalism and did not articulate a criminological theory based on social inequities in a capitalist system; that job would be left to neo-Marxist scholars.

Bonger posits the period before capitalism in Europe was characterized by the existence of *primitive communities* which were guided by an altruistic drive for survival – people were motivated by the needs of the whole, and this drive was transferred to the economic system. In this vein, Durkheim seems to appear in Bonger's work, in the proposition that a shared morality creates altruistic traits in society. People suffered or prospered together, based on natural forces in an era before machines made the weather, geography, and other factors less relevant. With the advent of the industrial revolution, the altruistic motivation was transformed into an egoistic one, in which people aggressively competed against each other, dehumanized others, and generally focused on themselves and their own welfare. Moving from nature, production became focused on needs that are fake and unnatural. From this economic change came an increase of crime in various sorts – economic, sexual, violent, and others (Curran & Renzetti, 2001).

According to Bonger, the capitalistic worldview of egoism (the focus on oneself rather than the whole) became adopted by most members of society, including the proletariat. Egoism, Bonger claims, promotes criminal behavior. The motivation for criminality, therefore, comes from a "criminal thought" that compels people to deviate from social norms. People's lives become determined by conditions of capitalism but despite these determinant factors, they are still held responsible for their behavior. Bonger's solution is the transition to a socialist society, which will reduce crime. In this new society, crime as currently experienced will not exist and physicians rather than judges will be needed to address deviations (Leonard, 1982).

In noting several of the critiques of Bonger's work which included, among others, economic reductionism and an inadequate understanding of true Marxist ideology, Leonard (1982) applauds his depiction of capitalism's effects, his attempts to describe a relationship between capitalism and crime, and his concern over economic exploitation.

### Profiling the Literature

### Criminality and Economic Conditions (1916)

In his most cited work, Bonger makes a comparison between the early pre-capitalist (or *primitive communist*) societies and the capitalist economic systems in Europe existing in the late 1800s and early 1900s. Since primitive communist societies were producing goods for instant consumption rather than money and the accumulation of wealth, the members were all working for the common interest of survival. As noted earlier, this common interest created a high level of solidarity and a strong sense of community, which resulted in high degrees of altruism and lower levels of deviance and crime. However, with the advent of capitalism in Europe, people became greedy and competitive, creating an egoist orientation that led to a lessening of shared values and an increase in crime. Plus, the enormous potential for goods produced creates false needs and a greater desire to obtain unnecessary products, by illicit means if necessary; this situation exists among those in the upper as well as the lower classes. The justice system, however, is more lenient on those in the higher economic strata. A second edition of this work was published in 1969, at a time when Marxism was becoming revisited by many scholars in its application to various disciplines, including sociology and criminology.

### An Introduction to Criminology (1936)

This criminology text written in 1936 is small compared to today's standards and certainly does not follow the same format. Bonger begins with a clear definition of criminology, which is the study of criminality "in its entire extent (this is theoretical or 'pure criminology') whilst side by side with their theoretical science, and founded upon its conclusions, we have what is called practical or applied criminology" (1936, p. 1). In this he acknowledges the pure and applied forms of the science. Bonger also describes the subfields of criminology, in the pure forms: 1) criminal anthropology; 2) criminal sociology; 3) criminal psychology; and 4) criminal psycho- and neuropathology; and in the practical forms: 5) applied; and 6) criminalistics.

Bonger proceeds with a historical perspective on the field, describing it as a "child of the nineteenth century" (1936, p. 26), beginning in the 1830s, with progressive reforms in the penal system and the rise of criminal sociology, but he also describes the field's precursors from antiquity to his present era. In the following chapters, he provides a discussion on the different schools: 1) "statistician sociologists" in which he explains the evolution of statistical methods in criminology; 2) the "Italian or anthropological school" of Lombroso and others; 3) the "French or environmental school" of Tarde and others; 4) the "bio-sociological" school in which a formula was given: "every crime = individual + environment" (p. 117); and 5) the "spiritualist school" with religion at its core. "Criminal psychology" deserves a separate chapter as does "crime as an applied science" in which Bonger outlines his philosophy on the treatment of chronic offenders as a policy matter: "criminals are among the most unhappy of our fellow-beings, and that, therefore is our duty to exercise the greatest humanity in our treatment of them" (p. 159).

## Race and Crime *(1943 – published posthumously)*

In this early work on the intersection of race and crime, Bonger begins with some definitions of race in use in the first half of the twentieth century, all which identify physical and inheritable traits as the primary characteristic; he then refutes these indicators of race as being superficial. He also adds ethnicity, nationality, and regionality in this pronouncement as well. Bonger uses statistical data from different countries, including the Netherlands, Germany, Poland, Finland, and the United States, to analyze the crime rates of these groups: "Negroes", "Jews", "Mediterraneans", "Alpines", "Nordics", and "East Baltics". Obviously, today definitions of race are quite different from these, but Bonger's use of statistical and comparative data offered a challenge to early criminologists who accepted biological explanations of criminality as evidenced by this comment: "crime occurs in all races, and, by the nature of things, is only committed by a number (generally quite small) of individuals in each race. In principle the races do not differ" (1943, p. 28).

## *Legacy*

Bonger's work is important as it moved criminology away from positivist notions of criminality as being based on biological traits and toward a focus on economic conditions, opening a new area of exploration into crime and deviance. Despite the many critiques of his approach, he cleared the way for other critical criminologists with a Marxist orientation such as Quinney, Chambliss, and the left realists, who followed him decades later. His comparison of pre-capitalist and capitalist periods also anticipates perspectives on modernity and late modernity that would emerge in the generations that followed.

## William J. Chambliss (1933–2014)

### *Introduction*

William J. Chambliss was a sociologist and criminologist who pioneered the field of critical criminology that budded in the 1960s. Michalowski (2016) suggests four primary contributions: 1) his challenge to current understandings of crime by introducing the political and economic interests in creating and enforcing law; 2) his development of a structural focus on law creation; 3) his seminal investigations into state crime; and 4) a deeply immersive ethnographic methodology that augments his theory. The thread connecting these contributions is Chambliss' commitment to uncovering the inequities that exist in the criminal justice system.

### Biographical Profile

Chambliss was born in 1933 in Buffalo, New York. His parents divorced when he was young, and his mother moved around as she was able to find work. She settled with the children in Los Angeles, California. Between his junior and senior years, Chambliss worked on a farm in Washington state where he encountered prison inmates who also worked there; from this experience he developed an interest in crime and its correction, and specifically how race figured in the criminal justice system. He enrolled at the University of Virginia but was unable to continue paying college costs, so he returned to California where tuition was free at the time (Burke, 2014). He attended the University of California, Los Angeles, where he studied under famed criminologist Donald Cressey before being drafted into the military and serving during the Korean War. Afterward, he attended Indiana University, where he studied for his Ph.D. under acclaimed addiction theorist Alfred Lindesmith which influenced his own research on the disparate drug laws that are based on race and class (Ferrell & Hamm, 2016). His experiences in Korea, in which he observed American and Korean soldiers commit many serious criminal actions such as rape, assault, and theft against the enemy with impunity, helped shape his belief that those in power make and enforce the rules (Chambliss, 1987).

Chambliss taught at four universities from 1962 until his death in 2014: The University of Washington, the University of California, Santa Barbara, the University of Delaware, and George Washington University, as well as participating in several visiting professorships around the world. He published several seminal books along with numerous book chapters and articles, mostly on critical criminology, to which he was a key contributor. His investigations into organized crime, corrupt governmental officials, and drug smugglers put him in some tenuous situations but he courageously carried out his research (Applebaum, 2014, Ferrell & Hamm, 2016). As much as Chambliss enjoyed the more mundane work of academia, such as reading through volumes of literature in criminology and deviant behavior, his true love was getting on the streets and dealing directly with persons involved with criminal behavior and its control, including participating in "ride alongs" with police officers (Applebaum, 2014).

### Profiling the Theory

Chambliss' work on critical criminological theory came against a backdrop of the protest movements of the 1960s. He used the ethnographic method to better understand the lived experiences of marginalized people on the street who engaged in criminal behavior (petty and serious crimes). He studied the structural forces that induce people to engage in criminal activity and, rather than engage in abstract sociological theorizing, he viewed deviance and crime as a "social force that flowed from courtroom to street corner, from corporate malfeasance to petty corruption, catching all involved in entanglements of law and crime" (Ferrell & Hamm, 2016, p. 167). Chambliss' early work was undergirded with the approach known as *legal realism*, which posits that law should be reflected in action rather than just abstract theory, and he hoped to produce a scientifically supported theory of law (Lilly, Cullen, & Ball, 2002).

The evolution of Chambliss' thought can be easily observed in his publications. His early writings, for example, reflected his basic ideas on conflict theory. In the early 1970s, he teamed up with law professor Robert T. Seidman to illustrate their position on the role of power and control in the legal system (Chambliss & Seidman, 1971). This text posited, among other things, that as societies become more complex, greater focus is placed on the criminal justice bureaucracy, guided and supported by the social elites who promote *law and order* policies that increase the stratification gap between the wealthy and the poor and working classes.

Chambliss' views began to change in the mid-1970s, as he began to question the system's ability to correct with any significant change. He joined some other social science scholars as they adopted a Marxist approach to crime and its control (Lilly, et al., 2002). In this line of thought, elites who run society determine the acts they want to criminalize because they benefit from them economically and from a safety perspective. The criminal justice system is exploitive and unless an overhaul is made of the system, it will continue to contribute to an unjust and unequal society.

### Profiling the Literature

### "A Sociological Analysis of the Law of Vagrancy" (1964)

This early essay from 1964 provides us with his views on how vagrancy laws have been used throughout history to remove people from public areas, not for concerns over threats, but for the economic benefit of the wealthy. This article chronicles the vagrancy laws in England in 1349 and analyzes their current relevance in America in explaining how such laws are meant to control society's *undesirables*, especially in relation to criminal behavior.

### On the Take *(1978)*

Originally published in 1978, the work had a second edition published in 1988 in which Chambliss provides this foundational statement of his theory:

> crime is not a by-product of an otherwise effectively working political economy; it is a main product of that political economy. Crime is in fact a cornerstone on which the political and economic relations of democratic-capitalist societies as constructed.
>
> *(p. 2)*

If Durkheim viewed crime as normal, Chambliss sees it as a keystone of our political and economic systems. This work is a result of an ethnographic study in Seattle, Washington conducted between 1962–1967, though he made subsequent analyses. In this book, he introduced the notion of how contradictions are embedded in the choices of law makers, law enforcers, and law breakers. In addition to his theoretical analysis, he offers prescriptions – the mobilization of citizen groups to oversee governmental operations and to decriminalize certain criminal activity (Chambliss, 1988). The book certainly has neo-Marxist overtones, however the prescriptions offered were progressive, but not revolutionary, a point maintained in the work.

### "The Saints and the Roughnecks" (1973)

This article is standard reading in college courses on deviance and criminology and involves Chambliss' two-year observation of two groups of high school boys – one from the middle class with significant resources, the other group from the lower, working class; the former he referred to as the "saints" and the latter as the "roughnecks". While the saints were expected to become respectable citizens and the roughnecks to become criminals, the activities performed by the saints as observed by Chambliss were often more deviant than the roughnecks. However, the saints' deferent appearance, the lack of visibility of their misdeeds, and the bias of the community worked to keep them out of trouble. Community expectations created a self-fulfilling prophecy for both groups, obviously benefitting the saints.

### "Toward a Political Economy of Crime" (1975)

This essay, written in the mid-1970s, represents a clear proclamation of Chambliss' approach to criminology. He unambiguously articulates the dramatic move in sociology from consensus-oriented approaches (functionalist, social disorganization, and differential association perspectives) to a more critical approach – an approach that is both reflective of and promoted by the same changes in criminology. Capitalistic societies, states Chambliss, create antagonisms between those in the *power elite* who own and control the modes of production and those who must be subservient to those interests, and who often resort to crime because of their circumstances. To support his position, he describes two studies he conducted – one in Nigeria and the other in Seattle, Washington, in which he exposes high degrees of governmental corruption. He supplements his conflict approach with the labeling perspective in this classic statement: "crime is a matter of who can pin the label on whom, and underlying this socio-political process is the structure of social relations determined by the political economy" (1975, p. 165).

### Law, Order, and Power (1971)

This work coauthored by law professor Robert Seidman describes the American justice system and seeks to "describe and to explain the characteristics and the shape of legal order" (1971, p. 13). It provides a comprehensive analysis of law and the legal system using judicial, sociological, philosophical, and anthropological perspectives. The two scholars present the claim that the legal system being based on a "*values consensus*" model of the whole society is a myth, and it is only the values of the lawmakers and the elites they support that are served, not those with fewer resources. The neutrality supposedly exemplified by the American legal system is therefore a myth. The authors advocate a *law in action* over a *law in the books* approach, one that supports the true ideal that justice is blind.

### Legacy

Regarding his contribution to the study of crime in various forms, Chambliss authored or co-authored almost two dozen books and an enormous number of book chapters, journal articles, and popular writings. He is also well-known for publication of several textbooks and reference works (one which contains an essay from one of the authors, LS). Chambliss was involved in several professional organizations, including serving as president of two major ones – the American Criminological Society and the Society for the Study of Social Problems, which now has a lifetime achievement award for exceptional scholars in his honor (Applebaum, 2014).

In the fields of the sociology of deviance and criminology, Chambliss' influence runs deep, and generations of scholars who identify as critical criminologists will reflect on his impressive body of work. Newer forms of critical criminology will also have a strong foundation upon which to build.

## Richard Quinney (1934–)

### Introduction

Richard Quinney is a well-established and prolific criminologist and sociologist who has sharp critiques of a criminal justice system that he believes is corrupted by capitalism. His early theoretical insights adopt a Marxist perspective in which he supports a revolutionary change to the justice system. Later formulations of his theory include new perspectives that focus on spirituality and peacemaking. His theorical contributions have taken different forms over the years but he continues to advocate for social justice reforms.

### Biographical Profile

Earl Richard Quinney grew up in rural Wisconsin and his upbringing provided him with a traditional, conservative perspective, which would later evolve to a critical approach as time passed. As a student he had interests in biology, psychology, and sociology and decided to attend Carroll College, a small liberal arts college in rural Wisconsin, from which he graduated in 1956. Because of his early interest in biology, Quinney was advised to consider a career in hospital management after graduation, so he enrolled in a master's program in that field at Northwestern University. After a bad experience with a summer job at a hospital, however, he was redirected to the sociology department and obtained his master's degree with academic work in sociology and criminology (Mutchnick, Martin, & Austin, 2009).

Originally interested in rural sociology, his attention turned to deviance and crime and he decided to enroll at the University of Wisconsin at Madison for his doctoral studies in sociology in 1957. Under the mentorship of esteemed criminologist Marshall Clinard, he completed his Ph.D. in 1962. While working on his doctorate, Quinney married Valerie Yow, an academic historian and the couple had two children. Quinney accepted a faculty position at the University of Kentucky and became involved in the Civil Rights movement. Over the next several years, he taught at several other institutions, published several well reviewed works, and adopted a counterculture lifestyle. After his moves, he ended up back in the Midwest as a faculty member at Northern Illinois University (Mutchnick, et al., 2009).

### Profiling the Theory

Although primarily known as a conflict criminologist, Quinney did not start out with a critical perspective. In fact, he initially adopted a functionalist perspective, notably in his work with mentor Marshall Clinard. By 1970, Quinney moved his emphasis from crime causation and instead of focusing on individual behavior, looked at the exercise of social control measures by the criminal justice system (Martin, Mutchnick & Austin, 1990).

Quinney's theoretical position can be placed into a type of ideology known as instrumental Marxism. This perspective posits that the powerful groups in society use the legal system to maintain their power and control over those without such power. If the poorer classes are controlled through legal processes, the rich maintain their class advantage and privilege. Definitions of crime and deviance are therefore created by the elites, using the criminal justice system as an instrument of control. Judges, prosecutors, and defense attorneys are instruments of a capitalistic state apparatus and while public defenders give the impression that the state supports those accused of crime by providing free representation to indigent citizens (Lynch & Groves, 1989), that representation is often of a lesser quality than that provided to those who can afford private counsel.

In addition to his conflict approach, Quinney also sees crime and deviance as being socially constructed concepts. Since the definitions of crime and deviance are created and maintained by those in power, these understandings become part of the dominant ideology that the rest of society comes to accept as fair. The problem is that individually based punishments neglect the broader social inequities of a capitalist system. It is the society that needs reform, not simply those who have violated actions deemed criminal by the powerful elites.

Quinney's later theorizing involves a mixture of spirituality and social justice in what has been called peacemaking criminology (Pepinsky, & Quinney, 1991). In this approach, crime is reframed as suffering and an inevitable consequence of living in a world where suffering can flourish. The politically popular "get tough" approaches to crime, according to Quinney, have been a failure and the use of more humane practices and efforts at reintegration into society are advocated.

### Profiling the Literature

### "Is Criminal Behavior Deviant Behavior?" (1965)

In this early article, Quinney begins with the position that violations of criminal law should be seen in relation to deviance. As society becomes more differentiated, the law becomes important as a formal system of order maintenance. A diversity of opinions about norms requires the government to step in as a mediator since there will not be a consensus about unacceptable human behavior. Not all laws are supported by all members of society and some are accepted more than others, in fact total agreement is impossible. In a democratic system, all people should have the ability to influence law, however, elites have greater influence and white-collar crime becomes especially problematic. According to Quinney, these and other factors should be taken into consideration by criminologists, who should advocate for changing laws when norms change.

### The Social Reality of Crime (1970)

Quinney, in his quest to "reinterpret criminology", proposes a theoretical approach to the sociology of crime that attempts to explain: 1) the process of crime definition; 2) the development of applications of these definitions; 3) the resulting behavioral manifestations; and 4) the culmination of criminal conceptions. Crime, from Quinney's perspective, is relative to different legal systems and should be viewed as "a *definition* of human behavior that is conferred on some persons by others...thus *crime is created*" (2001, p. 15, italics in text). These definitions of crime create a reality that is manifest in criminal justice policies, which are created by and benefit those with power. This results in conflicts between those with and those without power, a power which is regulated by governmental structures through the system of laws. Quinney provides an elaborate history of the development of laws and an analysis of the components of the criminal justice system – the police, the courts, and the correctional system. He then proceeds to an examination of the cultural (societal organizations) and the individual (action patterns), thereby formulating his theory at both macro and micro levels of analysis. He concludes the work with a view of crime through the lens of the public, along with its consequences, and a discussion on the "politics of reality" in which crime and its control become a political issue which "is used to the advantage of those who control the processes of government" (p. 316).

This book would become a classic in critical criminology and it elevated Quinney to the status of international crime scholar. Due to its wide circulation and to its challenge to traditional criminological theory, it was met with several critiques by conventional criminologists. However, the work's detailed and well-researched analysis made a major contribution to the field (Trevino, 2001).

## Critique of Legal Order: Crime Control in Capitalist Society *(1974)*

In this work, Quinney is clear in his assertion that "the legal system is an apparatus created to secure the interests of the dominant class. Contrary to conventional belief, law is a tool of the ruling class" (p. 52). This is accomplished through crime commissions, policy decisions in all areas of government, bureaucracies, police training agencies, and even propaganda campaigns through mass media. Echoing Marx, the problems of capitalism, Quinney posits, will bring about its own destruction but if an adequate socialist scheme is not created to replace it, society can fall to fascism. It is clear the events of the period – the Vietnam War, the Watergate scandal, civil and gender rights struggles, and the emergence of the counterculture movement – aid Quinney in formulating his ideas; he believes changes are coming that require a new radical criminology.

## Class, State, and Crime: On the Theory and Practice of Criminal Justice *(1977)*

In this work Quinney extends his neo-Marxist criminology. He advocates moving beyond analyses of individual motivations of deviant behavior and places the focus on "capitalist justice", which structures the legal system around attempts by those in power to maintain that power and "secure the existing capitalist order" (1977, p. 7). Quinney provides a clear description of Marxist theory and notes that as capitalism expands, the means of controlling the working class also expands through greater penal measures, especially for African American citizens, however, these punishments often exclude white-collar (capitalist) crimes. Quinney contends sociologists of the era tended to "furnish ideas that support the capitalist system" (p. 148) rather than challenge the prevailing system. Quinney is convinced capitalism will soon collapse and he envisions a socialist system emerging. He sees capitalist justice as being replaced by *popular justice*, though this concept is not fully explained. He also calls for social scientists to adopt and promote social theory based on the coming socialist system.

### *Legacy*

Quinney follows in the footsteps of early critical criminological theorists such as Bonger, and found a fraternity of ideas with Becker, Chambliss, and others who helped develop understandings of how criminal behavior is shaped by outside forces, especially economic ones. In an autobiography, Quinney explains his perspective has been driven by the role of political forces and his vision for future study should be "clearly within a framework that places it in the struggle for control of the social order" (Quinney, 1991, p. 52). And while Quinney's early calls for a reengineering of society have been unpalatable to many criminologists, his later theorizing that introduced spirituality and peacemaking have paved the way for theory and practice that accommodate approaches such as restorative justice and reintegration strategies (Cullen & Agnew, 1999) that focus more on correcting individual behavior than changing society.

## Ian Taylor (1944–2001), Paul Walton (1944–2012), & Jock Young (1942–2013)

### Introduction

Ian Taylor, Paul Walton, and Jock Young were critical criminologists who came of age in the turbulent 1960s, when social norms were challenged on many fronts, including prevailing perspectives on deviance and crime. Attending a conference on traditional criminology in 1968, the three (along with a few other like-minded *radicals*), formed the National Deviance Conference which sought to forge a "new criminology" with Marxist underpinnings (Taylor as quoted in Mintz, 1974). While they were certainly not the first to attempt this merger (consider Bonger, for example), and their voices were not the only ones heard in the 1960s that adopted a critical approach to crime and deviance, the three scholars co-authored a book entitled *The New Criminology: For a Social Theory of Deviance* (1973) which made huge waves in the sociology of deviance and criminology.

### Biographical Profiles

#### Ian Taylor (1944–2001)

Born in Sheffield, England, Ian Taylor was educated at Durham University and the University of Cambridge. He returned to Durham to complete his Ph.D. and joined the faculty at the University of Bradford. While on faculty at Bradford, he spent a good deal of time in Australia and Canada, where he met his wife. He authored several publications on a variety of subjects including sports, popular culture and, of course, crime. He took a position in Canada for several years before returning to England. In an obituary by Jock Young (2001), Taylor was described as a family man, eternal optimist, and committed socialist. He died of cancer at age 56.

#### Paul Walton (1944–2012)

Paul Walton was a professor who was employed at universities throughout several countries, including North America, Australia, and Europe. In addition to sociology, his work centered primarily on communications and journalism. He collaborated with scholars such as Andrew Gamble in works on Marxist ideology. He was part of a group of young theorists known as the Glasgow Media Group which published works (the *Bad News* series) that analyzed television newscasts. A charismatic figure, Walton had many interests and energetically worked to gain a better understanding of them (Andrew Gamble, personal communication June 23, 2001). He died in 2012.

#### William "Jock" Young (1942–2013)

William (Jock) Young was born in Scotland but moved to Aldershot, England where he attended a military school; he formed a group of students who rebelled against what they determined to be an oppressive educational system. After meeting a Marxist criminologist, he abandoned his plans to study biochemistry and enrolled in the sociology program at the London School of Economics, where he received his Ph.D. in 1972. In 1986 he became a faculty member at Middlesex University where he continued to research and publish, and at one point even served as an advisor to the London Metropolitan Police. In 2002, he joined the faculty at the City University of New York, where he was employed until his death in 2013 (Henninger, 2014).

### Profiling the Theory

Critical criminology has been described as "radical criminology" as well as "the new criminology", the title of the seminal 1973 work by the three scholars. Like Bonger and other critical theorists before them, they sought to introduce Marxism into the discussion on crime. This perspective grew out of the perceived limitations of labeling theory, primarily due to the neglect of the larger structural forces that lead to deviance and crime; they sought to correct these limitations (Leonard, 1982). In doing so they rejected the conservative crime theories that promoted increased police activity and harsher punishments (especially in poor inner-city areas). They also rejected the Marxist inspired *left idealist* theories that either focused on white-collar crime or glamorized working-class criminals as heroes who revolt against the political and corporate machines. The *new left realists* (as they are often called), adopt Marxist underpinnings but reject the idea that society must be fully overturned by social revolution; instead, they seek real-world, incremental solutions to deviance and crime.

In their approach, Taylor, Walton, and Young (1973) have, in their own words, created a theory "that would be adequate to move criminology out of its own imprisonment in artificially segregated specifics. We have attempted to bring the parts together again in order to form the whole" (p. 279). The *new* criminology, they claim, is not new at all as it seeks to address the same problems that occurred in the time of Marx and Engels; therefore, the focus should be to return the study of crime and criminals to center stage in the larger political and economic sphere.

The new criminology's critique of the study of deviance and crime has not been without its own critiques. Some argue that the application of Marxist theory is not at all compatible with the specific study of crime, others note a lack of empirical support for the theory, and others indicate the missing components that might have utility in a true critical criminology (Leonard, 1982). One should note that many of the critiques of Taylor, Walton, and Young's formulation have been leveled at Marxist criminologist since the time of Bonger.

### Profiling the Literature

### The New Criminology: For a Social Theory of Deviance *(1973)*

Taylor, Walton, and Young did not mean to break into new territory in a Marxist informed criminology when they co-authored this work, but that was the book's effect (Henninger, 2014). The book is intended as a critique of the traditional forms of criminological thought and the sociology of deviance, not as a textbook (Walton, as quoted in Mintz 1974), however, in its chronicling of the evolution of crime and deviance theory, beginning with the classical school theories to the critical approach, it resembles a criminology textbook, albeit a small one. It has been criticized for its inaccessibility to non-academics, especially those who work directly in the field (Leonard, 1982), and making it more accessible would have been valuable to getting their message to the masses (in *Communist Manifesto* fashion).

In its well-known description of the new criminology provided in the book's foreword, sociologist Alvin Gouldner explains that a new theoretical approach is needed that combines the critical nature of Marxist ideology with the Chicago School tradition of making deviance (and deviants) a major, not peripheral, aspect of study without judgement, but also without romanization. The reform of criminal theory proposed by the authors, Gouldner states, is needed to accomplish this end.

## The New Criminology Revisited *(1998) (Walton and Young)*

This work, edited by Walton and Young, further develops the theme of *The New Criminology*, updated for the 1990s. The compilation includes essays by not only Walton, Young, and Ian Taylor, but also John Braithwaite and Stan Cohen. Reflecting a sociological turn toward theories of late modernism, Young's essay "Writing on the Cusp of Change: A New Criminology for an Age of Modernity" claims that the explosion of theoretical developments in criminology since the post-World War II period find criminology in a new phase, this late modern era, when some of the normative moorings of the field have become ambiguous. Less cohesive than its predecessor, this edited volume still advances the cause of critical criminology.

## The Criminological Imagination *(2011) (Young)*

This book is Jock Young's ode to sociologist C. Wright Mill's concept of the *sociological imagination*, the idea that social problems must be extended from the micro level of analysis to the macro level; in other words, private troubles should be viewed as public issues. While Mills was focusing on all areas of social life, Young emphasizes the concept's utility in addressing crime and deviance. The book retains the critical focus as the new (now old) criminology, as did Mill's original conceptions.

## Critical Criminology *(1975) (Taylor, Walton, & Young)*

This work is a volume edited by Taylor, Walton, and Young that offers essays by critical criminology scholars, including Richard Quinney and William Chambliss, to further develop the ideas presented in *The New Criminology*. The editors penned the first chapter, profiling the development of critical criminology in Britain. One chapter, written by radical criminologist Tony Platt, is devoted to the potential for a critical perspective in the United States. The book was first published in 1975 when the idea of a Marxist-inspired criminology offered a direct challenge to traditional theoretical perspectives. In 2013, it was released by the publisher as a "revival edition".

## *Legacy*

The approach of the advocates of critical criminology, radical criminology, or left realism had a major impact on traditional forms of criminology that existed in the aftermath of World War II. As Sumner (1994) famously pointed out, the effect of *The New Criminology*, was that of a "political brick" being thrown through the windows of established criminology. It challenged conventional views of crime and opened the doors to other theoretical positions that included feminism, critical race approaches, intersectionality, green perspectives, and others.

In his reflections on the new criminology and on theorizing in criminology generally, Walton (1994) offered this sage statement: "this rejection and development of pre-existing paradigms turns out to be a task which each generation has to reconstruct rather than merely deconstruct" (p. 131). This is certainly something all theories that challenge the status quo must consider as they construct, and reconstruct, newer theoretical approaches.

## Donald Black (1941–)

### Introduction

Donald Black is an American sociologist who is known for publishing widely on the topics of variation and styles of law (Snipes, Bernard, & Gerould, 2010). Adopting a conflict perspective, Black believed that there was more law or less law in a society at any given time or place. For example, a homicide investigation sees more law than a minor car accident based on the response to the incident from law enforcement – and therefore the state. Black is unique though in that he shifted the focus from the criminal to the behavior of law. It is in this way that he developed, what he argues is a purely sociological theory of law.

### Biographical Profile

Beginning his academic career at the University of Indiana, Black was originally a psychology major before switching to sociology (Savage, 2002). Black was expecting the disciplines to be different, however, while working on his Ph.D. at the University of Michigan studying social organization with a minor social psychology, he was left wondering what the difference between the disciplines was (Savage, 2002). Black felt the majority of sociological theories included elements of psychology, something he was trying to move away from. From his perspective, seemingly alone in the field, he was looking for theoretical sociology absent from psychological principles. To that end, as a postdoctoral student at Yale University, Black decided to study the sociology of law, not from the perspective of people but from the perspective of the behavior of law (Savage, 2002). This was the intellectual launching point for Black's (1976) Theory of the Behavior of Law.

### Profiling the Theory

Under the same conflict paradigm as other theorists, Black (1976), suggests that the quantity of law varies in time and place such that there can be more law at some times and places and less law at others. Defining law as "governmental social control", Black argued that law is stronger when other social control is weaker – specifically, law is inversely related to other forms of social control such that when those other social controls weaken, laws are strengthened and when other social controls are strengthened, laws are weakened. Black also argued that laws varied in style. While mostly focused on penal law, Black also looked at compensatory law (payment between individuals for wrongs done), therapeutic law (rehabilitation for the offender), and conciliatory law (a compromise between the competing groups to bring about a resolution).

Black (1976) suggests that there are five dimensions of social life that interact with the law – stratification, morphology, culture, organization, and social control. Stratification refers to the vertical distance between the people in a social setting. This is typically measured by wealth and status of individuals and groups. Morphology refers to the horizontal aspect of social life such as the division of labor, intimacy and interaction with others – the degree to which they participate in each other's lives (Snipes, et al., 2010). Culture is the religion, recreation, science, and technology, of the society. Organization refers to the capacity of the society to take collective action. Finally, social control refers to the normative aspects of social life. While law is included in that, so too are ethics, etiquette, custom, and the treatment of the mentally ill.

Stratification is the primary variable that defines Black in the same category as other conflict theorists in that Black (1976) suggested the higher up the socio-economic ladder (or the wealthier), the greater the ability to use the law on one's own behalf. For example, an investigation of a wealthy murder suspect receives a lot more *law* than an investigation of a poor suspect. This is further demonstrated by Anatole France's (1894) statement, "The law, in its majestic equality, forbids the rich as well as the poor to sleep under bridges, to beg in the streets, and to steal bread." However, this is not limited to just the stratification variable. There are variable levels of law in morphology between individuals as well. Consider a married couple – for serious acts of violence or divorce, the law is not used against the other spouse. However, if a similar offense happened with a neighbor or stranger, the law may be employed (Black, 1976). These relationships, of more or less law, are true of societies with more or less culture, organization, and social control as well. Increases in culture, organization, and social control typically see decreases in law being used.

Using this theoretical framework, Black (1976) formulated 20 hypotheses about how law varies in quantity and style. However, he never performed a comprehensive test of these hypotheses (Snipes, et al., 2010). When a comprehensive test was attempted (Gottfredson & Hindelang, 1979a), the researchers found that the seriousness of the offense was the greatest predictor of the amount of law used. Black (1979) responded to this criticism stating that the level of seriousness we place upon certain acts is supported by the five previously mentioned variables, therefore supporting the theory. In response to this, Gottfredson and Hindelang (1979b) deemed the theory untestable and, to date, no comprehensive tests of the theory have been conducted (Snipes, et al., 2010). In fact, critics of Black's (1979) response to Gottfredson and Hindelang (1979a) suggested that Black weakened his theory by changing "what was a testable general theory about increments in the quantity of law into an untestable collection of ideas" (Braithwaite & Biles, 1980, p. 334) – an irony as Black has called for sociology to be a truly scientific discipline.

### Profiling the Literature

### The Behavior of Law (1976)

Black argues in the preface that "this book does not judge the variation of law, nor does it recommend policy of any kind. Rather, it is merely an effort to understand law as a natural phenomenon". The text attempts to explain difference in the law at given times and places and is Black's major theoretical work. Outlining how there can be more or less law in any given society at any given time, Black "integrates a vast range of ideas and empirical materials in the sociology and anthropology of law, boldly asserting general theorems which are related to rich and illuminating detail" (Rueschemeyer, 1978, p. 1040). However, critics of this text complain that, while Black certainly contributed to the scholarship of law, his theory building and lack of empirical validation left much to be desired (Rueschemeyer, 1978; Braithwaite & Biles, 1980; Sherman, 1978).

### The Social Structure of Right and Wrong (1993)

This text, a collection of essays, attempts to expand Black's theory of law violation to include all "right or wrong" behaviors. By differentiating between formal social controls (laws) and less formal social controls (e.g., communal shaming), Black attempts to explain how the structure of society dictates what is right and what is wrong. By ridding himself of any sort of psychological theoretical concepts, Black "presents right and wrong – meaningful social interactions – as meaningless behavior" (Frankford, 1995, p. 788) and overcomplicates the nature of societies by suggesting that only what can be directly measured (e.g., the number of traffic tickets given out) can be studied. In this way, he ignores concepts like motivation or personality as unmeasurable. Suggesting all social conflicts are basically the same (and in need of management), Black's text attempts to "locate conflicts and their directions within a 'social field' in order to explain and predict their outcomes" (Jackall, 1995, p. 1176). This "abstract and formalistic" argument (Jackall, 1995, p. 1176) is still an important theoretical work for those who are interested in the complex concepts of rightness and wrongness in a given society.

## *Legacy*

Black's work, while drawing some scientific controversy, has still been influential in the scholarship of sociology and criminology. Black's scholarship on deviance extends beyond that of explanations of why individuals commit crime – in fact, some scholarship (see Black, 1983) even suggests that crime should not be viewed as an inherently bad thing but rather as a way for citizens seek *self-help* as it was traditionally viewed in primitive legal societies. Black's scholarship extends to all areas of sociology, including the study of the field of sociology itself (see Black, 2000 for a theory of "Pure Sociology"). Regardless of his broad interests, there can be no doubt that Black has left his mark on the field of deviance.

## References

Akers, R.L., Sellers, C.D.S., & Jennings, W.G. (2016). *Criminological Theories: Introduction, Evaluation, & Application* (7th ed.). New York, NY: Oxford University Press.

Applebaum, R.P. (2014). Never afraid of living: William J. Chambliss 1933–2014. *Social Science Space*. https://www.socialsciencespace.com/2014/02/never-afraid-of-living-william-chambliss-1933-2014/

Bemmelen, J.M.V. (1955). William Adriaan Bonger (1876–1940). *Journal of Criminal Law, Criminology, and Police Science*, 46(3), 293–302.

Birmingham, R. (1970). Criminality and economic conditions: Willem Bonger. *California Law Review*, 58(2), 527–532.

Black, D. (1976). *The Behavior of Law*. Bradford, UK: Emerald Group Publishing.

Black, D. (1979). Common sense in the sociology of law. *American Sociological Review*, 44(1), 18–27.

Black, D. (1983). Crime as social control. *American Sociological Review*, 48(1), 34–45.

Black, D. (1993). *The Social Structure of Right and Wrong*. San Diego: Academic Press.

Black, D. (2000). Dreams of pure sociology. *Sociological Theory*, 18(3), 343–367.

Bonger. W.A. (1916). *Criminality and Economic Conditions*. Boston: Little, Brown, and Company.

Bonger, W.A. (1936). *An Introduction to Criminology*. Trans. E. van Loo. London: Methuen & Co.

Bonger, W.A. (1943). *Race and Crime*. Trans. M.M. Hordyk. New York: Columbia University Press.

Braithwaite, J., & Biles, D. (1980). Empirical verification and Black's "*The Behavior of Law*". *American Sociological Review*, 45(2), 334–338.

Burke, A.S. (2014). Chambliss, William J. In M. Miller (Ed.). *Encyclopedia of Theoretical Criminology*. Chichester, West Sussex, UK: Wiley Blackwell.

Chambliss, W.J. (1964). A sociological analysis of the law of vagrancy. *Social Problems*, 12, 67–77.

Chambliss, W.J. (1973). The Saints and the Roughnecks. *Society*, 11(1), 24–31.

Chambliss, W.J. (1975). Toward a political economy of crime. *Theory and Society*, 2(2), 149–170.

Chambliss, W.J. (1987). I wish I didn't know now what I didn't know then. *The Criminologist*, 12, 1–19.

Chambliss, W.J. (1978). *On the Take: From Petty Crooks to Presidents*, 2nd ed. Bloomington & Indianapolis: Indiana University Press, 1988.

Chambliss, W.J., & Seidman, R.T. (1971). *Law, Order, and Power*. Reading, MA: Addison-Wesley.

Cullen, F.T., & Agnew, R. (1999). *Criminological Theory: Past and Present, Essential Readings*. Los Angeles: Roxbury.

Curran, D.J., & Renzetti, C.M. (2001). *Theories of crime*, 2nd ed. Boston: Allyn & Bacon.

Ferrell, J., & Hamm, M.S. (2016). Thesis on Chambliss: Roughnecks and Saints. *Critical Criminology*, 24, 165–180.

Frankford, D.M. (1995). Social structure of right and wrong: Normativity without agents. *Law and Social Inquiry*, 20(3), 787–803.

Gottfredson, M.R., & Hindelang, M.J. (1979a). A study of the behavior of law. *American Sociological Review*, 3–18.

Gottfredson, M.R., & Hindelang, M.J. (1979b). Theory and research in the sociology of law. *American Sociological Review*, 27–37.

Henninger, A.M. (2014). Jock Young: Critical criminologist. *Dialectical Anthropology*, 38, 113–115.

Jackall, R. (1995). "*The Social Structure of Right and Wrong*". By Donald Black (Book Review). *Social Forces*, 73(3), 1176.

Leonard, E.B. (1982). *Women, Crime, and Society: A Critique of Criminological Theory*. New York & London: Longman.

Lilly, J.R., Cullen, F.T., and Ball, R.A. (2002). *Criminological Theory: Context and Consequences*, 3rd ed. Thousand Oaks, CA: Sage.

Lynch, M.J., & Groves, W.B. (1989). *A Primer in Radical Criminology*, 2nd ed. New York: Harrow & Heston.

Martin, R., Mutchnick, R.J., & Austin, W.T. (1990). *Criminological Thought: Pioneers Past and Present*. New York: Macmillan Publishing Company.

Michalowski, R.J. (2016). Guest Editor's Introduction. *Critical Criminology* 24, 161–162.

Mintz, R. (1974). Interview with Ian Taylor, Paul Walton, and Jock Young. *Issues in Criminology*, 9(1), 33–53.

Mutchnick, R.J., Martin, R., & Austin, W.T. (2009). *Criminological Thought: Pioneers Past and Present*. New York: Macmillan.

Pepinsky, H., & Quinney, R. (1991). *Criminology as Peacemaking*. Bloomington: Indiana University Press.

Peterson, G. (2010). Intellectual biography of Donald Black: The sociology of deviance and his deviant quest to purify sociology. *Intellectual Biography*.

Quinney, R. (1965). Is criminal behavior deviant behavior? *British Journal of Criminology*, 5(2), 132–142.

Quinney. R. (1970). *The Social Reality of Crime*. Boston: Little, Brown, and Co., 2001.

Quinney, R. (1974). *Critique of Legal Order: Crime Control in Capitalist Society*. Boston: Little, Brown, and Company.

Quinney, R. (1977). *Class, State, and Crime: On the Theory and Practice of Criminal Justice*. New York: Longman.

Quinney, R. (1991). *Journey to a Far Place: Autobiographical Reflections*. Philadelphia: Temple University.

Rueschemeyer, D. (1978). Book Review: *The Behavior of Law*. *American Journal of Sociology*, 83(4), 1040–1042.

Savage, S.P. (2002). The geometry of law: An interview with Donald Black. *International Journal of the Sociology of Law*, 30(2), 99–129.

Sherman, L.W. (1978). Book Review: *The Behavior of Law*. *Contemporary Sociology*, 7(1), 11–15.

Snipes, J.B., Bernard, T.J., & Gerould, A.L. (2010). *Vold's Theoretical Criminology*. New York: Oxford University Press.

Stichman, A. (2010). Bonger, Willem: Capitalism and crime. In F.T. Cullen & P. Wilcox, (Eds.). *Encyclopedia of Criminological Theory*. Newbury Park, CA: Sage.

Sumner, C. (1994) *The Sociology of Deviance: An Obituary*. Buckingham: Open University Press.

Taylor, I. (1971). Review of Criminality and economic conditions by Willem Bonger. *British Journal of Criminology* 11(2), 198–201.

Taylor, I., Walton, P., & Young, J. (1973). *The New Criminology: For a Social Theory of Deviance*. London: Routledge.

Taylor, I., Walton, P., & Young, J. (1975). *Critical Criminology*. Abingdon, Oxon: Routledge, 2013.

Trevino, A.J. (2001). Introduction. In *The Social Reality of Crime*. New Brunswick and London: Transaction Publishers, ix–xxi.

Walton, P. (1994). Re-examining the new criminology. *Current Issues in Criminal Justice*, 5(3), 326–331.

Walton, P., & Young, I. (1998). *The New Criminology Revisited*. Hampshire and London: Palgrave.

Wigmore, J.H. (1941). Willem Adriaan Bonger. *Criminal Law and Criminology*, 31(5), 657.

Wozniak, J.F., Cullen, F.T., & Platt, T. (2015). Richard Quinney's *The Social Reality of Crime*: A marked departure from and reinterpretation of traditional criminology. *Social Justice*, 41(3), 197–215.

Young, J. (January 23, 2001). Ian Taylor. Sociologist pioneering radical approaches to the study of crime, sport, and popular culture. *The Guardian*.

Young, J. (2011). *The Criminological Imagination*. Cambridge: Polity Press.

# 10

# GENDER AND CRIME

## Adler & Simon, Daly & Chesney-Lind, Messerschmidt

## Introduction

Gender has been described by early feminist criminologists as the attribute most correlated with criminal behavior, meaning crime has been committed by one group (males) at much higher levels than another (females). Developing from a conflict theoretical approach and inspired specifically by the second wave feminist movement (dubbed the "women's liberation movement" in the 1970s), the role of gender became a focus of many areas of social life, including crime and deviance. Freda Adler and Rita James Simon were pioneers in this new focus, followed by Kathleen Daly and Meda Chesney-Lind, among others. Later the gender focus was moved into the study of "masculinities" by James Messerschmidt.

A note on the terminology is in order: in sociological thought, the concept of sex refers to a person's biological classification as male or female, while the concept of gender refers to the prescribed role expectations based on sex. The term sex, however, also refers to an activity, comprised of various behaviors considered to be both "normal" and "deviant". Additionally, more recent understandings point to the role of identity formation attributed to sex and sexuality. To avoid confusion, the term gender is used in this section.

## Freda Adler (1934–) & Rita James Simon (1931–2013)

### Introduction

The second wave feminist movement of the late 1960s and early 1970s offered a new contribution to criminology. 1975 was a key year as Freda Adler and Rita Simon separately released two major works, Adler's *Sisters in Crime* and Simon's *Women and Crime*. Previous work in criminology and the sociology of deviance either ignored female criminality or focused on the differences between male and female offending. Cesare Lombroso and Guglielmo Ferrero (1894), for example, believed female crime was linked biologically through male characteristics, and since crime is less prominent in females, this supported the theory of atavism. Another theorist, Otto Pollak (1950) believed that female criminality was hidden as women can naturally conceal their behavior. With the impact of the second wave of feminism (and the so-called women's liberation movement) in the late 1960s and early

DOI: 10.4324/9781003036609-10

1970s, things began to change in criminology and the formulations of gender-based crime theories began. While the theories of Adler and Simon differ in some ways, they are included here as both represent what is known as the "liberation thesis".

## Biographical Profiles

### Freda Adler (1934–)

Born in Philadelphia, Freda Adler earned her B.A. in sociology at the University of Pennsylvania in 1956, studying under key figures at the time such as Thorstein Sellen, Marvin Wolfgang, and Otto Pollack; as mentioned above, Pollack was notable for some early work in gender and crime. After having three children, Adler returned to the University of Pennsylvania for graduate work in criminology and, in the male-dominated field, she was for a time the only woman in the program. She wrote her doctoral dissertation on unequal sentences given to African American offenders and received her Ph.D. in 1971. She became a research director in the field of addictions after graduation and before beginning her research of gender and crime. Her book *Sisters in Crime* gained her almost immediate fame and criticism. She became a well-known international scholar in feminist criminology, conducted research for the United Nations, and became a scholar in maritime criminology (Flynn, 1998). She joined the faculty at Rutgers University and currently holds the status of Professor Emeritus; she also holds a visiting professorship at the University of Pennsylvania. She has many publications, has held several professional posts, and received numerous awards for her work. In addition, she founded one of the country's first schools of criminal justice at Rutgers and is an internationally known criminologist (Rennison, 2014).

### Rita James Simon (1931–2013)

Rita Simon (Rita Mintz) was born on Thanksgiving Day, 1931, to parents who were of Jewish and Polish descent. She was born and raised in New York City and attended the same public high school as Ruth Bader Ginsberg; there she developed an interest in leftist politics. She entered the University of Washington in 1948 where she planned to major in journalism but switched to sociology. During this time, she married Ralph James and they entered graduate school at Cornell University in 1952. The couple moved to Chicago where Rita worked as a research assistant on a project at the University of Chicago law school. (Her work on this project would appear in one of her early books.) She completed her Ph.D. in sociology in 1957 at Chicago and began teaching there as an assistant professor the next year; this was the same year she and Ralph divorced. At Chicago, she met Ph.D. student Julian Simon and the couple married and moved to New York, where Rita, now Rita James Simon, worked for a social work program at Columbia University while also teaching at Yale. She and Julian both received academic positions at the University of Illinois until 1983 when she became a dean and later professor at the university. Julian died in 1998 (van der Does, 2008) and Rita died 11 years later.

## Profiling the Theory

As noted in the introduction section, traditional criminological theories either embraced biologically based stereotypes or were primarily explorations into why males commit crime and generally ignored female offending. Gender, however, is the strongest correlation of criminal behavior (i.e., men are more likely than women to commit crimes). In addition, the justice system is inconsistent in its enforcement and sentencing of crimes based on gender (Vold, Bernard, & Snipes, 2002).

These now antiquated ideas are addressed by Adler and Simon as they move the focus from biological determinism to an emphasis on social influences. Both believe that as increased equity between the sexes occurs (but certainly not full equality), a *gender convergence* results and explains an increase in female crime (Lynch & Groves, 1989). This idea, called the liberation thesis or emancipation thesis, posits that as social controls against women lessen, female criminality will correspondingly increase.

Adler (1975) posits that an increase in female assertiveness has created a substantial increase in female crime. She expects the following changes as women obtain greater equality: 1) women will be treated with more deference, which also leads to less protection; 2) there will be more women judges, police officers, and prosecutors, resulting in fewer decisions to arrest and prosecute based on sentimentalism and emotion and more on legal variables; 3) female crime (referring here to sex work) will be reduced and in cases where is still exists, will be prosecuted more vigorously and with less compassion.

Simon (1975) also believes that increased educational and occupational opportunities will allow greater access to socioeconomic power, which will result in an increase in female white-collar and financial crime. However, it will also lead to a decrease in violent crimes because as women become more upwardly mobile, they will also become less victimized and oppressed; this, she stated, will make them less likely to resort to violent activity (Cullen & Agnew, 1999).

### Profiling the Literature

### Sisters in Crime *(Adler) (1975)*

The title of this book is a rebuttal to Clifford Shaw's work *Brothers in Crime* (1938) which focuses on male crime. As an announcement of feminist theory's entrance into the field of criminology, Adler begins the work with lyrics from Helen Reddy's feminist pop anthem "I am Woman". She quickly follows by introducing the character Marge, a divorced, middle aged, middle class mother who is in prison for robbery – an exemplification, she claims, of a new type of criminal, resulting from the rise of female liberation and a resulting change in the criminal justice system. Adler describes how women, beginning in the 1960s, have become involved in criminal activity previously reserved for men, including violent assault, mugging, and political crime as well as *non-womanly* behavior such as family desertion; she even states the rate of female death by suicide is a result of the newly attained gender equality.

Adler describes the myth of biology since the days of Cesare Lombroso and the challenges to that biological determinism by Émile Durkheim, Sigmund Freud, and Margaret Mead, and notes how men have traditionally failed to accept women as equals – the worst offenders being the male police officers who refuse to accept the "changed woman" either as criminal violators or fellow officers.

In this work, Alder uses short case histories of women who have committed various sorts of deviant behavior, including gang activity, political protest, sex work, and drug use. The case histories add flavor to the book which is reminiscent of the work of some of the earlier Chicago School theorists. Adler also offers chapters that address race and class as they relate to female criminology, providing a more sociological examination, as well as an anticipation of forms of criminology that currently emphasize intersectionality. She also adds information on judicial and correctional measures as they relate to female criminality, before closing with reflections on the women's liberation movement and its consequences to women, currently and in the future.

Referencing a famous line from Marx, Adler's thesis can be summed up in her quote, "Women have lost more than their chains. For better and worse, they have lost many of the restraints which kept them within the law" (1975, p. 24).

## Women and Crime *(Simon) (1975)*

Simon's work is often compared with that of Adler's *Sisters in Crime* as they were both books on crime from a feminist perspective published in the same year of 1975. However, the two works are quite different in style and substance. Simon's book has about half of the page count as Adler's and is a much more empirical work. The book's primary purposes are twofold: 1) to provide statistical data regarding women's offending patterns and their treatment by the police, and 2) to prognosticate about things to come involving these patterns and treatment. According to Simon, women in criminal endeavors have taken on roles subservient to men and as they obtain greater opportunities in education and the workplace, they will find representation in certain criminal activities more than others. For example, women's involvement in white-collar and financial crimes will increase since they seek financial and social status as readily as men, but their involvement with violent crimes, most notably murder and manslaughter, will decrease as frustrations by women will diminish as their oppression lessens.

She explains, much like Adler, that historical crime has left women out of the discussion and when they were included in this discussion, biological inferiority was said to be the cause; in this vein she specifically mentions the work of Lombroso, Eleanor and Sheldon Glueck, and Sigmund Freud. Simon also gives a brief description of feminist political movements and the oppression of women in other "liberation" movements such as the American Federation of Labor (AFL), the Student Nonviolent Coordinating Committee (SNCC), and the Students for a Democratic Society (SDS).

Beginning in the third chapter of the book, Simon introduces many pages of data in the form of tables on female demography in different areas, the treatment of females in criminal courts for different crime types, and the number and types of parole allowances. She also includes comparative analyses of male/female differences in various countries. Her conclusion is that as women gain equality in other spheres of life, they will also be more represented in criminal activity, notably white-collar crime, but less in other types of crime.

In contrast to Alder's book, this work is supported by data from governmental sources, which gives it a more academic relevance. However, this academic focus also makes it less accessible to lay readers. Reading both works provides a better balance from which to view female criminality at a specific point of time.

## The Criminology of Deviant Women *(Adler and Simon) (1979)*

This is a text reader edited by Adler and Simon that is divided into five sections: 1) a historical perspective of female offending; 2) female crime; 3) women in the judicial system; 4) women who are incarcerated or on parole; and 5) a cross-cultural perspective of female criminality. The first section is a must read for students of feminist criminology and includes excerpts from the works of Cesare Lombroso and Guglielmo Ferrero, Willem Bonger, and Otto Pollak, and other key figures; Simon and Adler both provide information on feminist criminology's past and future and address the field from the perspective of the women's liberation movement. The second section addresses female criminality and deviance in several areas including sex work, shoplifting, organized crime, drug use, violence, and terrorism. The third section deals with women in the court system, as defendants and as victims of discrimination in an unequal court system. The fourth section addresses women in prison (forgotten offenders), sexual segregation and recidivism, and general experiences of incarcerated women and women on parole. The volume ends with a cross-cultural perspective of women in the criminal justice system, showcasing Adler and Simon's interest in, and knowledge of, crime in an international context.

## Legacy

Adler and Simon were pioneers in feminist criminology and it can certainly be said they broke the glass ceiling in the male-dominated field of criminology. And though the liberation thesis has not been supported by evidence in the time since they published their work, they helped move explanations of female crime from biological assumptions to social understandings and to place female criminality into the wider study of criminology (Cullen & Agnew 1999; Rennison 2014).

## Kathleen Daly (1948–) & Meda Chesney-Lind (1947–)

### Introduction

Kathleen Daly and Meda Chesney-Lind are groundbreaking criminologists whose work "Feminism and Criminology" (1988) focused on moving female crime and offending to the forefront of criminological theory and research. Often considered together because of this well-known work, they are individual scholars who have possessed different theoretical perspectives, different research agendas, and different interests in the field over the years. They are pioneers of criminology and their work has engaged and expanded feminist scholarship in criminology and paved the way for other scholars to follow.

### Biographical Profiles

#### Kathleen Daly (1948–)

Daly achieved her Ph.D. in sociology from the University of Massachusetts in 1983. She taught at the State University of New York, Yale University, and the University of Michigan from 1982 through 1995. In 1995, she received a Fulbright Award to study restorative justice in Australia. She decided to stay in the country and is now Professor of Criminology and Criminal Justice at Griffin University in Brisbane (Griffin University n.d.).

#### Meda Chesney-Lind (1947–)

Born in Woodward, Oklahoma, Meda Chesney-Lind was raised in Baltimore, Maryland. After her parents' divorce at age 16, she moved to Portland, Oregon, with her maternal grandparents. She met her soon to be husband at Whitman College where both had been active in anti-Vietnam War protests. She completed her Ph.D. at the University of Hawaii at Honolulu and later taught courses to female prison inmates though a community college program. Despite a demanding teaching load, she still found time to conduct research on female criminality and later joined the faculty at the University of Hawaii at Manoa (Burke, 2014).

### Profiling the Theory

Traditional criminology, from a feminist perspective, has accepted a patriarchal approach in which certain ideas about gender revolved almost exclusively around males, placing female crime and female treatment in the criminal justice system on the periphery. Chesney-Lind states that this traditional approach of "add women and stir" is outdated and that a new focus is required. The old idea that female crime (and female victimization) is rare and should not be included in criminological research and theory has come under scrutiny due to increases in female offending and a new realization of old patterns of female victimization, which until now have been kept under wraps by an oppressive patriarchal system. As Daly and Tonry (1997) note, examinations of crime regarding gender always shift the discussion to women, although "men are not less gendered than women"; they are the "norm, the universal non-gendered offender" (p. 204).

Five key issues are at the heart of feminist thought, as opposed to other social or political perspectives: 1) gender is a complex social product and represents more than just biological issues; 2) gender and gender relations play a key role in constructions of social life; 3) notions of masculinity and femininity are socially constructed from a patriarchal standpoint; 4) the production of knowledge has traditionally been androcentric; and 5) women should be a central focus of social inquiry, not peripheral to it. A feminist criminology agenda "draws from feminist theories or research, problematizes gender, and considers the implications of findings for empowering women or for change in gender relations" (Daly & Chesney-Lind, 1988, p. 505).

### Profiling the Literature

#### "Feminism and Criminology" (Daly & Chesney-Lind) (1988)

In this seminal essay, Daly and Chesney-Lind reflect on the status of feminist criminology from the 1970s and 1980s and attempt to reconcile the conflicts inherent in being both feminists and criminologists. They clearly define their objective – to appraise three areas: 1) the construction of a feminist theory of crime; 2) the control of male-to-female violence; and 3) gender inequality in the criminal justice system. The scholars offer a definition of feminism, address its distinctions from other ideologies, and discuss some myths about feminism. They offer critiques of earlier theorists, notably Adler and Simon. The work provides an excellent social-historical view of feminist criminology building in the late 1980s, addresses issues not only of that period but also of today, and invites critique and a broader discussion of the field of criminology.

#### "Gender, Race, and Sentencing" (Daly & Tonry) (1997)

This comprehensive article, coauthored with American legal and policy scholar Michael Tonry, addresses gender and racial disparities in adult arrest and incarceration policies. The authors note that when sentencing reform measures were implemented in the 1960s, the primary focus was on excluding race in sentencing considerations ("forbidden consideration") and later gender was also included in this strategy, despite the many differences that were not taken into consideration. The authors then consider both race and gender regarding arrest procedures, sentencing patterns and practice, and general policy considerations. Five recommendations for research and policy agendas are presented: 1) changing punishment considerations to locate women as subjects, in which women are the standards; 2) instituting less severe punishment methods; 3) considering the policy effects of disparate social conditions on different groups; 4) creating more moral evaluations of criminal justice practices; and 5) considering how equal treatment practices can negatively affect people of various gender and racial categories, as well as those of different class, age, and ethnic groups.

## "Beyond Bad Girls: Feminist Perspectives on Female Offending" (Chesney-Lind) (2004)

In this essay, part of a volume edited by Colin Sumner with William Chambliss as advisory editor, Chesney-Lind begins by explaining criminology's resistance in moving away from androcentric criminology because patriarchy is so deeply embedded in society. Regarding female victimization, she notes "the victimized woman does not challenge core notions of patriarchal ideology; she – the plundered waif – after all, needs male protection and assistance" (2004, p. 256). As female crime rates have risen and ideas about female victimization become unveiled, the focus must be shifted to a feminist vision of crime and delinquency. A focus on offenses by juvenile females, especially those involving violence or gang activity, is needed. Despite concerns over an increase in "bad girl" behavior, delinquency by young females has been "ignored, trivialized or denied" (p. 258).

Several recommendations (a "to do list") are made for criminologists: 1) enhancing research and theorizing with a focus on gender (and race); 2) continuing unintimidated in their academic work despite the backlash that comes in a patriarchal society; 3) focusing on the offending behavior of women and girls rather than just the societal responses to it; and 4) influencing policy making in this regard.

## "Restorative Justice and Sexual Assault: An Archival Study of Court and Conference Cases" (Daly) (2006)

This is an archival study of the experiences of 400 sexual assault cases in Australia which sought to ascertain: 1) the distinction made between court and conference options; 2) the disposition of cases to either of the options; and 3) the most appropriate option (from the victim's view). Traditional notions of justice suggest the conferences, which are a component of restorative justice policies and involve a meeting between the offenders, the victims and their supporters or representatives, would be problematic in cases of child sexual abuse due to concerns over the revictimization of those sexually offended. Daly addresses the critiques of the program in her findings that the conferences promote more disclosures of the crime by the offender than in traditional court systems; this both facilitates treatment outcomes and provides a greater sense of satisfaction for the victim due to the fact their offender confessed to the sexual assault.

## Fighting for Girls: New Perspectives on Gender and Violence (Chesney-Lind & Jones) (2010)

This edited volume provides insight into girls' violence and the criminal justice system. Noting there is an abundance of media images that depict aggressive "bad girls" who are becoming "more like boys", but a paucity of academic research about youthful female violence, Chesney-Lind and her coeditor Nikki Jones provide quantitative and qualitative empirical analyses by scholars that address juvenile female arrests, incarceration, intimate relationships, involvement with the educational system, life in violent communities, and others. Recommendations to alleviate the problem are made that require an attention to the social conditions encountered by girls that create the impetus for violence as well as the policy measures that sustain it.

## Legacy

Daly and Chesney-Lind have provided major advancements to the field of criminology. Although feminism has now become mainstream in the field with its own journals, research agendas, and divisions and sections in professional organizations, there is a threat to this subfield due to increased politicization and backlash against progressive movements; Chesney-Lind suggests there is now a greater urgency than before to produce gender-based research and theory (Groot 2014).

The feminist theorists have advanced new lines of scholarship, and their work has provided foundations for intersectional approaches, queer criminology perspectives, and other new arrivals to the field. Their influence on male violence against females is especially germane today considering the need for "Take Back the Night", "Me Too", "Times Up", and related victim's movements.

## James W. Messerschmidt (1951–)

### Introduction

James Messerschmidt is an esteemed criminologist, best known for his gender-based perspective known as masculinities theory. In his work, which is based on a structured action perspective, Messerschmidt adopts a socialist feminist approach and moves gender-based theories into a focus on the role of masculinity, especially regarding a concept known as hegemonic masculinity, into the study of crime and deviance. The social conditions of any given period must be evaluated, according to Messerschmidt, to fully understand and explain male behavior, especially criminal behavior.

### Biographical Profile

Messerschmidt was raised in a middle-class family with a dominant father who was abusive to him, his brother, and his mother. His mother was kind and loving and he credits her for influencing his interest in gender equality and activism. As an undergraduate student, he was a member of two radical student organizations and was involved in the anti-Vietnam War movement (American Society of Criminology, 2008). He received his B.S. from Portland State University, his M.S. from San Diego State University, and his Ph.D. from the University of Stockholm. He began his academic career at Moorhead State University in Kentucky but has been on the faculty at the University of Southern Maine since 1986 (University of Southern Maine, 2021). He has been in many grass roots social movement activities and considers himself an "academic activist" (American Society of Criminology, 2008).

### Profiling the Theory

Messerschmidt maintains that feminist theory has accomplished the goal of moving crime from the *malestream* focus on men and crime but has also excluded them from the overall theoretical framework – it is preferable, in his assessment, not to return to a focus on male criminality but rather to examine masculinity, as a structured concept, in its role in crime. Even feminist approaches in the past have adopted a belief in the natural differences between males and females, thereby thwarting any real discussion and analysis.

Hegemonic masculinity is key to this analysis and refers to a concept introduced by sociologist R.W. Connell (1987) and adapted from social philosopher Antonio Gramsci's conception of cultural hegemony – the power possessed by institutions to control the subordinate classes. In this gendered context, it refers to the broader cultural context of males, especially how upper-class white males, are expected to oversee most areas of social life, with all the benefits that come with that status; in this cultural scheme, all others must accept a subordinate status. Messerschmidt (1993) adds that "hegemonic masculinity emphasizes practices toward authority, control, competitive individualism, independence, aggressiveness, and the capacity for violence" (p. 83). If men follow this dominant ideology, they can easily act in ways that reflect the script of masculinity, especially if their opportunities for expressing masculinity are blocked – in this way, the theory takes on some of the characteristics of strain theories (Lilly, Cullen, & Ball, 2002).

The concept of hegemonic masculinities is based on the idea that there are "multiple masculinities", some that are non-hegemonic and others that are hegemonic, and which can be observed at three levels: 1) the local (face-to-face interactions); 2) the regional (societal); and 3) global. Hegemonic masculinities are constructed in different ways, such as a dominating type (in which other males considered feminine are insulted) and a benevolent, protective type. Messerschmidt also discusses a hybrid type of masculinity in which males of privilege adopt displays of either masculine or feminine traits to secure or hide their privilege and power (Messerschmidt, 2018). Therefore, there are different types and levels of masculinities that are constantly being reenacted at different levels. This has implications for deviance and crime.

In his theoretical formulation, Messerschmidt introduces structured action theory which posits that, through interaction, people create social structures which in turn affect behavior. Structure of class, race, and gender must be considered together in the backdrop of the different social settings in which some action is made. This approach, Messerschmidt reasons, is required to adequately situate his masculinities theory.

### Profiling the Literature

### Capitalism, Patriarchy, and Crime (1986)

Messerschmidt begins this work with the claim that criminology, in all its varieties, neglects the "sexual division of labor and its impact on crime" (1986, p. ix). And he seeks to correct that omission. His perspective is that of socialist feminism, and his goal is to further develop the theoretical perspective and apply it to it to deviance and crime. The core of the theory is patriarchy, especially as it relates to the male control of female sexuality and labor power ("in the market and at home", p. x). Messerschmitt states that the social feminist orientation to crime is comprised of two premises: the comprehension of criminality as related to patriarchy and capitalism, and the role of power in defining both the people in control of society (white capitalist class males) and the role of those without power (women and others in the working class). Powerless men (especially of lower class racial minority status) demonstrate masculinity through a "street toughness" and male bonding, both of which have the potential to victimize women. Likewise, the elites involved in white-collar and corporate crime victimize women and working-class men. The issue of sexual abuse is addressed – both the *legal rape* defined by criminal statutes, and *illegal rape* which involves intimidation, coercion, and harassment rather than physical force. These acts, according to Messerschmidt, can flourish in capitalistic society.

The book, which was written during the conservative Reagan era, ends with a proposal for policies that: 1) increase meaningful employment; 2) provide health care and other benefits; 3) decrease discrimination; 4) *democratize* the family such as those that support gender egalitarianism; 4) de-focus support for nuclear families in favor of other forms, including communal arrangements which re-structure the tasks of parenting, housework, and sexual behavior; and 5) provide more social services to citizens.

## Masculinities and Crime: Critique and Conceptualization of Theory *(1993)*

Though R.W. Connell's assessment in the foreword that the book is a "conceptual revolution in the social sciences" (1993, p. vii) might be an overstatement, this work makes a significant contribution to gender studies of crime. Acknowledging criminology's failure to adequately address crime from a gendered perspective, he points out the weaknesses in positivistic, strain, control, labeling, conflict, the newer critical theories of the time, and even some feminist approaches, that continue to conform to biologically based assumptions. After providing details on the development of the different types of feminism he formulates a theory that brings the behavior of men and boys (masculinity) to the forefront and describes how historically male control has developed through the economic division of labor. He describes how hegemonic masculinity is reflected in street crime, corporate crime, interpersonal violence, and the historical role of the state in maintaining male control, and how that has shaped criminology.

Goffman's (1959) work in impression management is detectable here in that males demonstrate masculinity by a variety of means, determined by the historical conditions that define the interpretations of masculine behavior. As times change, impressions of masculinity will likewise change.

## Crime and Structured Action: Gender, Race, and Crime in the Making *(1997)*

In this short book (less than 135 pages), Messerschmidt outlines his structured action theory. Social structure, he begins, consists of "regular and patterned forms of interaction over time that constrain and channel behavior in specific ways" (1997, p. 5); these structures are in constant interplay with gender, class, and racial divisions of labor and promote different actions based on the social settings in which they occur. People in these situations (actors) "self-regulate their behavior, and make specific choices in specific contexts" (p. 12). It is this process of *doing* gender, class, and race within these settings that should be the focus of inquiry.

Messerschmidt provides four case studies (borrowing from and expanding upon the method used by the early Chicago School sociologists) upon which to elaborate this theory, each contributing a chapter in the book. *Lynching*, described in the first case study, involves the "white supremacist masculinity" that was used during the Reconstruction era by white men to demonstrate masculine power over African American men and that which *protected*

White women. *Hustling*, the second study, is represented by African American activist Malcolm X, who adopted the masculine image of a *cool cat* during the period of the zoot suit culture in its flamboyant rejection of middle-class white society in the 1940s. The *bad girl* construction is considered next and is described through the lives of young females who are involved in street culture environments and defined by sexual scripts, but who also represent "male" deviance such as engaging in violence (*badness*). Finally, the *murderous managers* represent masculine dominance of occupational tasks, illustrated by the administrators who decided to proceed with the Challenger launch in 1986 which killed all seven crew members despite warnings from engineers to abort the mission.

## Legacy

Some feminist criminologists, including Kathleen Daly, feel a masculinities approach simply returns the focus to men, the primary complaint with traditional androcentric criminology. Messerschmidt's theory has also been criticized for: 1) the exclusion of females; 2) a narrow range of behaviors defined as masculine; 3) the lack of an explanation for conformity by marginalized males; and 4) the omission of other motivations of crime, such as enjoyment (Cullen & Agnew, 1999).

However, his work provides a needed addition to the field by extending a focus on gender to the role of masculinity in patriarchal society. In the structured action component of his theory, Messerschmidt's examination extends into other areas such as class and race, reflecting a newer focus in criminology on intersectionalities. Another area that is certainly ripe for examination is the masculine (some claim hyper masculine) nature of the criminal justice system itself. It is certainly easy to see how this notion fits into the criminal justice system as authority and control are key components of the system.

## References

Adler, F. (1975). *Sisters in Crime*. New York: McGraw-Hill.
Adler, F. & Simon, R.J. (1979). *The Criminology of Deviant Women*. Boston: Houghton Mifflin.
American Society of Criminology. (2008). *Dr. James W. Messerschmidt*. Division of Women and Crime. Retrieved January 29, 2021 from https://ascdwc.com/member-profiles-summer-2008/.
Burke, A.S. (2014). Chesney-Lind, Meda. In J.S. Albanese, *The Encyclopedia of Criminology and Criminal Justice*: Wiley Series of Encyclopedias in Criminology and Criminal Justice. Hoboken, NJ: Wiley.
Chesney-Lind, M. (2004). Beyond bad girls: Feminist perspectives on female offending. In C. Sumner (Ed.), *The Blackwell Companion to Criminology* (pp. 255–267). Malden, MA: Blackwell Publishing.
Chesney-Lind, M., & Jones, N. (2010) *Fighting for Girls: New Perspectives on Gender and Violence*. Albany: State University of New York.
Connell, R.W. (1987). *Gender and Power*. Sydney: Allyn & Unwin.
Cullen, F.T., & Agnew, R. (1999). *Criminological Theory: Past to Present, Essential Readings*. Los Angeles: Roxbury.
Daly, K., & Tonry, M. (1997). Gender, race and sentencing. *Crime and Justice*, 22, 201–252.
Daly, K. (2006). Restorative justice and sexual assault: An archival study of court and conference cases. *British Journal of Criminology*, 46(2), 334–356.
Daly, K., & Chesney-Lind, M. (1988). Feminism and criminology. *Justice Quarterly*, 5(4), 497–538.
Flynn, E.E. (1998) Freda Adler. *Women & Criminal Justice*, 10(1), 1–26.
Goffman, E. (1959). *The Presentation of Life in Everyday Life*. New York: Doubleday.
Groot, B.L. (2014). Chesney-Lind, Meda: Feminist model of female delinquency. In F.T. Cullen, & P. Wilcox (Eds.), *Encyclopedia of Criminological Theory* (pp. 153–156). Newbury Park, CA: SAGE Publications, Inc.

Griffin University. (N.d.) Professor Kathleen Daly. Retrieved online January 30, 2021 at https://www.griffith.edu.au/criminology-institute/our-researchers/professor-kathleen-daly.

Lilly, J.R., Cullen, F.T., & Ball, R.A. (2002). *Criminological Theory: Context and Consequences*, 3rd ed. Thousand Oaks, CA: Sage.

Lombroso, C., & Ferrero, G. (1894). *The Female Offender*. New York: Appleton.

Lynch, M.J., & Groves, W.B. (1989). *A Primer in Radical Criminology*, 2nd ed. New York: Harrow & Heston.

Messerschmidt, J.W. (1986). *Capitalism, Patriarchy, and Crime*. Totawa, NJ: Rowman & Littlefield.

Messerschmidt, J.W. (1993). *Masculinities and Crime: Critique and Conceptualization of Theory*. Lanham, MA: Rowman & Littlefield.

Messerschmidt, J.W. (1997). *Crime as Structured Action: Gender, Race, and Crime in the Making*. Lanham, MD: Rowman & Littlefield.

Messerschmidt J.W. (2018). Multiple masculinities. In B. Risman, C. Froyum, W. Scarborough (Eds.), *Handbook of the Sociology of Gender* (pp. 143–153). Handbooks of Sociology and Social Research. Springer, Cham.

Pollak, O. (1950). *The Criminality of Women*. Philadelphia: University of Pennsylvania Press.

Rennison, C.M. (2014). Adler, Freda. In J.M. Miller (Ed.), *The Encyclopedia of Theoretical Criminology*. Hoboken, NJ: John Wiley & Sons.

Shaw, C. (1938). *Brothers in Crime*. Chicago, IL: University of Chicago Press.

Simon, R. (1975). *Women and Crime*. Lexington, MA: Lexington Books.

University of Southern Maine. (2021). *James W. Messerschmidt*. Retrieved on January 29, 2021 from https://usm.maine.edu/criminology/james-w-messerschmidt-phd.

van der Does, L.Q. (2008). Rita James Simon: Reaching beyond the ordinary. *Women and Criminal Justice*, 13 (2–3), 13–28.

Vold, G.B., Bernard, T.J., & Snipes, J.B. (2002). *Theoretical Criminology*, 5th ed. New York and Oxford: Oxford University Press.

# 11

# RACE AND CRIME

## Du Bois, Work, Bell & Delgado

## Introduction

The theoretical perspectives introduced in this section involve the relationship between two important variables – crime and race. Today, race is correctly understood as a social construct, meaning race is based on a few physical attributes that are only important due to the social meanings placed on them. Race, therefore, is a means of categorizing people by certain traits, traits which in turn impact an individual's specific identity based on the construct. Racial stereotypes are common in society and often interfere with the effective administration of justice; therefore, a conflict approach has augmented racial perspectives on criminology.

The theorists and scholars in this section have produced theoretical advances, empirical research, and activism that put race at the center of discussions on criminality. African American scholar W.E.B. Du Bois has only recently been considered a legitimate founder of sociology and a key contributor to criminological theory, a fact that demonstrates the continuing legacy of racial discrimination. His call for a group of African American leaders to promote change (the "talented tenth") was answered by Monroe Work who provided empirical support for theories of race and crime. Du Bois also influenced a recent perspective known as critical race theory (CRT) which was started in legal studies and was extended into other areas such as criminology by scholars such as Derrick Bell and Richard Delgado.

## W.E.B. Du Bois (1886–1963)

### Introduction

William Edward Burghardt (W.E.B.) Du Bois was an African American scholar, primarily considered a classical sociologist, but whose work has elements of history, philosophy, political science, literature, and others. Considered the country's first sociologist of race (Lewis, 2000), he has not often been credited for his work on deviance and crime but, as will be discussed in this section, his contributions are substantial. His theory, research, and activism on race issues underscore most of his vast writings and certainly find a natural home in issues of race relations today. Though often excluded from academic criminological theory, it has been argued he should be considered among the pioneers (Gabbidon, 2001; Morris, 2015). The issues confronting American society would do

DOI: 10.4324/9781003036609-11

well to turn to the work of Du Bois during times when racial injustice and racial unrest are prevalent. As Morris (2015) proclaims, "we are in the age of Du Bois" (xix).

## Biographical Profile

Born in Great Barrington, Massachusetts, a primarily white community, Du Bois was raised humbly, but surrounded by the well-to-do. Perhaps Du Bois developed an early interest in deviance and crime due to some experiences as an impressionable teenager. The theft of some grapes by Du Bois and his friends from a prominent citizen's orchard might have resulted in him being sent to reform school if not for someone's intervention on his behalf; the experience likely taught him about the injustices in the criminal justice system. Another time, as a local correspondent for *The New York Globe* when he was 15, Du Bois expressed his interest in his towns' move toward enforcement in alcohol laws and his belief that Black people should become involved in the program (Gabbidon, 2001). These interests in equality and social action seem to have been carried with him throughout his life.

After graduating from his segregated high school at age 16, Du Bois attended Fisk College (now university) in Tennessee where he encountered prejudice and discrimination through the Jim Crow laws and voter suppression, and he lived in a land that witnessed the horrors of lynching. He graduated from Fisk in 1888 then attended Harvard University where he received a second bachelor's degree in 1890. Du Bois then received a fellowship to the University of Berlin where he studied under eminent European scholars and was finally not regarded as an outsider. He returned to Harvard to complete his Ph.D., the first African American to achieve this accomplishment. (Du Bois, [1920]1999; Tuttle, 1973).

After graduating, he accepted a position at Wilberforce University, rejecting an offer to teach at the Tuskegee Institute. At Wilberforce he met and married Nina Gomer, a student at the school, and they had a son, who died in infancy, and a daughter. After his marriage, he conducted a yearlong research project in Philadelphia, which would become a landmark community study. Du Bois then joined the faculty at Atlanta University (now Clark Atlanta University; Du Bois, [1920]1999; Tuttle, 1973).

Known as the "dean of black scholars" (Green & Smith, 1983), from 1890 until his death in 1963, Du Bois is generally well known for his contributions to conflict social theory, however, his contributions to criminological theory are becoming more recognized. In addition, Du Bois' empirical work is also of great importance and, while at Atlanta University, he helped open one of the first research schools for social science in the nation. He conducted one of the country's first crime polls in 1904, providing important data for Atlanta and other areas of the state of Georgia regarding African American perspectives on the criminal justice system (Gabbidon, 2000); this resulted in *Some Notes on Negro Crime, Particularly in Georgia* (Du Bois, 1904).

Du Bois helped found the precursor to the National Association for the Advancement of Colored People (NAACP), became editor of the NAACP's magazine, *The Crisis*, engaged in civil rights activities, traveled the globe as NAACP's delegate to the newly established United Nations, became a socialist, and continued to write extensively on racial prejudice and discrimination. He renounced his US citizenship after becoming frustrated over the lack of equality for people of color, and moved to Ghana, where he died in 1963 at age 95.

## Profiling the Theory

Du Bois rejects the biologically based theories of crimes committed by people of color, flying in the face of the prominent Social Darwinist ideology of the period (Collins & Makowsky,

1998; Morris 2015). Racial disparity and race relations were the key focus of his work. Du Bois begins his classic text *Souls of Black Folk* ([1903]1995) with this line: "the problem of the twenty-first century is the problem of the color line" (p. 41). The color line reflects the idea that African Americans, when visible to Whites, are perceived as a problem and who must experience emotional pain in silence as "non-persons" (Morris, 2015). All Du Bois' scholarly output was in some way connected, in "explaining, exploring, and deconstructing that color line" (Zuckerman, 2004, p. 5).

There exists, according to Du Bois, a *veil* that separates racial understanding (Morris, 2015). He also describes a *double consciousness* in which people of color perceive of themselves as honest, decent, law abiding people, while at the same time realizing they are seen by Whites as defective, unintelligent, and criminal. This "two-ness" creates a struggle in people of color and the labeling process becomes especially problematic.

Du Bois believed the way for people of color to receive equality was through academic education, political involvement, and reform engagement. He promoted leadership from promising members of the African American community, a group he called the "talented tenth". This group would create better economic, social, and political conditions for Black people, exemplified by scholars like Nathan Monroe Work. In this way, his ideas on racial progress differed from contemporary African American leader Booker T. Washington.

Du Bois' sought to disclose to the country the disparities in crime types and punishments based on race. The criminal justice system, as with the other basic institutions in American society, was aimed at controlling Black violators (or suspected violators). The convict lease system, which was simply an extension of slavery, is an example. Of special note was the abhorrent practice of lynching which Du Bois noted involved some type of (often perceived) insult from Black men toward Southern White femininity, while White men who attacked Black women often acted with impunity (Du Bois, 1914).

### Profiling the Literature

#### "The Negro and Crime" (1899a)

In this essay, Du Bois explains the emergence of "a Negro criminal class" as an expected outcome of a people who were granted freedom after such a long period living under stressful, oppressive conditions. He outlines the causal agents in the development of Black criminality: 1) the convict-lease system in which those that are incarcerated are leased out for their labor; 2) the differential treatment of a Black people in the justice system; 3) mob behavior by White vigilantes; and 4) the discriminatory segregation practices that promote the color line.

### The Philadelphia Negro (1899b)

This work is normally acknowledged as the first classic description of the circumstances of urban African American life; however, it is less understood as the first empirical sociological study in America (Morris, 2015). The study was commissioned by the University of Pennsylvania at the end of the nineteenth century to ascertain the problems and living conditions of African Americans in Philadelphia. Du Bois studied the people of a section of the city known as the seventh ward for a period of 15 months and conducted personal interviews and official statistics to give a clear picture of the situation. Du Bois sought to provide descriptions of: 1) the history of the people in the area; 2) their current condition as individuals; 3) their current history as a social group; and 4) their physical and social environment.

Du Bois uses his academic training in history and sociology to provide comprehensive information about the residents' family lives, education, health, occupations, and other aspects. Chapter 13 is entitled "The Negro Criminal" and provides valuable information such as comparisons between Black and White criminality, arrest data, incarceration information, and some interesting criminal case studies. This chapter is followed by another that addresses "Alcoholism and Pauperism" in which Du Bois makes connections between poverty, crime, and emancipation. At the end of the work, he describes the "duty" of African Americans to seek social reform, to prevent neighborhood crime, to support self-improvement strategies, and to provide outlets for youth. He also describes the duty of Whites to be civil and understanding of the plight of Blacks and avoid discriminating against them, though he notes the inherent difficulties in that request.

The work is widely regarded as marking a major turning point in American sociology and criminology. Du Bois ([1920]1999) would later state "nobody ever reads that fat volume on *The Philadelphia Negro*, but they treat it with respect, and that consoles me" (p. 11).

## Souls of Black Folk *(1903)*

Published in 1903, *Souls* is at once a sociological, historical, political, and literary classic – separate essays connected by an examination of race and race relations. Although not specifically a criminological work or even an empirical sociology text, it is included here as it includes some of Du Bois' primary theoretical concepts. It provides the concepts well known in the social sciences today including the color line, the veil, and double consciousness, mentioned in the theory section. His use of vivid metaphorical imagery is a way in which Du Bois connects his readers to the issues of race relations in America.

Du Bois includes a chapter that addresses his differences with African American leader Booker T. Washington on strategies for African American advancement – Du Bois sought rapid progress through academic education and direct confrontation by a group of young African American leaders, which, as stated previously, he called the "talented tenth" (top ten percent), while Washington sought a measured progression achieved through vocational training and appeasement with the White power structure.

## *Legacy*

It is difficult to overstate the impact of Du Bois to social science theory and social activism. He attempted to shed light on the extremely racist practices of his era, some practices that continue to exist today. Du Bois' work influenced what is termed critical race theory (CRT), which began in the 1960s and early 1970s to address the numerous and ubiquitous ways in which race affects social life, the ways in which vested interests keep racism viable, and how race is socially constructed and continues to stratify society (Delgado & Stefancic, 2007). Regarding crime and the criminal justice system, aspects such as differential policies and actions in policing, sentencing, and corrections, along with minority victimization and other issues, are at the forefront of CRT; all which had Du Bois' attention, many years earlier. The current issues that have prompted Black Lives Matter protests around America and the world reflect many of the same concerns of Du Bois.

Du Bois' theorizing on the convergence of race, gender, and class has defined him as the first sociologist to address what is now termed intersectionality (Morris, 2015), which is the idea that these social identifiers should be studied together as agents of oppression. A branch of criminology – intersectional criminology has developed on this framework.

It is fortunate that Du Bois produced a body of work specific to sociological criminology. For too long Du Bois has been excluded from the rank of the classic sociologists and criminologists; as Gabbidon (2001) notes, "whatever the reason for his interest in the issues of crime and justice, he left a legacy that can no longer be ignored" (p. 583).

## Monroe Nathan Work (1866–1945)

### Introduction

Monroe Nathan Work was a sociologist, administrator, and researcher who analyzed the conditions of race relations and racial inequality in America from the late nineteenth to the mid-twentieth century. He researched the intersections between criminality and poverty and was a key chronicler of the African American experience in his lifetime. Work was initially influenced by the activism of W.E.B. Du Bois and he answered Du Bois' call to become one of the "talented tenth" of young black scholars with a duty to challenge racial injustice. However, he also worked closely with Booker T. Washington at the Tuskegee Institute for three decades.

Despite working with high profile charismatic African American leaders, he was reserved, professorial, and quiet, barely moving his lips when he spoke (McMurry, 1985). When Work began his career, he did so at a time racial relations and the mistreatment of African Americans were at a remarkably high level. The promise of emancipation and reconstruction gave way to Jim Crow laws, disenfranchisement, a lack of opportunity, differential treatment based on race, and the horrific practice of lynching, all of which Work confronted directly through his academic work.

### Biographical Profile

Work was born in 1866 in Iredell County, North Carolina, one of 13 siblings whose parents were emancipated slaves by the time of Monroe's birth. The family relocated to Illinois in the 1860s and the next decade to Kansas, part of the first great wave of African American migration in the United States. His siblings left the family farm, leaving him to work the land and care for his parents, delaying his high school education until age 23. After high school, he taught at a private school and worked as a minister. Despite several setbacks, he entered the Chicago Theological Seminary and began studying the new discipline of Christian sociology.

In 1898, he entered the sociology department at the prestigious University of Chicago and worked in a variety of jobs to support himself, including delivering laundry on campus. After graduating with an M.A. in sociology and psychology the following year, he became one of the first African Americans to produce sociological works on race in the country, along with W.E.B. Du Bois, Kelly Miller, and author Richard Wright (Tucker, 1991). He moved to Savannah, Georgia in 1903 where he taught education and history at the Georgia State Industrial College (now Savannah State University); he took the position primarily to learn about the racial conditions in the deep south. There he met his wife Florence E. Hendrickson, a schoolteacher in the area.

He was hired by Booker T. Washington at the Tuskegee Institute as an administrator and researcher in 1909 until his retirement in 1938. *The Negro Year Book* was a laborious endeavor launched at Tuskegee by Washington, granting Work and the department of records and research US$1,000.00 to complete a study of the achievements of African Americans on a wide variety of subject areas. Work received accolades as editor of the yearbook, prompting

Richard Wright, Jr. to refer to him as a painstaking sociologist and historian. Washington planned only one edition of the book but, due to its popularity, several updates followed (Guzman, 1949). Work wanted to provide coverage of the incidents of lynching, and beginning in 1914 he began producing statistical data semi-annually through the Institute, which he sent to news outlets across the country, even in the Southern United States (McMurry, 1985).

After retirement, he continued to press for a better understanding of racial issues, attended seminars, worked with other researchers, and planned to update his book under a new name and move the focus to a global examination of colonization of people of all racial groups. Although he compiled much information, he did not finish the project before his death in 1945 (McMurry, 1985).

## Profiling the Theory

Work is better known as a researcher than a theorist, however his skillful methodology was developed from his academic training at one of the great research institutions in the country at the time. Chicago School of Sociology theorists W.I. Thomas and Robert Park were major influences, and the style of that school is implicit in his work. From them he learned and adopted the method of compiling large amounts of data, mapping, and using the communities in a manner like that of other Chicago School theorists. His methodology is also like that of Du Bois, especially in his focus on racial inequalities as sources of problems in communities of color. As Work notes,

> the fact that he [sic] is in this transitional state from a lower to a higher plane of development accounts for a part, at least, of his excess of crime. Within this transition the economic stress under which he [sic] has labored appears to be the main factor.
>
> *(Work, 1900, p. 222)*

Work accepts that other variables are at play, however he notes the salient effects of economic inequality.

Work was influenced by and worked with African American leaders W.E.B. Du Bois and Booker T. Washington, whose ideas were quite different regarding the measures that should be taken to promote racial equality. Though Du Bois supported measures that created a more rapid transition to, as Work noted, "a higher plane of development", Washington sought a slower pace of advancement, so as not to buck the White establishment and risk future gains. The opposing theoretical positions of Du Bois and Washington were adopted into Work's social thought because of his belief in the salient role of academic education to lift Black Americans into roles equal to Whites, with an accompanying belief that vocational training was also important to meet this end. In adopting and integrating these two theoretical positions, Work was certainly a "man with a foot in both camps" (McMurry, 1985, p. 52).

## Profiling the Literature

### "Crime among the Negroes of Chicago" (1900)

This article reflects a study conducted in the waning years of 1897 and the first half of 1898. After providing some basic national crime data, Work provides information on African Americans in Chicago at the time, then proceeds to illustrate crime data for this population.

Again, many variables were examined in his analysis of the data including "skin complexion"; it would be interesting to have more of his insights on the role of multiraciality regarding deviance and crime from a racial perspective, but no information exists in this report. Through statistics he shows increases in crime of Black Americans and in his last section he addresses the primary causes of crime – the difficult transition from slavery to freedom and the economic difficulties arising from this transition. According to McMurry (1985) the article inspired a business owner in California to invest in Chicago's settlement house program.

### "Negro Criminality in the South" (1913)

In this article, Work explains that prior to the American Civil War, crime by African Americans was low, but at the end of the war it increased, primarily due to the chaos and confusion of the time. Work provided statistics for Georgia and other southern states which revealed dramatic increases in the number of Black inmates after the war, but a decrease beginning around 1894–1895. He also noted a greater increase in lynching prior to this time. He discovered three factors related to Black crime in the South post war: 1) the use of the convict lease system in which inmates were used for labor; 2) severe punishments for petty crimes; 3) a lack of adequate facilities for juvenile offenders; 4) *ignorance* (he did not elaborate on this term); and 5) alcoholism. Work also saw hope in a few forms: Black citizens who sought to find sources for criminality, and efforts by political and academic organizations, such as the Southern Sociological Congress, to study African American crime and offer suggestions for reform.

### A Bibliography of the Negro in Africa and America (1928)

This project, under the guidance of Work, was in production for over 20 years, contained 75 chapters and 17,000 entries, and was considered by Robert Park "the most valuable aid thus far available to students of Negro life and of the Negro problem" (Park, 1929, p. 127). Work produced *The Negro Year Book* in 1912 and in that work, he added 408 references in a section called "A Select Bibliography of the Negro". After its publication, Work, as Director of Records and Research at the Tuskegee Institute, received grants to expand the bibliography project and created 10,000 references. Interest continued to grow to an international level so, along with additional funding, he visited European libraries and added another 7,000 (Park, 1929). This comprehensive study of African American life would have likely not been available without funding from philanthropic organizations (Moses, 1996).

### Legacy

Work is the only scholar who is directly connected to the scholarship and activism of both W.E. B. Du Bois and Booker T. Washington (McMurry, 1985). He was, as a biographer put it, "one of that select group of men of the Post Civil War period who caught a vision of the needs of their people and had prepared themselves to meet those needs" (Guzman, 1949, p. 428).

In his obituary in the *Journal of Negro History* (1945), it was mentioned that Work normally rejected public attention and was not generally well known, but was well respected, in academia. His academic work paved the way for others interested in race and criminality. As noted by his biographers, Work labored away from the spotlight in ensuring that America placed value on the lives of African Americans (Guzman, 1949; McMurry, 1985); his aim in this respect certainly mirrors the Black Lives Matter movement and others that would evolve in the coming century.

## Derrick Bell (1930–2011) & Richard Delgado (1939–)

### Introduction

Derrick Bell and Richard Delgado are different from other theorists that have been profiled thus far in that they did not coauthor or develop a theoretical idea in collaboration with one another in the traditional sense. However, together, they are considered two of the intellectual heavy weights in what is referred to now as Critical Race Theory (Bell, 1995). Focusing on race and racism, "critical race theory is a body of legal scholarship…a majority of whose members are both existentially people of color and ideologically committed to the struggle against racism, particularly as institutionalized in and by law" (Bell, 1995, p. 898). While Bell and Delgado are by no means the only important scholars on the topic (see a host of scholarship by Charles Lawrence, Mari Matsuda, and Patricia Williams), they have been selected for this section as their scholarship most closely matches the goals of this text.

### Biographical Profile

#### Derrick Bell (1930–2011)

Viewed by some as the most influential of all the critical race theorists (Bernstein, 2011), Derrick Bell came from humble roots. Born in Pittsburgh, Pennsylvania, Derrick Bell was the first in his family to go to college when he attended Duquesne University. Participating as an ROTC cadet, Bell went to Korea as part of the Air Force after graduation (Bernstein, 2011). When the Korean War ended, Bell enrolled in law school at the University of Pittsburg and become a Department of Justice attorney upon graduation. Bell only held this job for a few years before he resigned in protest at the Department of Justice's insistence that he terminate involvement with the NAACP – this would not be the last post he resigned. Bell resigned his post as Dean of the University of Oregon Law School when not allowed to hire an Asian American as a faculty member, and again from Harvard University over the school's refusal to hire and offer tenure to minority women (Cummings, 2012; Bernstein, 2011). A true believer in racial equality, it is clear that Bell was willing to personally sacrifice in order to stand up to injustice.

### Richard Delgado (1939–)

Born to a Mexican American father who came to America as an orphan, Delgado's early life was somewhat transient. He attended the University of Washington where he got his degrees in mathematics and philosophy before attending law school at the University of California, Berkeley. Publishing heavily with his wife, Jean Stefancic, Delgado built on Bell's work and extended the theory into the mainstream of American legal thought. Delgado is currently a professor of law at the University of Alabama.

### Profiling the Theory

After the 1960s Civil Rights Movement appeared to stall, Critical Race Theory (CRT) was developed to deal with the new forms of institutional racism, such as colorblindness (Delgado & Stefancic, 1993; 2007). Founded primarily by law professors of color, CRT directly challenged the law by exposing the racial inequalities supported by the US legal system

(Cummings, 2012). The origins of CRT were notably humble; never intending to start a movement, Black law professors got together to discuss how they could support each other and survive in a White-male dominated legal profession. These scholars realized that they were communicating, thinking, and writing in ways that were quite different from the academic mainstream – especially as it related to race and racism in America. While this movement considers many of the same problems as the original civil rights movement, it extends further to question the order of society, including legal reasoning and the purported *neutral* constitutional principles of law (Delgado & Stefancic, 1995).

CRT serves "the dual purpose of providing a race-based interdisciplinary theoretical framework for analyzing laws, policies, and administrative procedures that have a deleterious impact on racial minorities" (Cummings, 2012, p. 54). In this way, the emphasis in CRT is on storytelling and narrative as empirical evidence of the human experience and reality, and rejects the traditional pedagogy that was pervasive in legal scholarship. CRT argues that White elites will tolerate and encourage Black advancement only insofar as it also helps to advance White interests as well (Bell, 1980). For example, in one of Bell's (1980) most cited works, he suggests that Brown v. Board of Education (347 US 483 (1954)), the case in which the US Supreme Court overturned the segregation of schools, had less to do with racial freedom and more to do with the realization that the United States had just fought a war against Nazism, and was in the process of fighting communism, under the premise that "all men were created equal". Segregation was a direct affront to that principle and being used by the enemy to question US motives. Further, attempts to industrialize the South were being hindered by segregation; therefore, segregation had to end (Bell, 1980).

With this in mind, CRT has a few basic propositions in which one should view law and criminal behavior. First, racism is ordinary (Delgado & Stefancic, 1995). While this may be a simple statement, often when discussing racism, it is viewed as an aberration to the normal way of life. Further, by not acknowledging that it is ordinary, it suggests that it is not as serious of a problem and therefore there is not a serious need to address it. Second, the power dynamic of Whites over people of color serves both psychic and material purposes for the dominant group. By using terms like *colorblind* or coming up with *formal* means of addressing racism, we are only solving the most blatant problems of racism while ignoring the more subtle issues in society. For example, outlawing predatory mortgage loan practices, while positive for minorities, also has obvious benefits to those in power who give out loans and sell houses (Delgado & Stefancic, 1995).

A third proposition of CRT is that race and races are a social construction and are products of social thought and relations (Delgado & Stefancic, 1995). While it is true that certain races look similar and may be from similar ancestorial lands, these characteristics make up a very small percentage of the individual's genetic traits and focus on insignificant, subtle differences between groups as opposed to the humanness that all groups share – such as intelligence, morality, and personality. Society ignoring these characteristics in favor of surface level descriptions is of great interest to CRT researchers (Delgado & Stefancic, 1995).

A fourth proposition is that society racializes different minority groups at different times for different purposes (Delgado & Stefancic, 1995). For example, in considering the first Thanksgiving, Native Americans were viewed as friends who helped the early colonists survive in the new world – a belief still celebrated by many on a Thursday in November. However, a short time later, the same groups of people were viewed as savages that needed to be removed from American territories due to threats of violence. The view of these different races at different times, according to a CRT theorist, shows that these views are intimately tied to the interests of the dominant group (Delgado & Stefancic, 1995).

A fifth proposition of CRT suggests that each race has its own origin and ever-evolving history (Delgado & Stefancic, 1995). While this is true, it ignores the complex nature of individual origins in favor of a simplistic understanding of a group of people. It also ignores that everyone has "conflicting, overlapping identities, loyalties, and allegiances" (Delgado & Stefancic, 1995, p. 10) in favor of some singular oneness.

Finally, CRT proposes that due to these differing experiences and histories of people of color, people of color need to be allowed to explain to White people things that White people are unlikely to know (Delgado & Stefancic, 1995). For example, fire hoses and police dogs were routinely used on Black people by slave patrols and again by the police during the Jim Crow era. To that end, it makes sense that there may be a strong distrust of law enforcement by southern Black people compared to their White counterparts. By sharing these experiences with White people, minority scholars can help tell the story of how racism affects their lives in a direct way (Delgado & Stefancic, 1995).

While this theory is clearly broader than criminology or deviance issues, for the purpose of this section we will focus just on those specific topics. According to CRT, ideas of criminality and punishment for crimes have their origins less in right and wrong and more in who is committing the deviant act (Delgado & Stefancic, 2007). For example, in an empirical piece on who is more of a threat to society, Delgado (1994) showed that White people are significantly more dangerous to society than minorities in terms of undeclared wars, dangerous consumer products, or property loss due to white-collar crimes, and yet minorities are overrepresented in arrest rates and incarceration because certain acts have been made more punishable than others. In this way, those in power are able to use law as a hegemonic strategy to maintain their power by keeping other groups suppressed.

While CRT has become a popular theoretical idea in the legal and social scientific communities, it is not without its critics – both academic (Farber & Sherry, 1997) and legal (Posner, 1997). As CRT is a direct assault on the entire system of justice, both liberal and conservative, this pushback is unsurprising. However, suggestions of anti-Semitism and anti-Asian rhetoric plague the theory (Farber & Sherry, 1995; 1997). The argument is that if American society is structurally unfair to people of color, how can the theory explain the successes of Asian-Americans and Jewish-Americans (both of whom have been historically discriminated against) absent of their cheating to get ahead. In response, Delgado & Stefancic (1995) suggest that just because certain groups thrive does not make the system fair. Regardless of the criticisms, it is clear that CRT has had a large impact on the scholarship and thought about how law, criminality, and race all intersect in society.

### Profiling the Literature

### Race, Racism and American Law *(Derrick Bell, 1973)*

This work asks lawyers of minority defendants if they can truly stake their futures on laws. Noting that solutions to the problem of racial injustice include ideas like emigration and civil disobedience, Bell also examines the law, through "illustrative cases" (*Stanford Law Review*) that show that major rights are being infringed upon. Bell's book is the first "which offers a truly comprehensive coverage of the matrices of racism and law" (Higginbotham, 1974, p. 1046).

### Critical Race Theory: An Introduction *(Delgado & Stefancic, 1995)*

This text by Delgado and Stefancic is an essential read for anyone interested in the topic of CRT. Organized in a straightforward manner, it first defines CRT on the six major propositions listed above. Each chapter then goes into detail where the propositions are more clearly defined, and supporting evidence is given. Finally, and unique to texts of this type, there is a chapter addressing the criticisms of CRT from both the left and the right. The final chapter lays out the future of America and CRT's role in helping to shape that future.

## Legacy

There is no doubt that the work done by Bell and Delgado, while not directly connected in co-authorship, is connected in spirit. Derrick Bell's insistence on storytelling as opposed to formal legal analysis opened the door for many minorities, including female, Latino, and gay scholars, to express their experience with the law in ways that were not previously available (Bernstein, 2011). In describing Delgado, Stanley Fish stated, "Richard Delgado is a triple pioneer. He was the first to question free speech ideology; he and a few others invented critical race theory; and he is both a theorist and an exemplar of the importance of story-telling in the workings of the law" (Delgado & Stefancic, 2011, p. 222). In assessing his own legacy, Bell (2008) stated, "my efforts may have benefited my career more clearly than they helped those for whom I have worked." However, the copious scholarship and legal doc-trines that have come out of both men's work can leave no doubt to the erroneousness of that statement.

## References

Bell, D.A. (1973). Race, Racism and American Law. New York: Aspen.

Bell, D.A. (1995). Who's afraid of critical race theory. *University of Illinois Law Review*, 4, 893–910.

Bell, D.A. (2008). *Ethical Ambition: Living a Life of Meaning and Worth*. New York: Bloomsbury Publishing.

Bell Jr, D.A. (1980). Brown v. Board of Education and the interest–convergence dilemma. *Harvard Law Review*, 93(3), 518–533.

Bernstein, F.A. (October 6, 2011). Derrick Bell, Law Professor and Rights Advocate, dies at 80. *The New York Times*. http://www. nytimes.com/2011/10/06/us/derrick-bell-pioneering-harvard-law-p rofessor-dies-at80.html?pagewanted=all&_r=0.

Brown v. Board of Education of Topeka. 347 U.S. 483 (1954).

Collins, R., & Makowsky, M. (1998). *The Discovery of Society*, 6th ed. Boston: McGraw-Hill.

Cummings, A.D.P. (2012). Derrick Bell: Godfather provocateur. *Harvard Journal of Racial & Ethnic Justice*, 28, 51–66.

Delgado, R. (1994). Rodrigo's eighth chronicle: Black crime, white fears. On the social construction of threat. *Virginia Law Review*, 503–548.

Delgado, R., & Stefancic, J. (2007). Critical race theory and criminal justice. *Humanity and Society*, 31(2–3), 133–145.

Delgado, R., & Stefancic, J. (1993). Critical race theory: An annotated bibliography. *Virginia Law Review*, 461–516.

Delgado, R., & Stefancic, J. (1995). *Critical Race Theory: An Introduction*. New York: New York University Press.

Delgado, R., & Stefancic, J. (2011). Living History Interview with Richard Delgado & Jean Stefancic. *Transnational Law & Contemporary Problems*, 19, 221–230.

Du Bois, W.E.B. (1899a). The Negro and crime. *The Independent*, 51, 1355–1357.

Du Bois, W.E.B. (1899b). *The Philadelphia Negro: A Social Study*. Millwood, NY: Kraus Thomson-Organization.

Du Bois, W.E.B. ([1903]1995). *Souls of Black Folk*. New York: Signet.

Du Bois, W.E.B. (1904). *Some Notes on Negro Crime, Particularly in Georgia*. Atlanta, GA: Atlanta University Press.

Du Bois, W.E.B. (1914). *Morals and Manners among Negro Americans*. Atlanta, GA: Atlanta University Press.

Du Bois, W.E.B. ([1920]1999). *Darkwater: Voices from Within the Veil*. Mineola, NY: Dover.

Farber, D.A., & Sherry, S. (1995). Is the radical critique of merit anti-semitic?. *California Law Review*, 83 (3), 853.

Farber, D.A., & Sherry, S. (1997). *Beyond all Reason: The Radical Assault on Truth in American Law*. Oxford University Press.

Gabbidon, S.L. (2000). An early American crime poll by W.E.B. Du Bois. *Western Journal of Black Studies*, 24(3), 167–174.

Gabbidon, S.L. (2001) W.E.B. Du Bois: Pioneering American criminologist. *Journal of Black Studies*, 31 (5), 581–599.

Green, D.S., & Smith, E. (1983). W.E.B. Du Bois and the concepts of race and class. *Phylon*, 44(4), 262–272.

Guzman, J.P. (1949). Monroe Nathan Work and his contributions: Background and preparation for life's career. *The Journal of Negro History*, 34(4), 428–461.

Higginbotham Jr, A.L. (1974). Race, racism and American law. *University of Pennsylvania Law Review*, 122 (4), 1044–1069.

Lewis, D.L. (2000). *W.E.B. Du Bois: The First for Equality in the American Century 1919–1963*. New York: Henry Holt.

McMurry, L.O. (1985). *Recorder of the Black Experience: A Biography of Monroe Nathan Work*. Baton Rouge and London: Louisiana State University Press.

Morris, A. (2015). *The Scholar Denied: W.E.B. Du Bois and the Birth of Modern Sociology*. Oakland: University of California Press.

Moses, S. (1996). The influence of philanthropic agencies on the development of Monroe Nathan Work's *Bibliography of the Negro in Africa and America*. *Libraries & Culture*, 31(2), 326–341.

Park, R.E. (1929). Reviewed work: *A Bibliography of the Negro in Africa and America*. *American Journal of Sociology*, 35(1), 126–127.

Posner, R.A. (1997). The Skin Trade. *New Republic*, 217(15), 40–43.

*Stanford Law Review, Race, Racism, and American Law* by Derrick Bell: Book Review, 26 (3), 713–714.

Tucker, M. (1991). "You can't argue with facts": Monroe Nathan Work as information officer, editor, and biographer. *Libraries and Culture*, 26(1), 151–168.

Tuttle, W.M. (1973). *W.E.B. Du Bois*. Englewood Cliffs, NJ: Prentice-Hall.

Work, M.N. (1900). Crime among the Negroes of Chicago: A social study. *American Journal of Sociology*, 6(2), 204–233.

Work, M.N. (1913). Negro Criminality in the South. *Annals of the American Academy of Political and Social Sciences*, 49, 74–80.

Work, M.N. (1928). *A Bibliography of the Negro in Africa and America*. New York: A.K. Wilson.

Work, M.N. (1945). Obituary. *The Journal of Negro History*, 30(3), 354–355.

Zuckerman, P. (2004). *The Social Theory of W.E.B. Du Bois*. Thousand Oaks, CA: Pine Forge Press.

# 12

# CRIME OVER THE LIFE COURSE
## Glueck & Glueck, Sampson & Laub

## Introduction

The theorists in this chapter are not interested in crime in any one stage of life or at any one point in time. Rather, they are interested in the rise and fall of criminality in individuals throughout their entire lives. Studying individuals over decades long spans of time, the theorists in this chapter look for common crime initiating variables at various stages in an individual's life – for some individuals, this began in the womb.

Early theorists (Glueck & Glueck) did not have the advanced statistical and methodological sophistication to study these effects as later theorists (Sampson & Laub), but they were among the first to suggest that studying an individual over time may be a more fruitful area of research than comparing two groups of individuals at different life stages. These types of research designs have become a gold standard in the study of crime and deviant behavior and are some of the most popular modern-day research methodologies utilized by researchers to help explain the role of various crime enhancing and crime reducing situations in an individual's life.

## Sheldon Glueck (1896–1980) & Eleanor Glueck (1898–1972)

### Introduction

Sheldon and Eleanor Glueck were pioneers in the field of juvenile delinquency (Rubenser, 2002). Among the first to utilize longitudinal research design, the Gluecks were also some of the first researchers to stress the role of the family environment on juvenile delinquency. The Gluecks were ahead of their time in the consideration of the life-course perspectives toward deviance. Their work is viewed as a precursor to the *career criminal* paradigm that is dominant in the study of crime and deviance today.

### Biographical Profile

Sheldon Glueck was born in Poland and immigrated to the United States as a child. His educational training consisted of a bachelor's degree in humanities, an MA in law, and a PhD in social ethics (precursor to sociology) from Harvard (Laub & Sampson, 2011; Rubenser,

DOI: 10.4324/9781003036609-12

2002). Eleanor Glueck's educational training was equally diverse. Receiving her BAs in English from Barnard College and social work from the New York School of Social Work, she obtained her MA and Ed.D. in education from Harvard University (Laub & Sampson, 2011; Rubenser, 2002). This interdisciplinary education helped them develop their inter-disciplinary approach to delinquency and allowed them to publish extensively in journals of psychology, sociology, criminology, social work, education, law, and psychiatry. However, this did not come without any costs. "The Gluecks belong to no single academic discipline, and they are suffering from the declassee fate of aliens and intruders" (Geis, 1966, p. 188).

The Gluecks met when Sheldon's brother, Bernard, introduced the two (Rubenser, 2002). Bernard was a psychiatrist at Sing Sing Prison where Eleanor worked and was a graduate student of Bernard (Laub & Sampson, 2011; Rubenser, 2002). The two began a long career that saw them working and publishing together extensively. Sheldon's career was more traditionally suc-cessful than Eleanor's as he was appointed a Professor of Criminology at the Harvard Law School in 1932 (Laub & Sampson, 2011). This appointment at the law school was unique from a structural standpoint as most law schools at the time (and still today) do not value social scientific research. Further, without graduate students, there was no one to carry on his research agenda.

Eleanor Glueck's professional career was even more strained. Although well published and holding a doctorate in education, she was never offered a tenured faculty position or teaching position. Instead, she was offered the role of a research assistant in criminology, and later research associate – a title she retained until she retired – at the Harvard Law School. This position made her a glorified graduate student in criminology, causing her to be an outcast from mainstream academic life in and out of Harvard (Laub & Sampson, 2011). This proves that titles in academia are largely meaningless compared to the influential work that can be done in pursuit of knowledge.

## Profiling the Theory

In what has been described as the "most important early study of delinquency" (Snipes, Bernard, & Gerould, 2010, p. 352), the Gluecks compared 500 persistent delinquents with 500 non-delinquents over the course of several decades (Snipes et al., 2010; Laub & Samp-son, 2011). A key feature of this data collection and analysis is the "multi-factor" approach of data collected in various disciplines – to include biology, psychology, and sociology. The Gluecks argued that the list of causal factors includes variables from all domains, including physique and temperament and extending all the way to familial factors (Cullen, Agnew, & Wilcox, 2011).

To justify this truly interdisciplinary approach, the Gluecks argued

> When…research into the causes of delinquency emphasizes the sociologic, or ecologic, or cultural, or psychiatric, or psychoanalytic, or anthropologic approach, relegating the others to a remote position, if not totally ignoring them, we must immediately be on the guard…they involve, therefore, the participation of several disciplines.
>
> *(Glueck & Glueck, 1950)*

It is in this way that the Gluecks developed their causal explanation for crime, stemming from a variety of disciplinary traditions (Glueck & Glueck, 1950). They argued that criminals were morphologically different from non-delinquents such that the deviants were physically meso-morphic (muscular, solid); temperamentally energetic, impulsive, extroverted, and aggressive; attitudinally hostile, defiant, resentful, suspicious, and stubborn; psychologically direct and con-crete as opposed to using symbolic expressions, and less methodological in their approach; and socio-culturally reared in homes with little understanding, affection, or stability. While any one of these areas, if expressed to an extreme, could be a major causal factor in delinquency, the Gluecks argued that most delinquency is dependent on the interplay of all the conditions and forces taken together (Glueck & Glueck, 1950).

While this study was groundbreaking and one of the first longitudinal studies of deviance, it was not without criticism (Cullen et al., 2011; Snipes, et al., 2010) – specifically that their data was limited and their methods incomplete. Regardless of the criticisms, there can be no doubt that this theory was the first major step in the view that deviant individuals had different familial, physiological, and temperamental differences from non-criminals, and these differences were somewhat persistent over the life-course of individuals.

### Profiling the Literature

### Unraveling Juvenile Delinquency *(1950)*

"Undoubtedly the work for which the Gluecks are known best" (Laub & Sampson, 2011, p. 371), this text details the major theoretical work of the authors when they matched 500 delinquent boys to 500 non-delinquents. Controlling for age, neighborhood, ethnicity, and IQ (all common predictors of deviance), the authors found differences between delinquent and non-delinquent boys that were believed to be the causal factors of their criminality. It was in this text that the Gluecks also argued that no one discipline had a monopoly on the study of deviance (Cullen, et al., 2011). Since the social world was inherently interdisciplinary and complex, so too should be the study of social phenomenon, like crime. While the criticisms of the text were somewhat common, even at the time of publishing, one reviewer grounded the discussion.

> It's easy to think of what one would like to see done in a research like this. But one of us who attempts it would probably wind up doing approximately half as well as the Gluecks have done already – wishing, the while, that he were the author of this book.
>
> *(Gault, et al., 1951, p. 737)*

### Legacy

The legacy of the Gluecks, like all others in the text, can be seen in the criminological and sociological literature that has been developed since their contributions were initially made. However, what is most impressive about their legacy is the impact they had on the field absent any formal graduate students being trained under their influence (Laub & Sampson, 2011). While most researchers have generations of students to carry on their work, the Gluecks only had their short time in the academy to make a large enough influence to carry on their legacy. To say they succeed in that would be an understatement. Sampson and Laub are just two of the researchers who carried the torch of longitudinal and age-graded theory that the Gluecks proposed – and used the Gluecks data in so doing.

## Robert Sampson (1956–) & John Laub (1953–)

### Introduction

Called "among the most influential life-course criminologists working today" (Piquero, 2004, pp. 347–348), Sampson and Laub, building off the work of Sheldon and Eleanor Glueck, developed an age-graded theory of informal social controls that builds off Hirschi's (1969) social bonding theory and is widely studied in the field of criminology today (Akers, Sellers, & Jennings, 2016). Also referred to as developmental or life-course perspectives, Sampson and Laub are part of a theoretical tradition that suggests that variables play greater or lesser roles depending on the stage of life of the individual. The goal of these perspectives is to better understand the stability and change of deviant behavior in an individual throughout their life, as well as between individuals in different stages of life (Akers, et al., 2016).

## Biographical Profile

### Robert Sampson (1956–)

Born in 1956 in Utica, New York, Sampson witnessed the decline of industry that saw the population of his city declining with it (Marino, 2008). Always interested in the complexities of society, Sampson studied sociology for his undergraduate degree. For his graduate work, he attended SUNY-Albany where he began his study of crime, under the watchful eye of his dissertation advisor, Travis Hirschi. In 1994, Sampson became the program director for the Project of Human Development in Chicago Neighborhoods (PHDCN), one of the largest data sets on crime and deviance in America (Marino, 2008). This helped to solidify him as a major theoretical and quantitative criminologist. This dataset is still used today in a vast amount of criminological research due to its longitudinal, seven-year in depth study of youth and their caretakers. Sampson is still an active member of the Harvard faculty today.

### John Laub (1953–)

John Laub was born in 1953 in Chicago, Illinois (Wilkerson, 2010). He studied at the University of Illinois as an undergraduate (1975) and completed his PhD at SUNY-Albany in 1980. Teaching at Northeastern and the University of Maryland, Laub made such an impact on the field of criminology and criminal justice that in 2010 he was appointed by President Barack Obama to be the Director of the Department of Justice's National Institute of Justice (Wilkerson, 2010).

## Profiling the Theory

Laub and Sampson (1993) developed an age-graded theory of informal social controls. The theory, drawing heavily on Hirschi's (1969) bonding theory, suggests that individuals will experience abrupt *turning points* along with gradual changes that are natural with getting older (e.g., marriage, employment, etc.) to increase their social bonds to society. This is believed to be the causal difference between those who offend in adolescence and stop, versus those who persist in their offending. Those who cease offending have experienced these turning points in personal or occupational relationships, while those who continue their offending have not had such abrupt or significant turning points.

Cullen, Agnew, & Wilcox (2011) describe this another way. First, the offender experiences a turning point (e.g., marriage). Second, the turning point causes the offender to be subject to new, informal social controls (e.g., the opinions and encouragement of a spouse). Third, the routine activities of the offender shift from deviance orientated behaviors and hangouts (e.g., bars and clubs) to prosocial behaviors and hangouts (e.g., home with spouse), cutting the offender off from any deviant influences. The fourth step in the process is a commitment to this *new* life. As so much has been invested in this new life (be it a job or relationship), deviant behavior is too risky to pursue.

Notably, it is the stability of these changes that causes a stabilizing effect in conformity or deviance rather than simply the event occurring (Sampson & Laub, 2003; Akers, et al., 2016; Cullen, Agnew, & Wilcox, 2011). For example, a deviant individual might meet and fall in love with someone and have a lifelong marriage – or a deviant individual might meet and fall in love with someone but, for one reason or another, the relationship fails. The failed relationship will not have as strong a desistence effect on criminality as the successful relationship.

Sampson and Laub (1993) tested this theory using the data that was collected by the Gluecks in the 1950s – an often pointed out limitation to their work. Utilizing advanced statistical methods that the Gluecks did not have available to them at the time, Laub and Sampson (1993) tracked the stability and change of deviant behavior over the life course. In 2003, Laub and Sampson tracked down as many of the original cohort as possible, some of whom had reached the age of 70. Using this data, Sampson and Laub (1993) generally found support for their theory. In follow-up studies, other researchers generally found support for the notion that marriage and employment caused significant reductions in recidivism (Piquero, Brame, Mazerolle, & Haapanen, 2002; Uggen, 2000). However, others have criticized the data as being too old, only including males, and only including White people. All of these suggest that the data, and therefore the theory, may not be generalizable to other groups that were excluded from the analysis (Akers, et al., 2016; Snipes, et al., 2010; Kubrin, Stucky, & Krohn, 2009).

### Profiling the Literature

### Crime in the Making: Pathways and Turning Points through Life *(1995)*

A text that has been described as "imaginative and forthright, a well-argued re-search monograph with broad theoretical and methodological implications" (Modell, 1994, p. 1389), *Crime in the Making* is a methodological update to the data collected by the Gluecks decades before. Called the "benchmark for current and future longitudinal studies of crime and delinquency" (Chilton, 1995, p. 357), Sampson and Laub find a surprising continuity of criminal behavior over a 30-year period and then attempt to explain the difference in adult criminality using a social bonding framework. Attempting to bridge the divide between sociological criminologists who reject individual based explanations of crime and those who focus on individual differences at the cost of social processes, Sampson and Laub develop an explicit theory of informal social controls that link an individual's family and occupational ties to their peers, explaining that delinquency in childhood and adult social bonds, such as job stability and marital attachment, independently explain significant variations in adult criminality (Modell, 1994; Chilton, 1995).

### Shared Beginnings, Divergent Lives: Delinquent Boys to Age 70 *(Laub & Sampson, 2003)*

Arguing that to truly explain crime throughout the life course, data is needed on childhood, adolescences, and adulthood, and as the title suggests, this text examines the lives of delinquent boys through to the age of 70 (Sweeney, 2005). This "must read for all those interested in the longitudinal patterning of criminal activity" (Piquero, 2004, p.348) follows up on their previous book and collects new data on the same population used by the Gluecks so many decades before. This new methodological follow-up has been argued to be "required reading to illustrate the effort and energy required to track down individuals and conduct follow-up interviews aimed at gathering retrospective data after 35 years" (Michalski, 2007, p. 416). This revolutionary work has given the field "an excellent example of the thinking and research methods of modern criminology along with a rich source of data on the life course of people who were once labeled as delinquent" (Chambliss, 2005, p. 1814).

## Legacy

It is difficult to define the legacy of people who are still active in the field. However, the legacy of Sampson and Laub has already been cemented. Defined as some of the most influential life-course theorists today (Piquero, 2004), Sampson and Laub's use of long-itudinal data to explain differences between deviants and non-deviants is considered a new gold standard in the study of crime. Further, Laub's presidential appointment as the Director of the Department of Justice's National Institute of Justice (although his term is over) has further shown the pair's research and perspectives on crime and deviance has made an impact far outside the traditional academic circles in which these topics are studied.

## References

Akers, R.L., Sellers, C.D.S., & Jennings, W.G. (2016). *Criminological Theories: Introduction, Evaluation, & Application* (7th ed.). New York, NY: Oxford University Press.

Chambliss, W. (2005). Book review: *Shared Beginnings, Divergent Lives: Delinquent Boys to Age 70*. *American Journal of Sociology*, 110(6), 1811–1814.

Chilton, R. (1995). Book reviews. *Crime in the Making: Pathways and Turning Points Through Life* by Robert J. Sampson and John H. Laub. *Social Forces*, 74(1), 357.

Cullen, F.T., Agnew, R., & Wilcox, P. (2011). *Criminological Theory: Past to Present: Essential Readings*. New York: Oxford University Press.

Gault, R.H., Bates, S., Sellin, T., Hooton, E.A., Anderson, J.E., Winnet, N.S., ... & Dession, G.H. (1951). "Unraveling juvenile delinquency": A symposium of reviews. *Journal of Criminal Law and Criminology (1931–1951)*, 41(6), 732–759.

Geis, G. (1966). Review of *Ventures in Criminology*, by Sheldon Glueck and Eleanor Glueck. *Journal of Criminal Law, Criminology, and Police Science*, 57, 187–188.

Glueck, S., & Glueck, E. (1950). *Unraveling Juvenile Delinquency*. New York: The Commonwealth Fund.

Hirschi, T. (1969). *Causes of Delinquency*. Berkley, CA: University of California Press.

Kubrin, C.E., Stucky, T.D., & Krohn, M.D. (2009). *Researching Theories of Crime and Deviance*. New York: Oxford University Press.

Laub, J.H., & Sampson, R.J. (2011). Sheldon and Eleanor Glueck's *Unraveling Juvenile Delinquency Study*: The lives of 1,000 Boston men in the twentieth century. *The Origins of American Criminology: Advances in Criminological Theory*, 1, 369.

Laub, J.H., & Sampson, R.J. (1993). Turning points in the life course: Why change matters to the study of crime. *Criminology*, 31(3), 301–325.

Laub, J.H., & Sampson, R.J. (2003). *Shared Beginnings, Divergent Lives: Delinquent Boys to Age 70*. Cambridge, MA: Harvard University Press.

Marino, M. (2008). Profile of Robert J. Sampson. *Proceedings of the National Academy of Sciences*, 105(3), 842–844.

Michalski, J.H. (2007). Book Review. *Shared Beginnings, Divergent Lives: Delinquent Boys to Age 70*. *The Canadian Journal of Sociology*, 32(3), 415–418.

Modell, J. (1994). Book Review. *Crime in the Making: Pathways and Turning Points Through Life*. *American Journal of Sociology*, 99(5), 1389–1391.

Piquero, A.R. (2004). Book Review. *Shared Beginnings, Divergent Lives: Delinquent Boys to Age 70*. *Journal of Criminal Law and Criminology*, 95(1), 345–364.

Piquero, A.R., Brame, R., Mazerolle, P., & Haapanen, R. (2002). Crime in emerging adulthood. *Criminology*, 40(1), 137–170.

Rubenser, L. (2002). Glueck, Eleanor Touroff (1898–1972), and Sheldon (1896–1980). In McShane, M.D., & Williams III, F.P. (Eds.). (2002). *Encyclopedia of Juvenile Justice*. Newbury Park, CA: Sage Publications.

Sampson, R.J., & Laub, J.H. (1995). *Crime in the Making: Pathways and Turning Points through Life*. Cambridge, MA: Harvard University Press.

Sampson, R.J., & Laub, J.H. (2003). Desistance from crime over the life course. In J.T. Mortimer & M. J. Shanahan (Eds.) *Handbook of the Life Course* (pp. 295–309). Boston, MA: Springer.

Snipes, J.B., Bernard, T.J., & Gerould, A.L. (2010). *Vold's Theoretical Criminology*. New York: Oxford University Press.

Sweeney, M. (2005). Book Review. *Shared Beginnings, Divergent Lives: Delinquent Boys to Age 70*. *Social Forces*, 83(4), 1767–1768.

Uggen, C. (2000). Work as a turning point in the life course of criminals: A duration model of age, employment, and recidivism. *American Sociological Review*, 65(4), 529–546.

Wilkerson, F.B. (2010). Profile: John Laub. *Medill News Service*. https://dc.medill.northwestern.edu/blog/2010/08/19/john-laub-profile/#sthash.8FS96deE.dpbs

# INDEX